A HISTORY LOVER'S GUIDE TO BALTIMORE

To Jim

A History Lover's Guide to

BALTIMORE

Brennen Jensen and Tom Chalkley

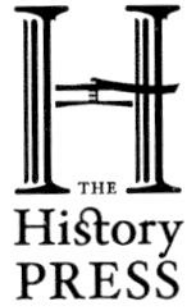

Published by The History Press
Charleston, SC
www.historypress.com

Copyright © 2021 by Brennen Jensen and Thomas Chalkley
All rights reserved

First published 2021

Manufactured in the United States

ISBN 9781467145763

Library of Congress Control Number: 2021934129

Notice: The information in this book is true and complete to the best of our knowledge. It is offered without guarantee on the part of the authors or The History Press. The authors and The History Press disclaim all liability in connection with the use of this book.

All rights reserved. No part of this book may be reproduced or transmitted in any form whatsoever without prior written permission from the publisher except in the case of brief quotations embodied in critical articles and reviews.

CONTENTS

ACKNOWLEDGEMENTS

The following fine people helped make this book possible. They either provided information, helped us access sites, reviewed chapters for accuracy and readability or provided photographs. Perhaps a combination of things. Thanks, hon!

Joseph Abel, Bradley Alston, Rafael Alvarez, David Armenti, Frank Armiger, Raymond Bahr, Jim Burger, Art Cohen, Nathan Dennies, Caprice Di Liello, Elizabeth Doerr, Nick Fessenden, Mike Franch, Jackson Gilman-Forlini, Craig Hankin, Matt Hood, Greg Houston, Jonathan Jensen, Lynn Williams Jensen, Anita Kassof, Chris Myers, Jill Orlov, Klaus Philipsen, Larry Pitrof, Eli Pousson, Jayna Powell, Ruth Quinn, Joseph Romeo, Charles Schlauch, D.W. Shelton, Kathryn Skare, Patrick Smith, Aisha Springer, Barbara Taylor, Maeve Thistel, Dan Van Allen, Charlie Vascellaro, Jessie Walker, Jode Watkins, Sherri Weaver and Deb Weiner.

INTRODUCTION

This colonial-era port town has been dubbed America's southernmost northern city and the northernmost southern. As you will discover in these pages, Baltimore's water-lapped, mid-Atlantic setting has done much to shape its destiny. Other nicknames you might hear include "Mobtown," coined in the 1800s after the citizenry's penchant for rowdy street action, and, more benignly, "Charm City," born of a 1970s public relations campaign.

By any name, here you'll find nearly three hundred years of history to explore and interpret through hundreds of historic sites, monuments, attractions and museums. Baltimore presents a happy hunting ground for history buffs.

A History Lover's Guide to Baltimore is divided into twelve chapters dealing with different aspects of the city's life and times—its origins, wars, religion, industry, built environment and more. Each chapter begins with an essay providing a broad-brush chronology of the subject matter in its Baltimore context. Following the essays are descriptions, pictures and historical notes about sites where visitors can see (and, in many cases, enter) the monuments, relics, buildings, streets, green spaces and rooms where people lived and history happened.

Alas, it's impossible to perfectly cater to every interest or ensure that each historic factoid is tucked away in an ideal place. Baltimore and the once-separate community of Fell's Point both date to the 1700s, with Chapter 1 dealing primarily with the former; the Point's story is told largely in Chapter 2, detailing maritime history. The African American chapter focuses primarily on sites and figures related to the political and

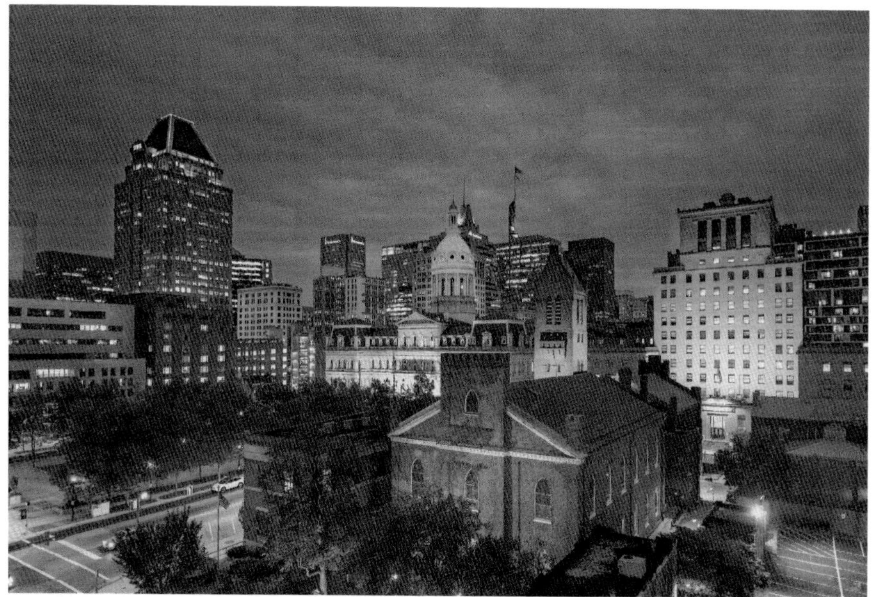

Domed City Hall and the diverse Baltimore skyline at dusk. *Courtesy of iStock/Ferrantraite.*

social struggles of Black Baltimoreans, from the abolitionist movement through the civil rights era. Not to discount the challenges many Black musicians and athletes faced, but these figures are discussed in the general chapters on entertainment and sports. If historic buildings are your thing, there's a whole chapter dedicated to Baltimore's built environment—with the caveat that notable buildings are discussed in other chapters as well, particularly the many religious structures discussed in Chapter 4.

A ready solution to such organizational challenges—and one that would make your authors very happy—is to read the book cover to cover before visiting Baltimore. But barring that, make note of the cross-references that pop up, use the index and explore at your own pace and whims.

In addition to navigating history, you have to navigate the town. To help with that, each site in the book is identified by address and by its broad geographic location, as outlined in the accompanying map, as well as contact information and web addresses. For the map, we've adapted our broad breakdown of city areas from a scheme devised by Peter Fitzgerald at Open Street Map (openstreetmap.org). While there are many ways to divide up any city, these nine broad divisions are a good fit for our subject matter. Because Baltimore started at the harbor and grew out from there, most of the oldest sites will be found in neighborhoods clustered around the

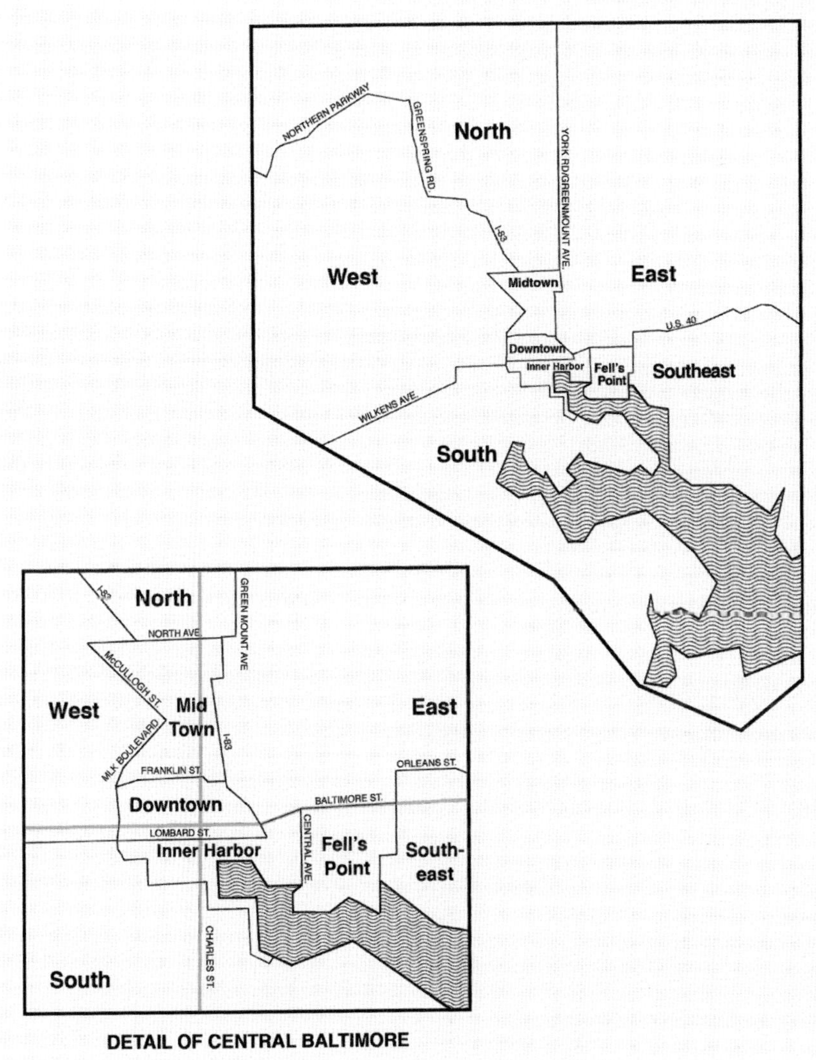

To help with orientation, historic sites are listed by the geographic divisions on this map. *Courtesy of Tom Chalkley.*

water. The city's central north–south corridor, defined by Charles Street and its parallel arteries, is also rich with places of historic and cultural interest. Farther from the center, historic sites are a bit more spread apart.

For newcomers to Baltimore, it's useful to know a few general rules. Streets designated "East" or "West" are divided by Charles Street. In the same way, streets tagged as "North" or "South" are named and numbered in relation to Baltimore Street. For example, 2500 North Charles Street is twenty-five blocks north of Baltimore Street, and 5 West Biddle Street is on the first block west of North Charles Street. Numbered east–west streets, beginning with 21st Street, start above North Avenue.

Also, note that Baltimore is an independent city largely surrounded by Baltimore County. There are many historic sites "out in the county," as Baltimoreans refer to the land beyond the city line, but this book focuses on the city.

This introduction ends with a collection of citywide historic resources and sites and is a good place to start getting acquainted with the "Monumental City"—another nickname from the 1800s. Happy hunting!

YOUR GUIDE TO HISTORY

Visit Baltimore
401 Light Street • Inner Harbor
(877) 225-8466 • www.baltimore.org

This nonprofit agency runs the sleek visitors' center on the west end of the Inner Harbor and a handsomely designed website, both of which offer a wealth of information and guidance for visitors, event planners and hometown tourists. For the history sleuth in particular, the website's "What to Do" section has links to "History and Monuments" and "Museums and Attractions."

Maryland Center for History and Culture
610 Park Avenue • Midtown
(410) 685-3750 • www.mdhistory.org • Admission Fee

Founded in 1844 as the Maryland Historical Society, this museum, research library and press is the state's oldest continuously operating cultural institution and the largest entity focused on preserving and celebrating Maryland history—home to 350,000 objects and some 7 million books and documents. Its teeming collection and expansive exhibit space cut across every chapter of this book, beginning with its fine collection of paintings depicting both prominent colonial figures and early Baltimore. Military buffs will want to check out the collection of weapons, uniforms and banners from

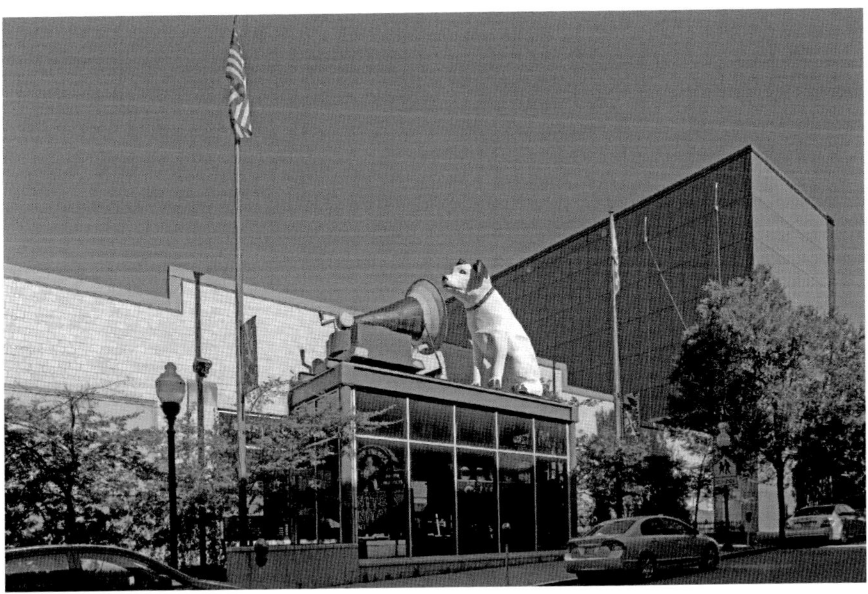

"Nipper" sits atop the Center for Maryland History and Culture. This oversized example of RCA's old canine mascot once adorned a local electronics firm. *Courtesy of Visit Baltimore.*

the state's various campaigns. The African American holdings include one of the largest collections of paintings by Joshua Johnson, the country's first professional Black artist, and a hoard of photographer Paul Henderson's decades-spanning imagery of the civil rights era. Baltimore's prominence as a center of furniture making is presented in an entire gallery brimming with pieces. The Center also has numerous artifacts on a storied pair of Baltimore belles and their romantic entanglements with royalty: Betsy Patterson Bonaparte, jilted bride of Napoleon's kid brother Jérôme, and Wallis Warfield Simpson, the Baltimore socialite who became the Duchess of Windsor after Britain's King Edward VIII, forbidden by his family to marry the twice-divorced American, abdicated the throne for her in 1936.

Baltimore City Historical Society

(410) 685-3750 x379 • www.baltimorecityhistoricalsociety.com

This association of Baltimore history buffs promotes the study, presentation and appreciation of the city's history. It sponsors monthly history talks and other events and has a lively presence on social media.

Baltimore Heritage
(410) 332-9992 • www.baltimoreheritage.org

Founded in 1960 when bulldozer "urban renewal" was in full swing, this nonprofit organization advocates for the preservation of the city's historic and culturally significant places, buildings and neighborhoods. When not fighting to save history, it celebrates it with all manner of programming and outreach: neighborhood walks, building tours, online videos and lectures. Its website has a wealth of building-by-building information, and there is even a free interactive, GPS-enabled history and self-guided walking tour app for the iPhone and iPad.

Baltimore Heritage Area Association
(410) 878-6411 • www.explorebaltimore.org

This state- and city-sponsored nonprofit organization oversees the work of the Baltimore National Heritage Area (BNHA), the state-recognized collection of historic zones that incorporates much of the central city and a number of scattered sites. Among its many projects, the BNHA offers history tours through its "urban ranger" program and its network of self-guided walks and trails. The BNHA website is itself an excellent place for armchair tourism, cataloguing many of the historic locations that are in this book, along with handsomely illustrated articles about historical characters, social movements and events. Working in partnership with schools, community-based groups and history-oriented organizations, BNHA supports a variety of educational and cultural programs and provides grants for a variety of history- and heritage-related projects, such as exhibits, events, preservation work and interpretive markers.

Chapter 1

BALTIMORE TOWN

SIXTY ACRES AND A DREAM BESIDE THE PATAPSCO

Although destined to become the country's second-largest city by 1830, Baltimore was a late bloomer—a civic newbie alongside the likes of Boston, New York, Philadelphia and Charleston, all of which date to the 1600s. And Baltimore didn't arise organically from a location naturally fortuitous for trade but rather was created by lawmakers in 1729 as a real estate speculation.

Colonial-era Maryland at the time was an agrarian backwater with economic activity centered largely on self-sufficient tidewater plantations. Its sleepy capital Annapolis (founded in 1649 and called Providence in its earliest days) was but an overgrown village and served as the principal urban center for an agrarian colony with little natural need for townships. To shake up this moribundity and spur development and trade, the Maryland Assembly set about birthing towns by legislative writ as far back as 1683. Many of these would-be communities never made the jump from paper charter to proper towns, but Baltimore is one that did—eventually. An act passed in 1729 acquiring sixty acres on the north shore of the Patapsco River from brothers Charles and Daniel Carroll. It was then carved up into sixty lots; streets and lanes were laid out, and the roughly acre-sized parcels were offered up for sale with the stipulation that purchasers must erect buildings on them within eighteen months.

They called it Baltimore Town. The name comes from the Calverts, a clan of seventeenth- and eighteenth-century English nobles whose Irish peerage made them the "Barons of Baltimore," an Anglicization of the Irish-Gaelic

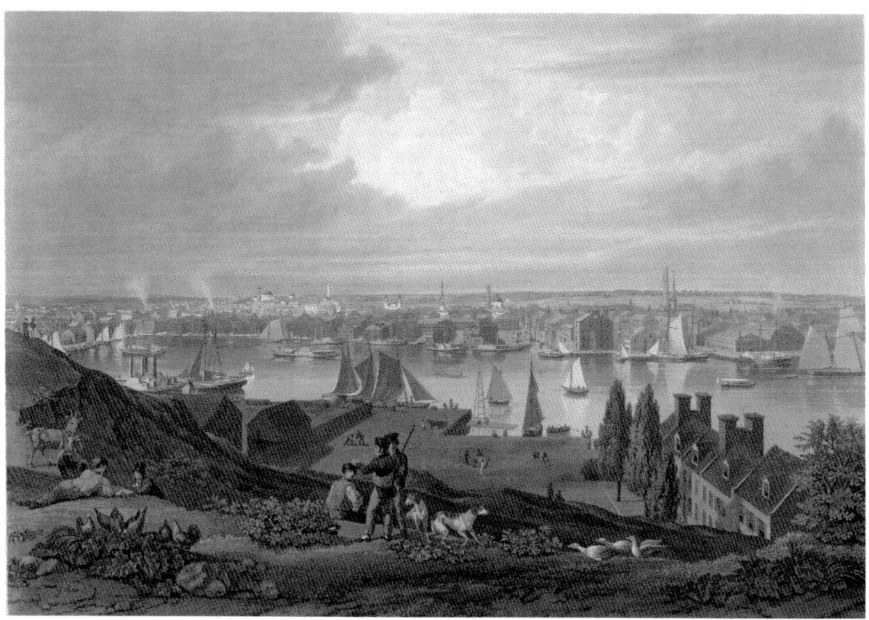

Artistic depiction of Baltimore viewed from Federal Hill, circa 1830. *Courtesy of Library of Congress.*

name of their estate, *Baile an Thí Mhóir e*, meaning "Town of the Big House." Cecil Calvert, the second Lord Baltimore, was the first proprietor of the Province of Maryland, a position he held from 1632 to 1675. (His first-lord father, George Calvert, is the one who had applied to King Charles I for a charter to the lands, but he died a few weeks before it was granted; neither Calvert ever set foot in what would become Maryland.)

Sales were slow, and only seventeen lots were purchased after nearly two years—several had already been defaulted on. You could argue that it wasn't the wisest location—the acreage was hemmed in by steep slopes to the north and marshland to the east. And there was competition. In 1732, Jones Town was chartered on ten acres east of Baltimore Town on the other side of a sizable stream known as the Jones Falls (after David Jones, who had settled nearby in 1661). A clutch of buildings already existed there, which is why Jones Town is also known as Old Town. Meanwhile, ship's carpenter William Fell, whose brother Edward was living in Jones Town, began settling a peninsula just southeast of Baltimore Town where he'd set up shop in 1726. He named it Fell's Prospect, and the deeper waters off its shores facilitated shipping and shipbuilding. (William Fell's son Edward would formally lay out the town of Fell's Point in 1763.) By the 1740s, Baltimore

Town was but a clutch of houses huddling around muddy streets behind a wooden stockade of the sort associated now with the Wild West—erected here, reports suggest, to protect the fledgling town from marauding pigs, not Native Americans. (In any event, shivering Baltimoreans eventually pulled it down one winter for firewood.)

While tobacco was the state's principal cash crop (and enslaved labor the crop's principal workforce), Baltimore Town never became a major port for this commodity. Instead, wheat became the town's first successful export after Scotch-Irish trader Dr. John Stevenson successfully sent a shipload to Ireland in 1750. Grain farming wasn't dependent on enslaved hands and wasn't as hard on the soil as tobacco, and it facilitated development away from the tidewater areas. Milling the grain before shipment was a logical next step, and soon Baltimore and environs were finding a mercantile footing. Marshes were drained and bridges built to connect the trio of settlements. Roads, crude as they were, fanned out from the upstart outpost on the Patapsco.

The city added new acreage—some virginal and some already developed. Fell's Point, which had grown into a bustling port and center of the maritime trades, was incorporated into Baltimore Town in 1773. (Baltimore had absorbed Jones Town back in 1745.) Its shipyards developed fast and maneuverable crafts that would come to be called Baltimore clippers. By the Revolutionary War, Baltimore had nearly seven thousand inhabitants, although its streets were still unpaved rivers of mud—something the delegates in the Continental Congress complained about when the threat of British attack drove them here from Philadelphia in 1776. For two wintery months, the de facto nation's capital was a three-story Baltimore tavern and inn known as the Henry Fite House. Here, delegates granted George Washington "extraordinary powers" to wage war. Later dubbed Old Congress Hall, it was home to financier and philanthropist George Peabody for a time and burned down in the Great Baltimore Fire of 1904. (The Baltimore Civic Center erected over the site in 1962 witnessed its own British invasion: a Beatles concert in 1964.)

With Baltimore unscathed by actual fighting and with its nimble ships making mincemeat of the Brits' would-be naval blockade, the war boosted the city's fortunes and set it up for peacetime prosperity. Yes, the streets finally got paved in 1782—streetlights were added two years later. A boomtown atmosphere prevailed. "I heartily enjoy the flourishing situation in which I find the town of Baltimore," remarked the Marquis de Lafayette, the French aristocrat and victorious general of the Continental Army when feted here in 1784. George Washington called Baltimore "the risingest town in America"

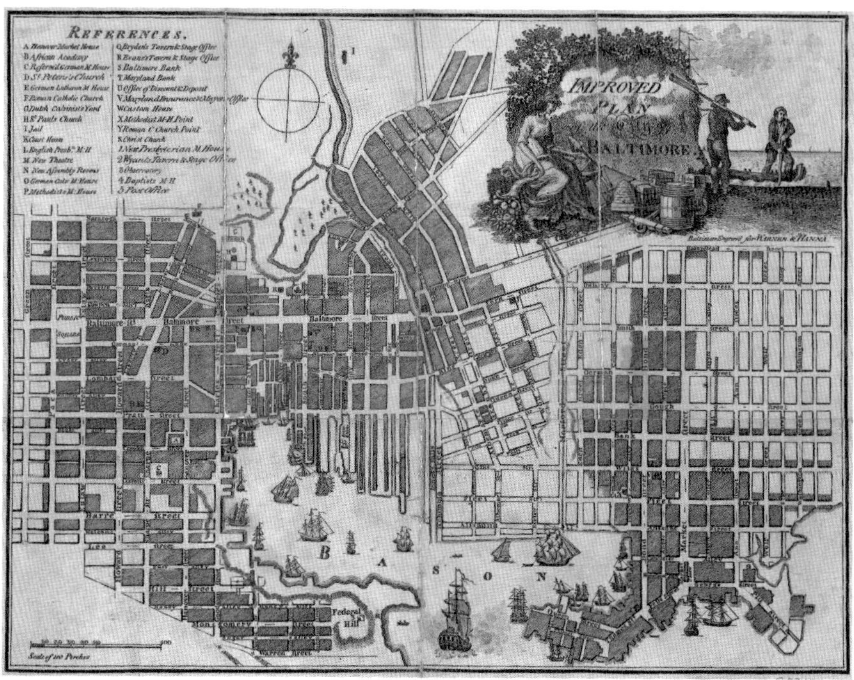

An 1804 map of Baltimore. Fell's Point and its distinctive "hook" jut into the harbor in the lower right. *Courtesy of Library of Congress.*

in 1798. One is hesitant to correct the Father of Our Country, but that's not quite right. One year earlier in 1797, the Maryland General Assembly finalized an act upgrading Baltimore Town to Baltimore City, giving its citizens greater political autonomy.

The growth only continued. During the first decade of the nineteenth century, the city's population increased 75 percent to more than forty-six thousand—moving in on Philadelphia as the nation's second city. In 1806, ground was broken on the nation's first cathedral, today's Basilica of the Assumption. Along with shipping and shipbuilding, industrial activities included textiles, sawmills, ironworks and brickyards. White-collar trades developed as well. Irish-born linen merchant Alexander Brown arrived in 1800 and soon established Alex, Brown & Sons, the nation's first investment bank. (Two centuries and innumerable mergers and acquisitions later, a financial entity by that name continues to flourish.)

But soon enough, war drums sounded anew. And Baltimore would not be able to avoid being bloodied this time.

YOUR GUIDE TO HISTORY

Carroll Mansion
800 East Lombard Street • Inner Harbor
(410) 605-2964 • www.carrollmuseums.org • Admission Fee

Maryland-born Charles Carroll of Carrollton, the only Catholic to sign the Declaration of Independence, lived in this circa 1808 house for a dozen years and was the last and longest-lived signer when he died here in 1832 at age ninety-five. Well, he wintered here with his daughter and son-in-law (who actually owned the place) and spent the fair-weather months on his sprawling plantation, Doughoregan Manor, near Ellicott City, Maryland, where hundreds of enslaved workers toiled. (It is owned by the Carroll family to this day and never open to the public.)

There's not much to see within this stout, dormered Federal house, as period furnishings are few. As you're guided along the creaky floors, the most fascinating things are the tales of what the building's been through in its two hundred–plus years. A tony address in Carroll's day (when it was looked after by enslaved domestics residing in the attic), the environs later took a socioeconomic nosedive; at various times, the house served as a distillery, saloon, immigrant tenement, sweat shop and vocational school. Up until 1954, it was a recreation center with basketball hoops hung on walls of the high-ceilinged parlor where Carroll had once entertained Alexis de Tocqueville and the Marquis de Lafayette. It's also a joint attraction with the Phoenix Shot Tower, a short walk away (discussed in Chapter 8), where Carroll laid the cornerstone in 1828.

Federal Hill
Neighborhood adjacent to Federal Hill Park • South
https://fedhill.org

Two blocks west of Federal Hill Park, the 100 block of East Montgomery Street is paved with stones and lined with houses dating to the early nineteenth century and one, at least (the wooden house at 130 East Montgomery), from the end of the eighteenth. The towering outlier at 125 East Montgomery began as a volunteer firehouse in 1854. This and a number of the surrounding blocks are showcases for the careful and costly restoration of private homes in a neighborhood subject to both federal and

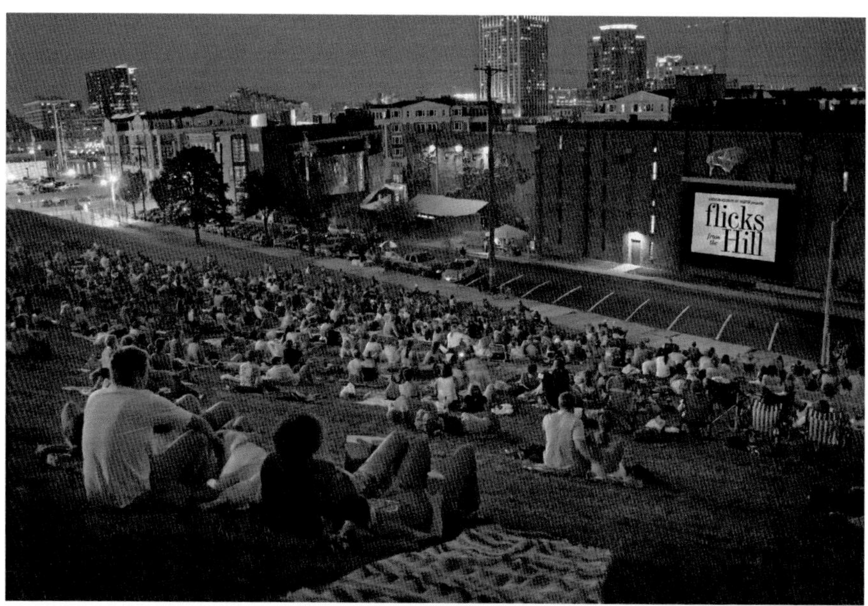

The American Visionary Art Museum turns a Federal Hill slope into an impromptu movie theater. Explorer John Smith made note of this prominent hill in 1608. *Courtesy of AVAM/Nick Prevas.*

local historic preservation rules. The stone pavement (restricted to that one block of Montgomery Street) is made not of cobblestones but rather of so-called Belgian blocks, rough brick-sized chunks of granite that arrived in Baltimore as ballast in wooden sailing ships. They have been worn smooth by two centuries of traffic. One noteworthy home here is the self-proclaimed, aptly numbered "Little House" at 200½ East Montgomery Street, not quite nine feet wide. The entire neighborhood extending to the east and south of the park is now popularly known as Federal Hill. The neighborhood commercial area, lining Light Street, is anchored by the venerable but much-updated Cross Street Market.

Federal Hill Park

300 Warren Avenue • Inner Harbor

This roughly ten-acre grassy promontory on the south side of the Inner Harbor is one of the city's most distinctive natural features. English explorer John Smith made note of a large clay hill back in 1608. It picked up its name in 1788 after it was the setting for a huge, boozy gathering to celebrate

Maryland's ratification of the U.S. Constitution. Green and groomed today, for much of its life the hill had a battered and cliff-like look. Over the years, it was mined for clay and other minerals and even tunneled into for underground beer storage. Beginning in 1785, ship spotters in an observation tower used a system of flags to give downtown merchants advance notice on what vessels were tooling up the harbor. It was made a park in 1880, and benches beneath shade trees provide unparalleled city views (and a chance to catch your breath if you scramble up the steep banks). The park includes a Civil War–era cannon (pointing down on the city, as it would have when the Union forces occupied the hill in 1861), a statue of Major General Samuel Smith and a monument to Major George Armistead, leaders of the Battle of Baltimore in 1814 (with Smith in charge of land defenses and Armistead commander of Fort McHenry).

Davidge Hall

522 West Lombard Street • Downtown
(410) 706-7454 • https://medicalalumni.org/davidge-hall • Free

Erected in 1812, the domed, Neoclassical Davidge Hall is North America's oldest medical education building in continuous use. It was the inceptive building of the College of Medicine of Maryland (now the University of Maryland School of Medicine) and a possible inspiration for Thomas Jefferson's famed Rotunda at the University of Virginia. The handsome brick structure, designed by Robert Cary Long Sr., Maryland's first native-born architect, sports a portico with eight Doric columns. But some of its more curious architectural features are less obvious, having been designed in darker days and with sinister events in mind: cadaver riots.

Human dissection was an increasingly important component of medical education early in the nineteenth century, although it was viewed as distasteful—even sacrilegious—by some of the public. It didn't help that grave robbing was a major source for medical school cadavers at the time. The building's namesake, Dr. John Beale Davidge, who would become the medical school's first dean, erected a private anatomy theater in 1807, only to see it destroyed by an angry mob in its first week. Five years later, Davidge Hall was laid out with potential riots in mind: first-floor windows are few, the main door is stout and a designated dissection area is tucked away on an upper floor served by a back stair that teachers and students could retreat down should anti-dissection mobs storm the front.

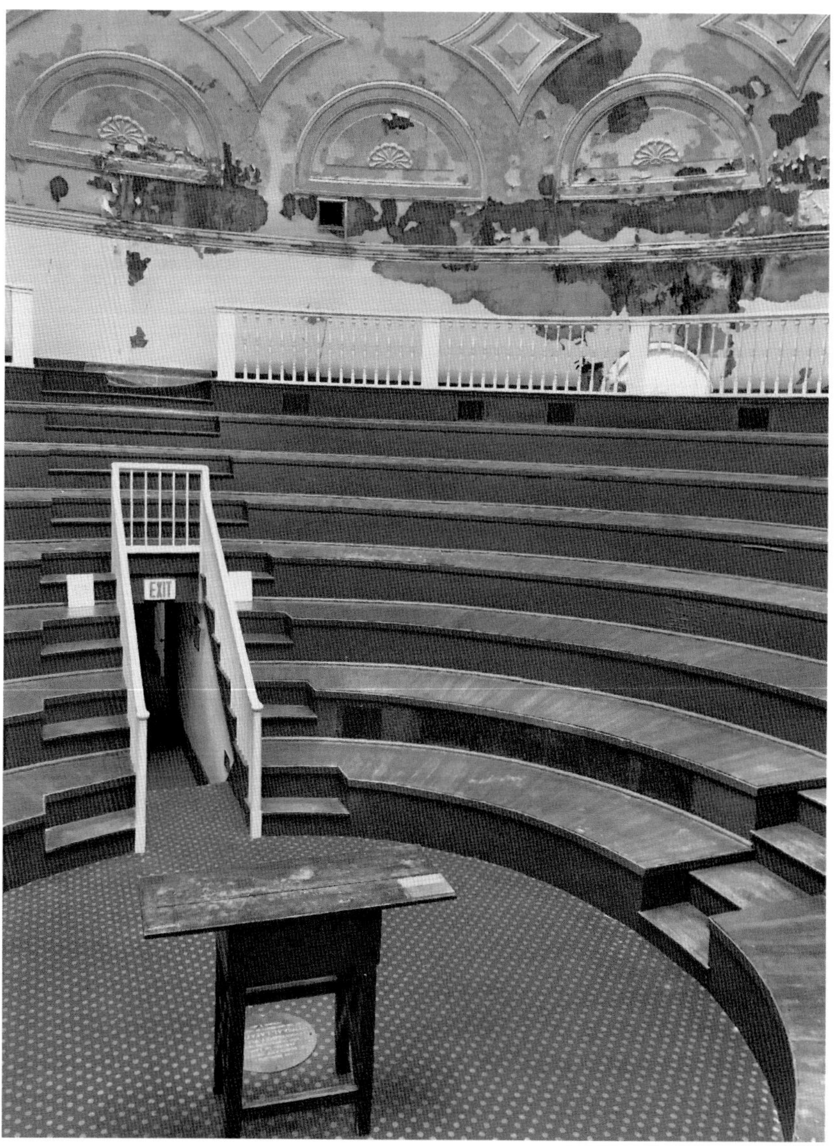

The University of Maryland Medical School's Davidge Hall features a domed room where medical students have been taught since 1812. *Courtesy of Brennen Jensen.*

The building's main features include the first floor's bi-level and semicircular Chemistry Hall, which accommodates about two hundred. Above this sits the building's show-stopper: Anatomical Hall, an amphitheater tucked under the ornate dome and skylights. A brass plaque in the floor marks where French Revolutionary War hero Marquis de Lafayette stood to receive an honorary degree in 1824. A mini-museum of sorts rambles through the perimeter, with mummified body parts once used for training along with a complete desiccated cadaver named Hermie. A barrel of the type once used for shipping cadavers is also displayed (the bodies were submerged in whiskey as a preservative and deodorant). Additional artifacts and stories relate to prominent alumni, such as Dr. Samuel Mudd, who went to prison for treating Lincoln assassin John Wilkes Booth's broken leg.

Ultimately, no cadaver riots occurred at Davidge Hall, although the edifice was involved in the country's only known case of "burking"—murder committed in order to sell the victim's body. (We owe the word to one William Burke, a Scotsman who killed more than a dozen people for this purpose in 1828.) In 1886, a medical school custodian named William Perry convinced two lowly accomplices to stab and bludgeon a destitute Baltimore woman to death and presented the corpse at Davidge Hall's door. Instructors purchased her for fifteen dollars but quickly grew suspicious of the body's fresh wounds and alerted the police. Only one of the foul trio was convicted and hanged for the crime.

Davidge Hall is slated to undergo a badly needed renovation; call to confirm if it's open.

Dr. Samuel D. Harris National Museum of Dentistry

31 South Greene Street • Downtown

(410) 706-0600 • www.dental.umaryland.edu/museum • Admission Fee

No, George Washington's dentures were not made of wood. A variety of materials was used for the Father of Our Country's multiple sets of false choppers, including human and animal teeth and sundry metals including gold, brass and lead. The set of Washington's dentures on display here is made of hippo tusk and dates to about 1789 (the reason why this singular attraction ended up in this chapter). They are among the forty thousand items in the museum's holdings that provide an interactive and kid-friendly telling of dentistry's history. The museum—an affiliate of the Smithsonian Institute—is part of the University of Maryland School of Dentistry, which began as the Baltimore College of Dental Surgery in 1840 and is considered the oldest dental college in the world.

Lexington Market
400 West Lexington Street • Downtown
(410) 685-6169 • www.lexingtonmarket.com

Dating to 1782, when it was first conceived on a grassy hill donated by Revolutionary War hero and statesman John Eager Howard, Lexington Market bills itself as the country's oldest public market. Known as Western Precincts Market in its earliest days, it was renamed in honor of the Battle of Lexington and quickly became the central and largest of the city's system of public markets (now numbering six, down from a high of eleven). One of the few remnants of the nineteenth-century market is the series of numbers engraved on curbstones on nearby Lexington Street, indicating market stalls rented by farmers for their market wagons. One of the oldest vendors, Faidley's Seafood, sells fresh and frozen seafood and has a raw bar and a counter where you can get one of the best crab cakes in the world. It can even sell you a muskrat (an Eastern Shore delicacy). As of this writing, the market is undergoing a $40 million makeover.

Peale Center for Baltimore History and Architecture
224 North Holliday Street • Downtown
www.thepealecenter.org

Constructed in 1814, this simple Federal-style building is packed with history. It was the first purpose-built museum in the Western Hemisphere. Its founder, the artist and entrepreneur Rembrandt Peale, used it to display works of art, including his own paintings, as well as natural specimens and new inventions. In 1816, the museum hosted the first demonstration of gas lighting; soon thereafter, Rembrandt Peale founded America's first gas light company, the direct ancestor of today's Baltimore Gas & Electric (BGE). From 1830 to 1875, the Peale building served as Baltimore's City Hall while construction of the present-day City Hall dragged forward. From 1878 to 1887, it housed the city's first public secondary school for African American children. Then, after a period of decline and neglect, it was renovated and reborn as the Baltimore City Municipal Museum in 1930. Since then, the museum has gone through at least two more cycles of neglect and rediscovery. It has most recently been reincarnated as a showcase for unsung history, storytelling and local urban arts and performances.

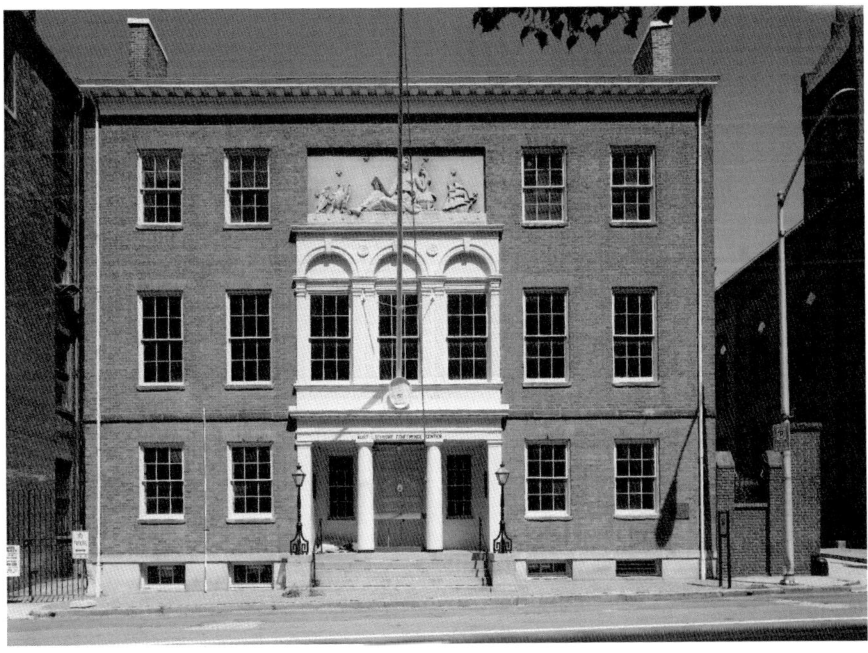

The Peale Center for Baltimore History and Architecture resides in the oldest purpose-built museum building in the Western Hemisphere. *Courtesy of Library of Congress.*

St. Paul's Rectory

24 West Saratoga Street • Downtown • Exterior Only

When erected in 1791 on one of the highest points in Baltimore Town, this handsome brick house had commanding views of the harbor. Today, the Federal-period edifice, with its Palladian window and pedimented entrance, is hemmed in by centuries of development as an eighteenth-century orphan and historical anomaly. For some two hundred years, it was home to the rector of St. Paul's Episcopal Church about one block east. Later leased out as commercial office space, it has since returned to church use. Former resident Sally Bruce Kinsolving, poet and wife of Reverend Arthur Barksdale Kinsolving, cofounded the Maryland Poetry Society here in 1923 and began friendships and regular correspondence with such literary luminaries as William Butler Yeats and Robert Frost. Carl Sandburg was known to have stayed here.

Homewood Museum

3400 North Charles Street • North
(410) 516-5589 • https://museums.jhu.edu • Admission Fee

Perched on a hill overlooking North Charles Street, the Homewood mansion was built in 1801 by Charles Carroll of Carrollton as a gift for his son, Charles Carroll Jr. The elder Charles, famed as a signer of the Declaration of Independence, was reputed to be the richest man in Maryland; the junior Charles, dissolute and alcoholic, nevertheless had refined tastes in architecture. Huge amounts of the old man's money were lavished on this jewel of a mansion until the elder Charles's patience wore out. A century later, long after the Carroll household dissolved, the Homewood mansion provided both the name and the stylistic model for the Johns Hopkins Homewood campus. Most of the oldest campus buildings, and many of the newer ones, emulate the mansion's red brick walls, white marble trim and hip roofs punctuated by rounded dormers. The Homewood mansion is now a museum, beautifully restored and decorated with period antiques and period-appropriate colors and fabrics. Regular tours are led by docents who are well versed on the house, its contents and the lives of its inhabitants—both the dysfunctional, super-rich Carrolls and their enslaved African American servants.

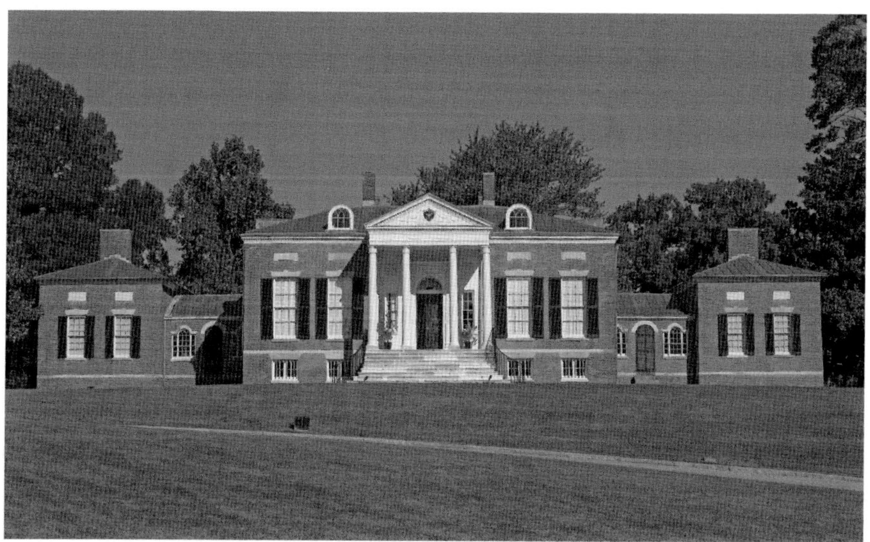

The Homewood Museum showcases the 1801 mansion that Declaration of Independence signer Charles Carroll of Carrollton gave his ultimately dissolute son. *Courtesy of the Homewood Museum/JHU.*

Columbus Monument

Harford Road at Parkside Drive • East

Baltimore's oldest monument stands not in a grand downtown square but rather in Heinz Park, five miles northeast of the harbor. Built of bricks and concrete in 1792, it marked the 300th anniversary of Christopher Columbus's first landing in the Western Hemisphere, the so-called discovery of America. It was the brainchild of an agent of the French government who came to America during the Revolutionary War and stayed on as a consul general. Settling in Baltimore, he built his estate, Belmont, at what is now the intersection of North Avenue and Harford Road. At a dinner party, the Frenchman learned that the "New World" lacked a single memorial to the Italian explorer. He built the forty-four-foot obelisk in his front yard and fitted it with a commemorative marble tablet. The monument was uprooted in 1963 and hauled up Harford Road to its present location. Now, in an era when Columbus's fame as an explorer is eclipsed by his notoriety as the first European practitioner of genocide, it and two other Columbus monuments in town have been vandalized.

Dickeyville

Neighborhood around the intersection of Pickwick and Wetheredsville Roads • West
www.dickeyville.org

Delightful Dickeyville is a historic mill town seemingly preserved in amber at the western edge of the city. While milling began here in colonial days, the oldest structure in this National Register Historic District is a stone house from the 1790s. It is joined by handsomely restored buildings in a hodgepodge of styles and materials—brick, stone and gleaming-white clapboard—dating mostly from the 1800s. Serene now, this community, earlier named Franklinville and then Wetheredsville after the Wethered family converted the area's primitive paper mill to textile work in 1829, has been beset by fire, floods and economic downturn. When the Dickey family took over the mills in 1871, the name changed again.

The path to its present state of pleasantness began in 1934, when pretty much the entire village was sold at a foreclosure auction for $42,000. A mortgage company scooped up the place and launched previously hatched plans to repurpose it as a purely residential enclave of English-village charm. A few new houses were unobtrusively added to the mix. The community

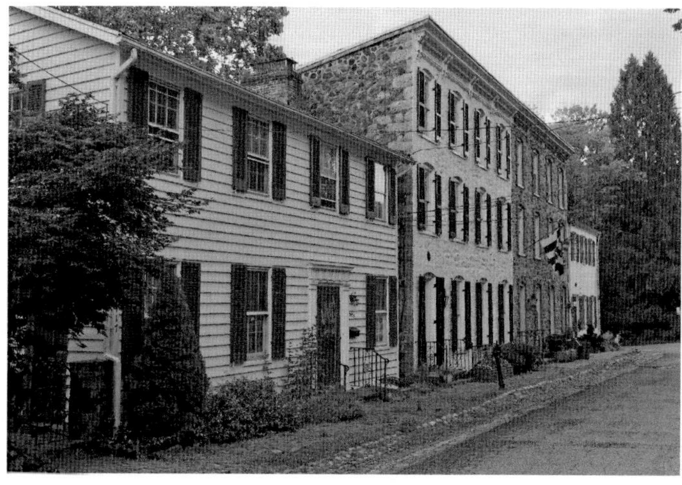

The well-preserved mill town of Dickeyville dates to the colonial era. *Courtesy of Brennen Jensen.*

association has prepared a self-guided walking tour with tales about nearly every address. (Just ignore its surely tongue-in-cheek suggestion that the throwback village was named after the "The Dickey Bird Song.")

Mount Clare Museum House

1500 Washington Boulevard • West
(410) 837-3262 • www.mountclare.org • Admission Fee

Baltimore's most significant colonial-era building was completed circa 1763 by Charles Carroll the Barrister (a descriptor employed to distinguish himself from his distant relative, founding father Charles Carroll of Carrollton). Located a few miles outside Baltimore Town when built, the Georgian-style home's sprawling acreage included a brickyard and one of the largest ironworks in colonial America. The wings of the houses seen today date to 1907, replacing originals demolished sometime between 1840 and the Civil War (when Union officers were quartered within). The house museum features period furniture and fittings, including many items that belonged to the Carroll family. It was recently renovated and retooled to include a more comprehensive look at all who lived in and around the city's oldest house, including the many enslaved people.

Chapter 2

FELL'S POINT AND THE WATERFRONT

SHIPPING AND SHIPBUILDING PUTTING THE CITY ON THE GLOBAL MAP

What is more than 270 years old and still bustling? The Port of Baltimore. Nearly $60 billion worth of cargo came through it in 2019, placing it among the nation's top ten ports for freight value. And Baltimore has long been the national leader in what's called "roll-on/roll-off cargo," which includes cars, trucks and various farm and construction machinery that (as the name suggests) are driven on and off ships. Some 800,000 vehicles routinely come through the port each year. If you own an imported car, there's a good chance it's been through Baltimore.

However, visitors to the city might never see this working side of the waterfront. The waters overlooked by the downtown skyline, Fell's Point and other popular residential areas are largely the domain of pleasure boats today—from fancy yachts and sailboats down to kayaks and paddle boats. Lined with condos and restaurants, this waterside is about leisure, not labor. The towering container cranes, deep-sea cargo vessels, coal heaps (yes, much to environmentalists' chagrin, Baltimore is a sizable coal exporter) and acres of vehicles are downstream in less touristed stretches of the Patapsco cutting across the city-county line. And as discussed in Chapter 1, the city's still-booming sea trade all began back in 1750 with a single shipload of wheat.

Along with shipping, shipbuilding is another important component of Baltimore's maritime story. But this industry hasn't just changed and relocated like port activities—it has dried up entirely. The city's shipyards got started in colonial-era Fell's Point and reached a peak during World

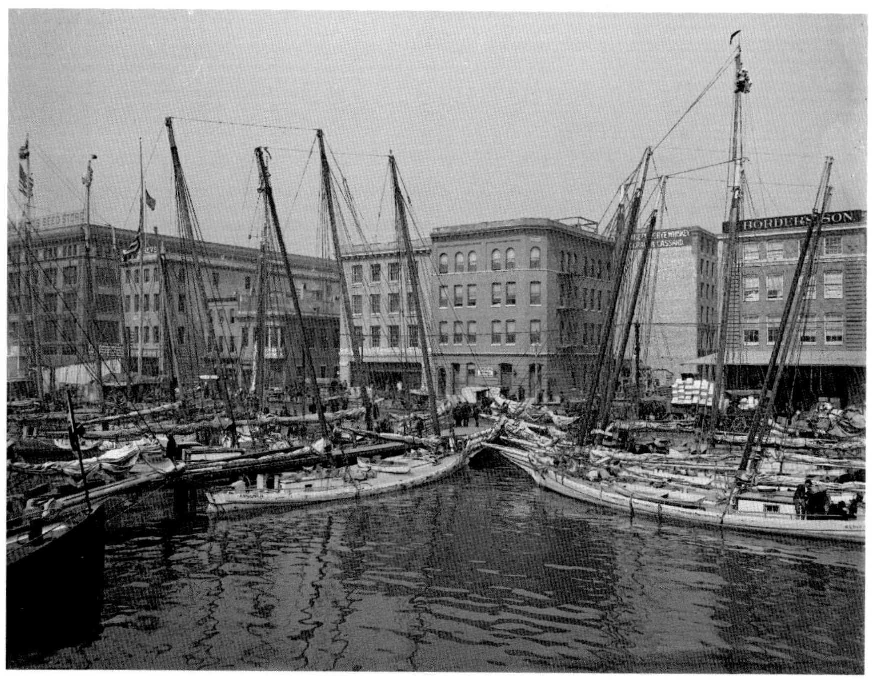

Sail-powered oyster boats crowd a bustling, circa 1905 Inner Harbor. *Courtesy of Library of Congress.*

War II, when twenty-seven thousand workers helped launch nearly five hundred munitions-carrying Liberty ships and Victory ships (as discussed in Chapter 3). As late as the 1950s, Bethlehem Steel's Sparrows Point Shipyard just across the city line launched more tonnage of new ships than any facility in the world. Even up to the 1970s, an Inner Harbor subsidiary of this shipyard sprawled beneath Federal Hill Park and employed some one thousand workers. The end came pretty swiftly after U.S. government subsidies helping American shipbuilders compete against cheaper (and often subsidized) foreign shipyards were phased out in the 1980s. General Ship Repair, a nearly one-hundred-year-old ship repair business near the Domino Sugars plant, is a maritime industries outlier.

One particular product of the city's shipyards that lives on, if largely in the imagination when one envisions the glorious age of sail, is the Baltimore clipper—what some consider the first uniquely American vessel. Alas, maritime history is sometimes murky and its terminology confusing. Fast, three-masted clipper ships, sometimes called China clippers if they engaged in Asian tea trade, plied the seas right up until steam power killed off sail in the latter half of the nineteenth century. And Baltimore built many of these, including the pioneering, 493-ton, 143-foot-long *Ann McKim*, launched from Fell's Point in 1833. But true Baltimore clippers can be thought of as these crafts' smaller, earlier cousins—two-masted schooners around 100 feet long whose V-shaped hulls made them speedy if cramped for cargo space. These nimble, heavily sheeted craft might have emerged in the eighteenth century in response to the sailing conditions at hand: a shallow, often windless Chesapeake Bay.

Their speed and maneuverability came to the fore in wartime. As is discussed in Chapter 3, armed early versions of these clippers harried the British in the Revolutionary War and again, even more effectively, in the War of 1812. Clippers broke through British naval blockades, and an armada of privateers (armed commercial vessels let loose to attack Crown shipping) captured some 2,500 enemy ships during the thirty-two-month war. But in peacetime, the original Baltimore clipper's limited cargo space saw them fall out of favor for high-seas trade. Sadly, the jaunty craft that helped our nation win and preserve its freedom ended up largely in the hands of smugglers and scofflaws—most ignobly, as slave ships. Although the United States outlawed international slave trade in 1808, Baltimore clippers could outrun naval enforcers, allowing the practice to continue.

As iron steamships replaced wooden sailing vessels, shipbuilding largely left Fell's Point and headed farther down the Patapsco or across it to Locust Point. Fewer goods landed in Fell's Point as well, save for regional produce and oysters feeding the growing canning industry. One of the last overseas commodities carried into Fell's under sail was coffee, brought up from South America in majestic three-masted barks as late as 1900. Baltimore was a leading coffee port for much of the 1800s and also led in another, quite different South American commodity: guano for fertilizer.

Baltimore was globally better positioned than its northern competitors for South American and West Indies trade (islands where flour was traded for sugar). But more importantly, the city is also some 150 miles up the Chesapeake Bay from the Atlantic and so closer to western U.S. cities—from Pittsburgh to Cleveland to Chicago and beyond—than other Northeast ports, particularly the coastal harbors of New York and Boston. This translated into the city enjoying lower overland shipping costs for goods coming through its port, formalized as the "freight differential" by the Interstate Commerce Commission, which set national transportation costs. The city enjoyed this leg up on other ports from the nineteenth century until 1963, when the Supreme Court struck down such price controls.

Passenger ships arrived in Baltimore as well. In 1868, the SS *Baltimore*, an early steamship of the North German Lloyd shipping line, docked in Locust Point at a pier built and served by the B&O Railroad and discharged 141 immigrants. Well over 1 million more would follow through 1914, making Baltimore the third-largest port of immigration after New York and Boston. The German line made regular transatlantic runs between Bremen, Germany, and Baltimore, with many of the passengers—Germans initially, followed by eastern Europeans in later years—immediately boarding trains for points west.

As the twentieth century wore on, the Inner Harbor lost much of its maritime bustle. For instance, up through the 1950s, banana-loaded freighters used to discharge their tropical cargo near where the National Aquarium is today—picture brawny stevedores trundling weighty bunches on their shoulders. But after Wilmington, Delaware, opened a state-of-the-art fruit port, such trade moved north. When the Baltimore Steam Packet Company ended overnight passenger steamship service between the Inner Harbor and Norfolk, Virginia, in 1962, it was the oldest steamship company in the country—plying the waters since 1840. Its nickname, "The Old Bay Line," lives on now as a popular brand of seafood seasoning.

Talk of reimagining an increasingly idle and decaying harborside for recreation and tourism started in the 1960s, and old warehouses and wharves began to get cleared out. Plans to send an expressway careening across the waters came and (thankfully) went. The waterside's potential was proven after several well-attended Baltimore City Fairs were held there in the early 1970s, and again in 1976, when some 100,000 visitors came to see an armada of tall ships in port for bicentennial celebrations. A "build stuff and they will come" mentality took hold, led by Mayor William Donald Schaefer, whose long City Hall reign mixed playfulness with pugnacity. The Maryland Science Center opened in 1976, the Baltimore Convention Center a few blocks west arrived in 1979 and the National Aquarium debuted in 1981. A linchpin for it all came when Maryland-born mega-developer James Rouse opened a pair of dining and shopping pavilions called Harborplace in 1980. Baltimore's shiny new waterfront soon drew more annual visitors than Disney World. Fell's Point, meanwhile, rallied to fend off a disastrous freeway plan and was reborn as a quaint but tidy magnet for tourists and pub-crawlers.

These days, Harborplace is a tad long in the tooth, and there is ready chatter in civic circles about redeveloping the environs. In any event, waterside development has steadily moved eastward to fill the gap between

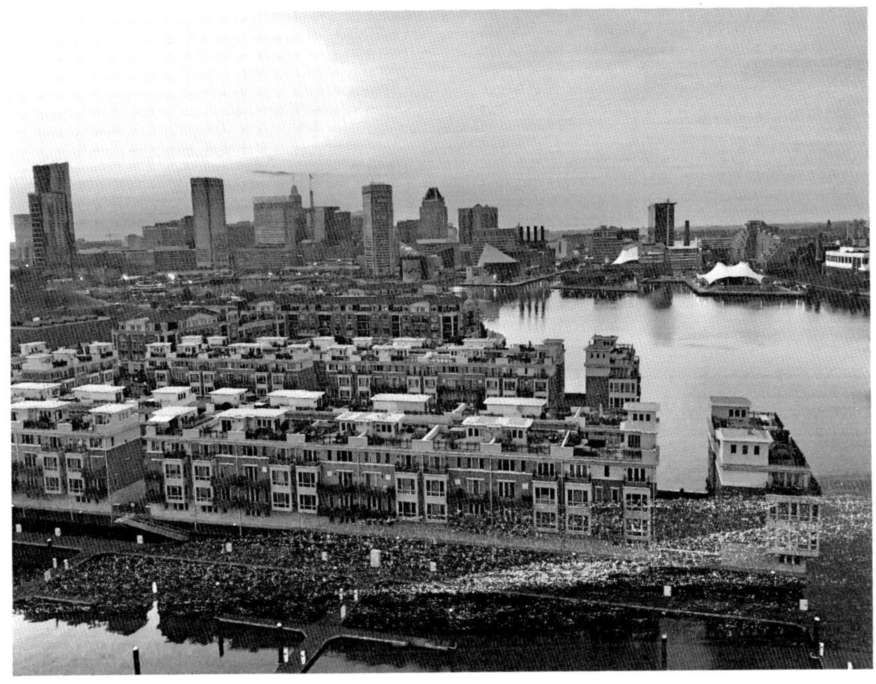

Rooms with a view. The city's waterfront is now a place to live, more than a place to work. *Courtesy of Brennen Jensen.*

the Inner Harbor and Fell's Point with shiny high-rises, including the Harbor East community, begun in the 1990s, and Harbor Point (on the problematic site of a former chromium plant), which broke ground a decade later. Along the south side of the harbor, upscale residential redevelopment has followed a similar downstream trajectory. Housing projects have proliferated, leapfrogging over still-viable harbor's-edge enterprises, notably Domino Sugars, General Ship Repair and the former Proctor & Gamble campus (now used by sporting goods giant Under Armour), to reach the eastern end of Locust Point, just shy of Fort McHenry, where a grain elevator became a condominium tower.

Waterfront boosters had wanted the improvements to include the water itself, envisioning an Inner Harbor that was swimmable and fishable by 2020. Although there have been improvements, this goal remains elusive. So, enjoy the harbor waters from the promenade or a boat, but don't swim in the harbor. Not yet anyway.

YOUR GUIDE TO HISTORY

Harbor Waterfront Promenade • Water's edge from Canton to Key Highway

https://planning.baltimorecity.gov/promenade-information

Sixty years ago, the waterfront of Baltimore's harbor was crowded with work boats, tugs, industrial barges and dry docks. Unless you had business there, you stayed away. Then came the radical makeover of the 1960s and '70s. The water's edge is now traced by a nearly continuous brick walkway, the Harbor Waterfront Promenade. Popular with local walkers and runners, the Promenade offers a unique water-level perspective on the city and the harbor that created it. It passes right by such historic sites as the Thames Street waterfront, the Frederick Douglass/Isaac Myers Maritime Park, the Seven Foot Knoll Lighthouse, the submarine *Torsk*, the USS *Constellation*, Federal Hill and the Baltimore Museum of Industry. In addition to historic sites, many restaurants and bars are located within a few steps of the Promenade. Altogether, the Promenade follows the periphery of the Inner Harbor for about five miles, from Canton Waterfront Park on the north side of the harbor to Key Highway on the south. Ongoing development means detours are not uncommon. On the south side of the harbor, the route winds through a condominium complex and comes to a stop at Key Highway, but dedicated promenaders can follow a long-term temporary route down half a mile of sidewalk. The red brick pavement reappears along the shoreline by the Baltimore Museum of Industry.

Harborplace

201 East Pratt Street • Inner Harbor
973-226-1950, x3 • www.harborplace.com

As Baltimore's waterfront transitioned from work to fun in the 1970s, Maryland-born mega-developer James Rouse—shopping mall pioneer and father of the planned city of Columbia, Maryland—proposed Harborplace, a pair of eating and shopping pavilions connected by a broad brick promenade. The idea was to create a "festival marketplace" inspired by Boston's historic Faneuil Hall Marketplace, which Rouse had helped develop earlier. Putting pivotal public land into private hands was controversial, and the plan was narrowly approved by city voters in a 1978 ballot referendum. It opened in 1980 and became a massive success. Millions came to browse and eat, and Rouse and his mayoral enabler, William Donald Schaefer, earned global atta-boys. But in a fate befalling other urban tourist developments, a certain corporate chain store sameness settled in, along with proliferating vacancies amid a retail sector facing increasing headwinds. Civic leaders are now discussing how to renovate the pavilions. Nevertheless, the waterside brick promenade continues to be Baltimore tourism's ground zero and an excellent place to stroll amid some of the city's most popular attractions. Pass-the-hat street performers—think jugglers on unicycles—entertain during warm weather months, when the harbor waters fill with rented paddle boats (some shaped like "Chessie"—a mythical Chesapeake Bay beast akin to the Loch Ness Monster).

Historic Ships in Baltimore
301 East Pratt Street • Inner Harbor
(410) 539-1797 • www.historicships.org • Admission Fee

This five-in-one attraction allows visitors to tour an 1854 sloop-of-war, an eighteenth-century lighthouse, a 1930s Chesapeake Bay lightship and a Coast Guard cutter and navy submarine that both saw action in World War II. The maritime artifacts are of different eras and functions, but to walk through them is to viscerally understand the privations the sailors or keepers endured—cramped quarters, isolation and the dangers of enemy fire and/or foul weather. The three-masted USS *Constellation* has been an Inner Harbor fixture since the 1960s. It is the last solely sail-powered ship the U.S. Navy built and the only floating and intact vessel from the Civil War era. Wander its decks, where the sailors loaded and fired its many cannons and slept in thickets of hammocks hung from the ceiling.

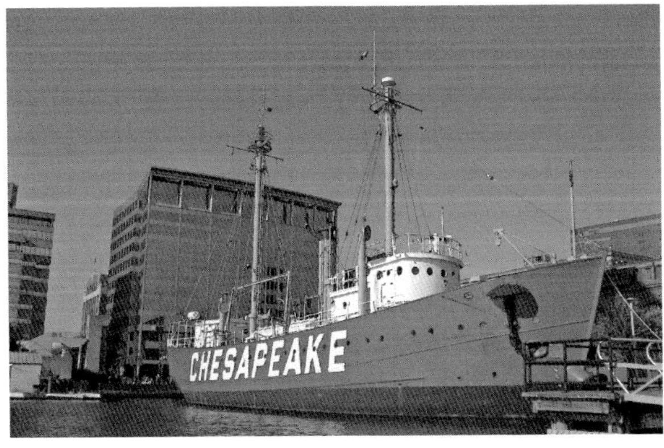

Lightship *Chesapeake* launched in 1930 and served as a floating lighthouse in the bay. *Courtesy of Historic Ships of Baltimore.*

Little Italy

Neighborhood bordered by President Street to the west, Pratt Street to the North, South Eden Street to the east and Fleet Street to the south • Inner Harbor/Fell's Point
www.littleitalymd.org

This cozy ethnic neighborhood of Italian restaurants and bocce courts was home to a mixture of immigrants until the 1870s, when Italians came to dominate. One reason is its proximity to the former President Street Station (today's Civil War Museum), where Italian immigrants who'd come through Ellis Island arrived by train from New York City. (Baltimore's immigrant pier, served by a German steamship line, catered more to northern and eastern Europeans.) Also, many Italian immigrants worked as fruit and vegetable peddlers, and the neighborhood enjoyed proximity to the city's wholesale produce market and docks. The ornate brick St. Leo's Catholic Church (22 South Exeter Street) was completed in 1881 as one of the nation's first houses of worship catering specifically to Italian immigrants. When Baltimore's epic 1904 fire bore down on the neighborhood, parishioners pleaded to St. Anthony for protection; the flames changed direction, and an annual weekend-long St. Anthony Festival honors this saintly intervention. Speaker of the House Nancy Pelosi grew up in Little Italy as a member of the politically dynastic D'Alesandro family, which includes one other member of Congress and two Baltimore mayors.

Maryland Science Center

601 Light Street • Inner Harbor
(410) 685-2370 • www.mdsci.org • Admission Fee

If your concept of history includes prehistory, natural history and cosmic history, this museum is deeply historical. Located on the southwestern corner of the Inner Harbor, its standing exhibits include reconstructed Maryland dinosaurs, a planetarium and observatory, a Chesapeake Bay aquarium, an IMAX theater and hands-on, wow-inspiring experiences with physics, electricity, chemistry and engineering. With a strong emphasis on participatory science education, the Science Center offers an enjoyable, mind-expanding place to spend an afternoon with or without children. The IMAX theater shows all kinds of IMAX movies, not necessarily on scientific themes.

National Aquarium in Baltimore
501 East Pratt Street • Inner Harbor
(410) 576-3800 • www.aqua.org • Admission Fee

The National Aquarium in Baltimore kicked off the neo-aquarium movement upon its 1981 debut. This aquatic pioneer continues to rank in the upper echelon of watery attractions because of its innovative design and exciting expansions, including the $75 million "Australia: Wild Extremes" exhibit, which added sixty-four thousand square feet and one thousand animals in 2005 as it dramatically re-creates a Down Under river gorge. Look for a curious mural by the aquarium's main entrance unveiled in 2019, titled *Schaefer's Splash.* It depicts the day back in July 1981 when Mayor William Donald Schaefer made good on his pledge to swim in the seal pool if the aquarium missed its scheduled opening date (which it did by about two months). Clad in an old-timey bathing suit, the mayor took the plunge clutching an inflatable duck.

Port Discovery Children's Museum
35 Market Place • Inner Harbor
(410) 727-8120 • www.portdiscovery.org • Admission Fee

Guided by a play-to-learn philosophy, this tri-level attraction offers all manner of interactive and hands-on exhibits and play areas. The famed Walt Disney Imagineers had a hand in putting it together when it opened in 1998. Before it was filled with the sounds of youthful laughter, for most of the twentieth century the brick walls here echoed with the sounds (and held the smells) of fish mongering as home of the city's lively wholesale fish market. The building, with its large arched entranceways, was built in 1907, replacing a structure destroyed in the Baltimore Fire of 1904. The fish left for a suburban facility in 1984, closing the book on the city's earliest market area, where food had been sold since colonial days.

The Power Plant
601 East Pratt Street • Inner Harbor
(410) 752-5444 • https://cordish.com/portfolio/power-plant-and-pier-iv

This bulky brick complex with quadruple smokestacks is as much of an Inner Harbor icon as its neighbor the National Aquarium. Having undergone conversion from sooty industry to neon-spangled tourist attraction, it is Baltimore's most visible example of the adaptive reuse of older structures. Built in 1900 by the United Railway and Electric Company, it originally served as a power-generating station for the city's electric streetcar system. The plant's solid brick-over-steel construction helped it survive the great fire of 1904, and the complex kept expanding until 1909. The facility was later acquired by the Consolidated Gas, Electric Light and Power Company, precursor of the present-day BGE, which adapted the plant to generate steam for the company's downtown steam-heat customers. After BGE retired the outdated behemoth in 1973, city government decided to keep it standing and acquired it for redevelopment.

William Donald Schaefer Statue

Just North of the Baltimore Visitor Center • Inner Harbor

Nicknamed the "Do It Now" mayor for his sometimes brash and imperious ways, this colorful politico was a four-term Baltimore mayor (1971–87), two-term Maryland governor (1987–95) and state comptroller (1999–2007). He is remembered most as mayor—an irascible gadfly, unflappable city cheerleader and backroom deal-cutter. A veteran city councilman before assuming City Hall's big chair, Schaefer served during Baltimore's painful job-shedding de-industrialization and witnessed the groundswell of middle-class residents fleeing to the suburbs. He is perhaps best known for successfully developing the Inner Harbor into a glittering tourist-focused showpiece in the 1980s. Narratives of Baltimore as a come-back kid filled the national press, with *Esquire* magazine proclaiming Schaefer the nation's best mayor in 1984. Critics charged then (and some still do) that while funneling dollars to waterside projects, the city's population continued to plummet and schools and neighborhoods far from tourist sites were left wanting. (Subsequent mayors have so far done little to change these dynamics.) Still, Schaefer is widely remembered for his singular personality and unabashed love of the city. Save for when he was in the Governor's Mansion in Annapolis, the lifelong bachelor lived mostly in a modest Baltimore row house (with his mother, until she died in 1983). This bronze statue of Schaefer—arm outstretched to the waterfront he transformed—was erected in 2003 and created by local sculptor Rodney Carroll.

Fell's Point

Broadway and adjacent blocks, from the Harbor north to Pratt Street

"Fell's Point" was originally the name for a hook-like promontory that jutted into the Baltimore Harbor, pointing westward, creating a sheltered basin in the area now called Harbor East. The point took its name from the brothers William and Edward Fell, who settled in the area in the early 1700s and purchased adjacent land; the next generation of Fells laid out streets and established Fell's Point as an independent town in 1763. Ten years later, the town of Fell's Point merged with Baltimore Town to form a unified Town of Baltimore, although Fell's Point maintained—and continues to maintain—a distinct identity. Lying two miles east of today's Inner Harbor, closer to the Chesapeake Bay, Fell's Point has much deeper water. That and the sheltered basin above the "hook" made Fell's Point a landing for the biggest ships of its time and a major center of shipbuilding.

The Fell's Point neighborhood grew up alongside the shipyards of the eighteenth and nineteenth centuries. Wealthy shipbuilders, captains and merchants lived here, as did sailors and a significant number of free African Americans, many employed in the vital but low-paid work of caulking wooden ships. Up through most of the last century, the Point was

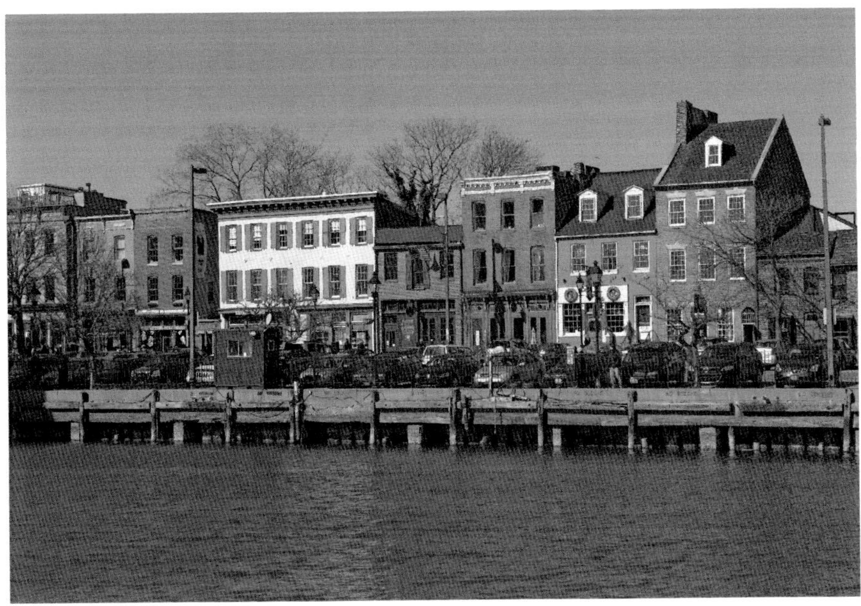

Old salt: Thames Street in Fell's Point oozes maritime charm. *Courtesy of Elizabeth Doerr.*

a rowdy stomping ground for seamen and stevedores, and the community retained much of its maritime character. Stone-paved Thames Street, with its embedded train tracks, hints at the old-school working port days. (It's pronounced here with the soft "th," as opposed to the English river for which it's named; if anyone asks where "Tems" Street is, you know they are not from Baltimore.) Another vestige of the rough-hewn waterfront era is one of the highest concentrations of bars in the city. The brawling seamen have been replaced by chattering pub-crawlers taking selfies, and one-time shot-and-a-beer taverns now offer fanciful cocktails and artisanal dining. A potent symbol of this scrubbed new face is the swanky Pendry Hotel (1715 Thames), carved out of a Beaux-Arts recreation pier where tugboats tied up in recent memory. Green-and-white "Eat Bertha's Mussels" bumper stickers have spread all over the world and originate from one of the oldest of the new Fell's Point places. Bertha's (734 South Broadway) has been offering up bivalves and free jazz jams in its cozy bar since 1972. Cat's Eye Pub (1730 Thames Street) is another live music venue dating to the 1970s, blessed with unpolished charm and eclectic sonic offerings.

As you stroll this waterfront community—now one of the city's toniest and most touristed—consider how 1960s highway planners sought to obliterate much of it and other old neighborhoods for various highway connections and exit ramps. Fell's Pointers played a leading role in a successful citywide campaign to scuttle the plans, and among those bluntly opposing the marauding roadways was a diminutive East Baltimore native with a thick Baltimore accent named Barbara Mikulski. "Babs" eventually parlayed her early taste of political power into a thirty-year career in the U.S. Senate, becoming the longest-serving female senator. (Alas, the efforts came too late for a large chunk of West Baltimore that disappeared in the construction of the permanently unfinished "Highway to Nowhere" parallel to Franklin Street.)

While the historic neighborhood was saved, not much remains of the old working waterfront: old warehouses and ship chandleries have been converted to mixed office and retail space, with varying degrees of concern for their historic legacy. The neighborhood's nautical character is now remembered chiefly in bar names, souvenirs and a diesel-powered "pirate ship" that conducts tours and hosts parties. Nonetheless, history lingers along Thames and Fell Streets, which face the harbor, and on nearby streets still paved with stone blocks that came to Baltimore as ships' ballast. Many of those side streets bear names from old England: Shakespeare, Lancaster, Essex. If you like your history spiked with colorful and fantastical yarns, sign up for one of the organized ghost tours plying the neighborhood. Many of the community's narrow shops and row houses date to the early 1800s; a handful are earlier still, including the oldest bar and the oldest private house in Baltimore.

Baltimore American Indian Center and Heritage Museum
113 South Broadway • Fell's Point
(410) 675-3535 • www.baltimoreamericanindiancenter.org • Free

In the 1940s, the opportunity for wartime jobs drew thousands of Native Americans to Baltimore, most of them members of the large Lumbee tribe of southeastern North Carolina. By the war's end, a large Lumbee community had assembled in the Washington Hill/Upper Fell's Point area. The neighborhood came to be called "The Reservation" by some residents. As Baltimore's heavy industries shrank in the 1960s and '70s, the Lumbee community's income plummeted and social needs surged. In 1968, inspired by Native American activism across the United States, leaders among Baltimore's Lumbees created the American Indian Study Center, which later became the Baltimore American Indian Center. The community itself has shrunk dramatically, as most of its members have moved away, some returning to North Carolina homelands. BAIC has shifted its focus to serving as a center for Native American social and cultural events. Its small, informal museum displays Native American artifacts and ceremonial items from many parts of the country. Call for hours.

Captain Steele House
931 Fell Street • Fell's Point • Exterior Only

This handsome three-and-a-half-story brick row house, built around 1790, is one of the best-preserved eighteenth-century residences in Baltimore. Captain John Steele was a prosperous shipbuilder whose wharf was located close by. Although the house was broken up into rental units for many years, much of its original woodwork and mantelpieces survived until 1968, when a new owner bought the house and set about restoring it to its pre-1800 glory. It's a simple but stately example of early Baltimore's Georgian style, which was based on English style books.

Caulkers' Houses

612 and 614 South Wolfe Street • Fell's Point • Exterior Only
www.preservationsociety.com

These tiny houses, now stabilized in a state of near collapse, are among the oldest buildings in Fell's Point, having been built at the tail end of the eighteenth century. From 1842 to 1854, these were the homes of poor but free African American workers who caulked the wooden ships that were built in the Point's numerous shipyards. (Caulking involves driving cotton or rope fibers into a ship's wooden seams to make them watertight.) Originally, these houses were built with wooden frames, with plastered brick filling the wall space between the timbers. Wooden siding was added later. Today, the houses are an archaeological site where mismatched crockery, coins, toys and other small artifacts have been discovered under floorboards and dug up from abandoned privies, shedding light on an all-but-forgotten community. On special occasions, the archaeological team offers fascinating tours of this stabilized ruin. Just a few steps to the north, at 604 South Wolfe Street, is a house dated to 1799, of similar design, which has been fully restored and is privately owned.

Early Wooden Houses

700 Block of South Ann Street • Fell's Point • Exterior Only

Very few wooden houses survive from early Baltimore, but these pastel-painted homes were built around 1803. They are separated from one another by just enough space to allow a person to walk through.

Fell Family Graveyard

Between 1607 and 1609 Shakespeare Street • Fell's Point

The southern side of Shakespeare Street, off the square in Fell's Point, is occupied by a continuous row of nineteenth-century houses, interrupted by a very small eighteenth-century burial site. A single stone—commemorating brothers Edward and William Fell, William's son Edward and grandson William—sits in a fenced yard about half the size of a small bedroom. Although a sign identifies the site as a cemetery, it's not known exactly which or how many Fells are interred here, but the elder Edward is known to have died in his native England and is buried across the Atlantic from Fell's Point. The brothers first arrived in the area around 1725 and 1730, respectively, and between them accumulated more than one thousand acres of low-lying shoreland. Edward Fell, son of William, laid out the first streets in 1761, naming many of them after his family: Ann, Aliceanna, Fell and Bond. (Anna Bond, wife of the younger Edward, was also his first cousin.)

Robert Long House

812 South Ann Street • Fell's Point
(410) 675-6750 • www.preservationsociety.com

The oldest urban residential building in Baltimore, the much-restored Robert Long House is the headquarters of the Society for the Preservation of Federal Hill and Fell's Point. The two-and-a-half-story brick house was built by Long, a prominent Fell's Point merchant, in 1765. Largely rebuilt by the society after protracted vacancy and a fire, it is decorated with period furniture and offers a glimpse of how the merchant class lived prior to the Revolution. Contact the society about tours.

The Horse You Came In On

1626 Thames Street • Fell's Point
(410) 327-8111 • www.thehorsebaltimore.com

The saloon at this location, known by its present name since 1972, has been serving alcohol since 1775, making it the oldest bar in the city of Baltimore. It claims the additional distinction of being the only establishment in Baltimore to have served liquor before, during and after Prohibition. With less evidence, the western-themed watering hole also claims to have been the bar where Edgar Allan Poe drank his last booze before collapsing in the street and being carted to the Washington College Hospital, one mile north, where he died. (The physician who examined Poe at the hospital said that he had "not the slightest odor of liquor on him.") A number of Fell's Point bars are said—or, again, claimed—to be haunted; in the case of the Horse, the house yarn invokes Poe's specter. The storied bar is tourist-friendly and offers live music.

Upper Fell's Point

Broadway and adjacent blocks between Pratt and Baltimore Streets • Fell's Point

Just a few blocks north of Fell's Point proper, you find a commercial corridor that has been rescued from obsolescence by entrepreneurial Hispanic immigrants. Fleeing war, crime and poverty in the 1980s, Central American refugees were made welcome in Southeast Baltimore. Many took "the land of opportunity" at its word and, after working for years in construction and service professions, started their own enterprises, such as the *restaurantes*, *bodegas*, churches and other Spanish-speaking institutions that have taken hold along Broadway and in other parts of East Baltimore, particularly Highlandtown.

Lazaretto Lighthouse

Mertens Street, off Clinton Street • Southeast • Exterior Only

The original Lazaretto Lighthouse was built in 1831 to mark Lazaretto Point at the narrow entrance to Baltimore's Inner Harbor. In 1926, the old tower was demolished and replaced by a steel mast topped with an electric light. The present-day lighthouse, an exact reconstruction based on original blueprints at the Library of Congress, was erected in the late 1980s by the Rukert Terminals Corporation, which has provided shipping services in the area since 1921. The lighthouse and its locality get their names from the lazaretto, or quarantine hospital, that used to occupy this headland, taking in sailors, ship passengers and others who showed signs of infectious diseases. The Rukert company's replica lighthouse is most easily seen from Fort McHenry, across the harbor or from a boat; from the landward side, it is somewhat hidden behind the tall silos of the Lehigh Cement company, but it's reachable via Mertens Street, off South Clinton Street. Watch out for large trucks.

Baltimore Immigration Museum

1308 Beason Street • South

(443) 542-2263 • www.immigrationbaltimore.org • Free

Opened in 2016, this still-evolving museum tells the story of Baltimore's position as the third-most popular port of entry for immigrants in the nineteenth and early twentieth centuries, when some 1.5 million new Americans disembarked nearby. It is housed in the last remaining immigrant house in the city—transitional facilities set up to provide temporary lodging to newly arrived immigrants. This one operated within a pair of conjoined three-story houses erected in 1904 by the former German Evangelical United Church of Christ next door. Nearly 4,000 immigrants passed through the facility until its closure in 1915. Most immigrants who landed here—of which Germans, Irish, Jews and Poles were the largest groups—quickly boarded trains for other locations, although some stayed to become Baltimoreans. Museum volunteers can help you research an immigrant ancestor who landed in Baltimore.

Pride of Baltimore II

1240 Key Highway • South
(410) 539-1151 • www.pride2.org • Admission Fee

Launched in 1988, *Pride of Baltimore II* is a replica circa 1812 Baltimore clipper (technically, a topsail schooner) built largely by hand in Fell's Point.

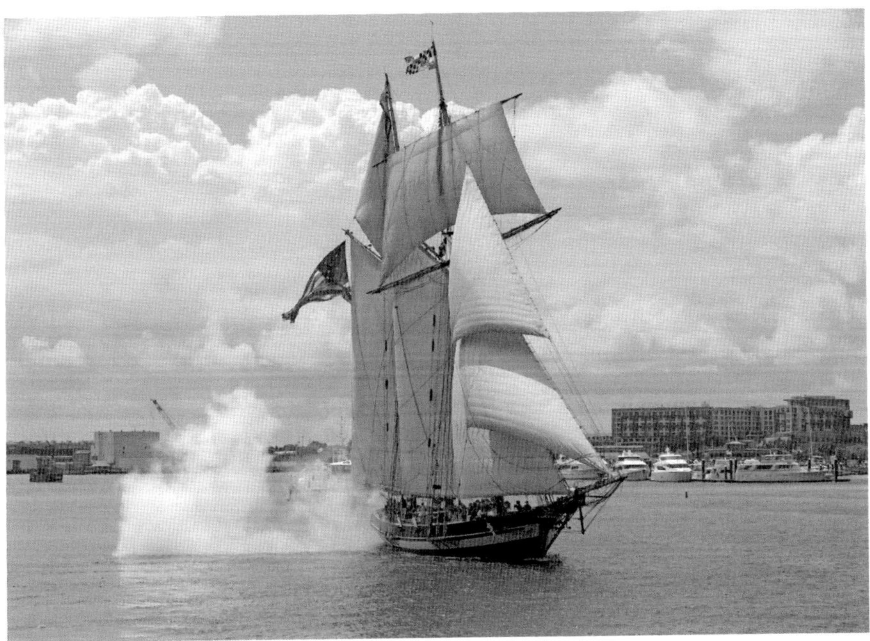

Pride of Baltimore II is a replica circa 1812 Baltimore clipper. *Courtesy of* Pride of Baltimore II.

The one-hundred-foot-long wooden vessel with twin raked masts serves as a floating goodwill ambassador, with a crew of twelve sailing it around the globe. When not out at sea or in the Great Lakes, *Pride II* is open for deck tours, day sails, educational programs and special events. The vessel replaced *Pride of Baltimore*, launched in 1977, which sailed more than 150,000 miles before capsizing and sinking in a sudden squall north of Puerto Rico in 1986 with the loss of four of its crew. A memorial to its sinking stands in Rash Field (between Federal Hill Park and the harbor). Mindful of this previous tragedy, *Pride II* incorporates additional modern safety features.

Silo Point

1200 Steuart Street • South • Exterior Only

This 2009 redevelopment project answers the question, "Can anything be turned into condominiums?" with a resounding "Yes!" More than 220 condo units on twenty-four floors were created within an unprepossessing, three-hundred-foot-tall grain elevator complex that the B&O Railroad had built in 1924. Once equipped with the world's tallest and fastest elevator and some ten miles of conveyors moving millions of bushels of corn, soy and wheat, when the complex discharged its last load of grain in 2001, the book closed on more than 250 years of grain exportation in Baltimore, the city's first successful enterprise.

Chapter 3

THE ROCKET'S RED GLARE

A CITY AT ARMS...A CITY SUPPLYING ARMS

The "Battle of Baltimore" might not carry the same historical gravitas as the pivotal clashes on American soil at Lexington, Yorktown or Gettysburg. You might not even be aware that you're celebrating this War of 1812 victory every time you face the flag at the start of a sporting event. Baltimore's finest hour is chronicled in our national anthem, "The Star-Spangled Banner," where the "bombs bursting in air" line and others describe a brutal British naval bombardment of the city's Fort McHenry. That Baltimore spurned this water assault, and its companion land invasion, is a point of civic pride, particularly as the victory happened on the heels of one of the most ignoble moments in American history: the British sacking of Washington, D.C., when the Capitol and White House were put to the torch.

Baltimore has been bloodied by war. And shaped by it. Although no battles of the nation's founding conflict, the Revolutionary War, occurred in or around Baltimore, the city made important contributions to the struggle for independence—initially by sea. Two of the first ships of the newly minted Continental navy were the converted merchant sloops *Wasp* and *Hornet*, both fitted out for war in Fell's Point in 1775. The twenty-eight-gun frigate *Virginia* launched from the Point in 1776 as one of the first purpose-built American warships. During the war, Baltimore sent nearly 250 commissioned and armed merchant ships, known as privateers, into service to disrupt enemy shipping.

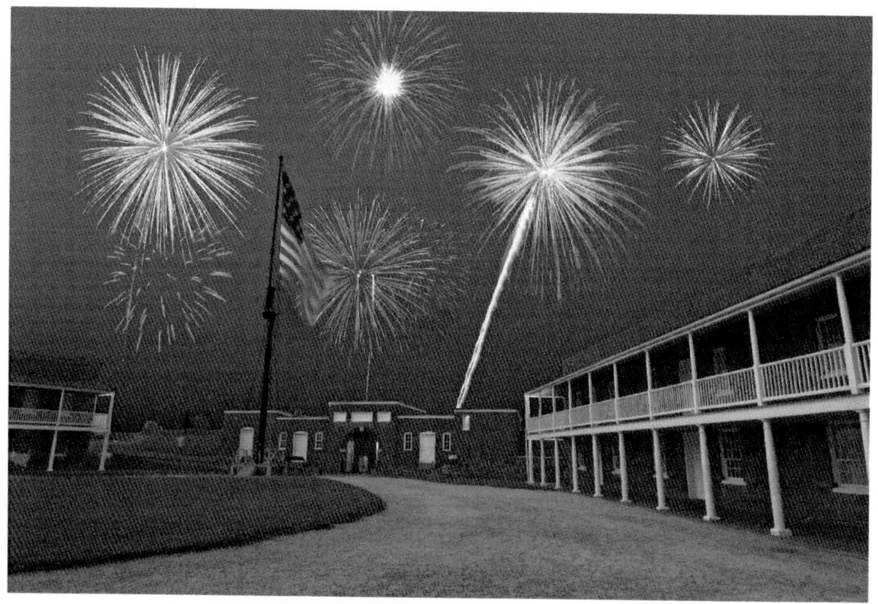

Fireworks over Fort McHenry. *Courtesy of Maryland State Archives.*

Washington himself called the state's dependable, disciplined troops his "old line," giving rise to Maryland's nickname, the Old Line State. One of the greatest leaders of the storied line was John Eager Howard, a soldier turned statesman born at his prominent family's (long-demolished) Baltimore County estate, The Forrest, in 1752. His steely demeanor and bravery during bayonet charges are well chronicled, and he achieved the rank of lieutenant colonel. After the Battle of Cowpens, South Carolina, in January 1781, Howard came off the battlefield clutching seven captured British officers' swords. Wounded at the Battle of Eutaw Springs in September 1781, he returned to Baltimore and began a political career that included stints as congressman, senator and Maryland governor.

From much farther afield came Polish-born Casimir Pulaski, a distinguished cavalryman who defended his homeland against Imperial Russia. Benjamin Franklin was so impressed with the gallant Pole when the pair met in France that he invited Pulaski to join the American Revolution. Pulaski arrived in 1777, vowing to "live or die" defending freedom, and in his very first engagement, at the Battle of Brandywine, he's credited with helping save George Washington's life. He came to Baltimore the following spring and raised a cavalry—Pulaski's Maryland Legion—which saw considerable action before Pulaski was mortally wounded during the Siege of Savannah.

Peacetime was brief for the young nation. You can be forgiven if your understanding of the War of 1812's origins is murky. The roughly three-year-long conflict has been described as America's Second War of Independence and grew largely out of Britain's protracted conflict with France (and a pesky fellow named Napoleon), as well as the Crown's use of the world's most powerful navy to disrupt American trade. (Britain also began providing arms and encouragement to the Native American nations fighting the country's westward expansion.) Most of the larger land battles occurred along the U.S. frontier with Canada, and Britain brought military forces up the Chesapeake Bay mainly for diversionary purposes. While sacking fledgling Washington was a symbolic victory, Baltimore was a strategic military target—the nation's third-largest city and a shipbuilding center disparaged in the British press as a "nest of pirates."

The Battle of Baltimore began in the wee hours of September 12, 1814. The British began landing the first of more than four thousand troops and eight horse-drawn artillery pieces at North Point, the terminus of a slender peninsula in the mouth of the Patapsco River about a ten-mile march from Baltimore (to this day the largest foreign force to ever invade American soil—if you don't count the Confederates). British commander Robert Ross, an Irish-born veteran of the Napoleonic Wars, led the mile-long column of men, boasting at dawn that he'd "sup in Baltimore tonight—or in hell."

The first certainly didn't happen, and the second depends on your theological beliefs. During an early skirmish, Ross was mortally wounded by sniper fire and toppled from his horse. Teenage American privates Henry McComas and Daniel Wells, themselves killed in the fray, are traditionally but dubiously credited with felling the general. The British pressed onward, ultimately clashing with American troops at a place called Bolden's Farm about five miles from the city. After heated fighting, the American forces retreated. But with night falling, the Brits didn't pursue and spent a rainy night camped on the battlefield.

Around six o'clock the following morning, the marine portion of the battle kicked off as the British fleet began firing on Fort McHenry, the star-shaped redoubt where Major George Armistead and one thousand troops guarded the city's water approaches. Fleet and fort exchanged fire for a few hours until Vice-Admiral Alexander Cochrane relocated his armada some two miles downriver—beyond the reach of the fort's cannons. From here, his five bomb ships (armed with mortars firing thirteen-inch exploding iron spheres) and a rocket ship (deploying Congreve rockets, terrifying if rather inaccurate incendiaries) besieged the fort ceaselessly.

At this point, you may be wondering how the Battle of Baltimore ended up being worthy of celebration, marked as it is by retreating American troops and underpowered cannons within a sitting duck fort. But then the victory was really not about muskets or cannons so much as picks, shovels and civilian *esprit de corps*. On the morning of the thirteenth, with the sound of the fort's bombardment as a backdrop, British forces resumed their advance on Baltimore but were soon in for a rude awakening: a line of dug-in defensive works confronted them, stretching for more than a mile—from the shores of Harris Creek up, across and beyond Hampstead Hill (modern-day Patterson Park)—manned by some twenty thousand defenders. Militia forces, yes, but also civilians—brewers, bakers, chandlers, laborers—both Black and White. The British had largely walked into Washington, but Baltimoreans, under General Samuel Smith's leadership, were having none of it. The invaders' only hope now was neutralizing Fort McHenry to allow the fleet to assault the city with additional troop landings and supporting fire. The naval bombardment continued into the night.

Watching it all was Frederick, Maryland lawyer Francis Scott Key, perched at the rails of a U.S. truce ship that had sailed out to the British to negotiate the release of a prisoner. His poem "The Defense of Fort McHenry" became our national anthem when paired with a melody (an English drinking song, as it happened). By dawn's early light, he saw that a star-spangled banner waved above the fort—in fact, an oversized flag woven in Baltimore purposefully employed by a defiant Armistead. The flag was still there, but the bested British soon weren't. They weighed anchor and fled, bound for New Orleans.

Alas, this winning spirit of civic unity was badly frayed by the time of the Civil War, when Maryland brother fought Maryland brother. The era's politics are complicated, but in general, Baltimore's more recent arrivals—such as the German and Irish immigrants streaming in—saw greater economic opportunity in a *United* States; they had little connection to slavery or the Southern cause. More established Baltimoreans, especially the moneyed set with business or familial ties to the South (or Maryland's own plantations), felt differently. Bottom line: Maryland was a slave state *and* a border state, a combination that would put Washington, D.C. (carved out of Maryland), in a precarious position should the state secede.

After Confederate artillery fired on federal forces holed up in South Carolina's Fort Sumter, forcing a bloodless surrender on April 13, 1861, President Lincoln ordered militia forces from Massachusetts and Pennsylvania southward to Washington, D.C. (now under threat from a newly seceded

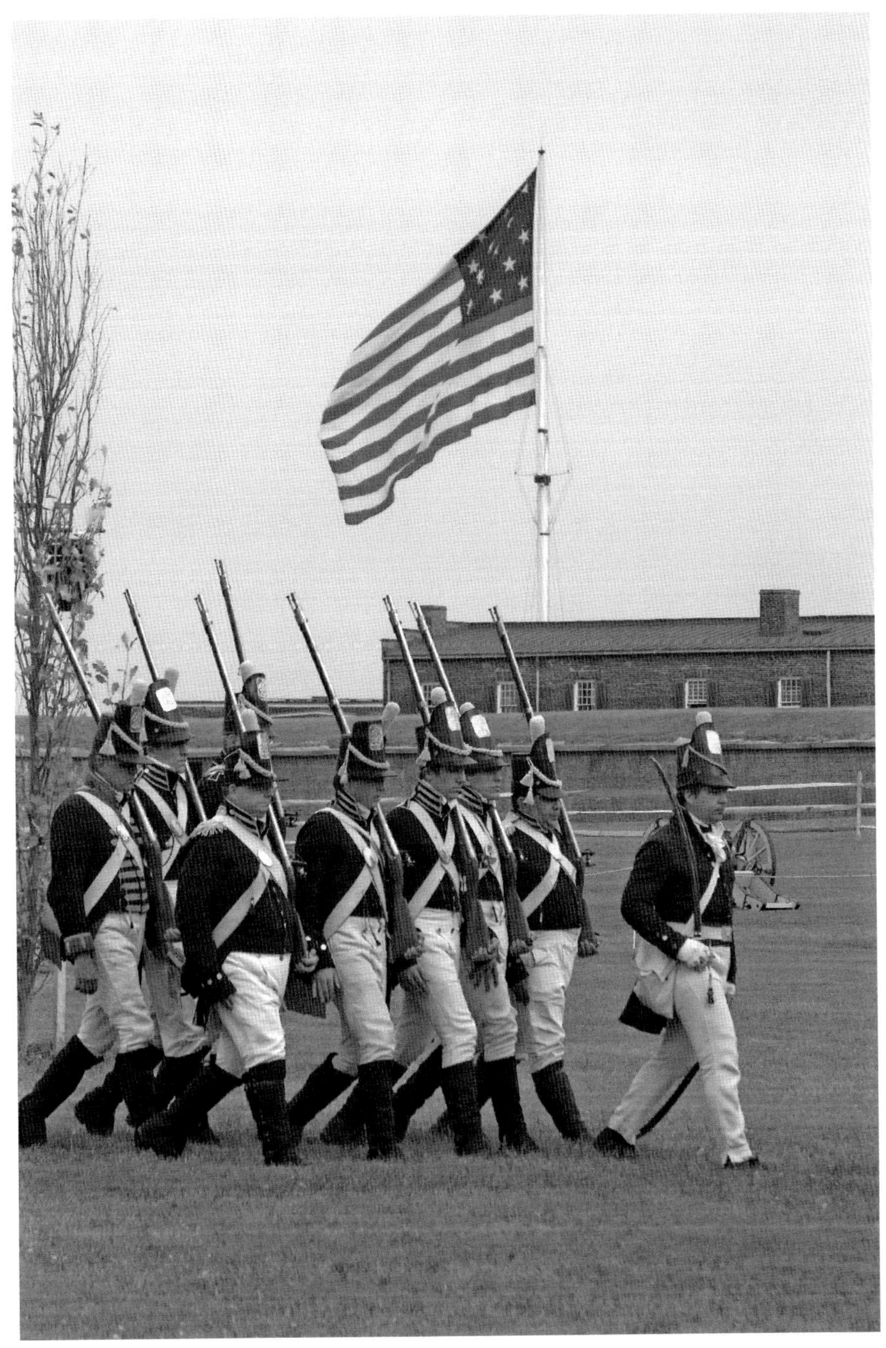

War of 1812 reenactors at Fort McHenry. *Courtesy of Maryland State Archives.*

Virginia). They had to pass through Baltimore, and in railroading's less-connected early days, this meant arriving at one station and leaving from another—a through-the-streets transfer process that put them at the mercy of violent mobs of Confederate sympathizers.

Nicholas Biddle, it is widely believed, has the sad distinction of shedding the first blood in America's bloodiest conflict. The sixty-five-year-old African American man was an orderly for a Pennsylvania militia officer, and though not officially enlisted, he had served so long and capably that he was allowed to wear a uniform. As the Pennsylvanians made their way on foot between Bolton Street Station (long demolished) and Camden Station, crowds taunted the men. Insults gave way to projectiles. Biddle, a uniformed Black man, was subject to intense acrimony and suffered a bone-deep gash on his head from a heaved paving stone. The bloodied and bruised men ultimately boarded their southbound train, and Lincoln himself greeted them upon their arrival.

But the next day, bloodshed *and* death reigned in the Pratt Street Riots. A thirty-five-car train arrived at President Street Station carrying the armed Sixth Massachusetts volunteer regiment and several unarmed companies of Pennsylvania volunteers. As the Massachusetts men made their way along Pratt Street to Camden Station (initially by horse-drawn train cars, later on foot), they were attacked by Southern sympathizers. Bottles and brickbats gave way to bullets. The troops returned fire. Pro-Union groups soon joined the melee as well. Meanwhile, the hapless Pennsylvanians were attacked as they waited in their train cars at President Street Station. Before police could restore order, and the troops either made their way south or retreated northward, at least a dozen civilians were dead, along with four soldiers. Scores were wounded on both sides. Baltimore mayor George William Brown declared the city's position as one of "armed neutrality" and forbade additional Union troops from passing through the city. He asked President Lincoln to honor this position, but for good measure, Brown had train bridges north of the city burned.

But Maryland and Baltimore were just too important and strategic for Union leaders to indulge the mayor. Events unfolded quickly. The Federal garrison atop Federal Hill was strengthened with one thousand men, and its cannons were pointed down at the city. Martial law was declared and the writ of habeas corpus suspended (meaning people could be detained without charge). Union general Benjamin Butler had overstepped his authority with some of these actions and was recalled to Washington, although he was subsequently promoted. Train bridges were restored and put under guard. Parts of Fort McHenry became a jail, and Mayor Brown himself was among the imprisoned, along with Frank Key Howard, editor of a pro-Southern newspaper and grandson of Francis Scott Key. The fort's flag that so cheered and inspired his grandfather in 1814 was to him now a symbol of despotism. One year later, in September, Maryland's Battle of Antietam was the single bloodiest day of the Civil War—indeed, the bloodiest day in American military history—with more than twenty-two thousand casualties.

Baltimore was never war-torn again—although that is not to say the city wasn't affected by wars in distant lands. Even before America got involved in World War I, the city's ethnic German population felt the sting of anti-German sentiment whipped up in the press. The city's largest immigrant group suddenly started keeping its head down. German-language public schools were closed along with some German-language newspapers, and more than a few folks named Schmidt became Smith. German Street, a bank-lined artery in the business district, was renamed Redwood Street in 1918 after Lieutenant George Redwood, the first officer from Baltimore killed in the war. (Ironically, the last American killed in the war was Baltimorean Henry Gunther, a German American man shot in France one minute before the Armistice went into effect.)

Of course, the nation was back at war with Germany within a generation (and with Japan and Italy as well). Civilian industries of all sorts hurriedly switched to making weapons and war materiel. President Roosevelt christened the SS *Patrick Henry* at the Bethlehem-Fairfield shipyard in September 1941. It was the first of the Liberty ships—the "Ugly Ducklings of the Sea Lanes"—built to deliver munitions through treacherous waters. Eighteen shipyards on the East, Gulf and West Coasts turned out these fourteen-thousand-ton cargo vessels (and their faster, more modern siblings known as Victory ships), but Baltimore built the most. At peak production, some twenty-seven thousand men and women built ships here, including six thousand African Americans. The *Patrick Henry* was followed by 383 other Liberty ships and 94 Victory ships. The shipyard was able to turn out a new ship every thirty-five hours. Meanwhile, just north of the city in Middle River, thousands of workers at the Glenn L. Martin Company produced more than 5,000 B-26 Marauder bombers.

Depression-era joblessness became a distant memory as workers poured into the city, many from the rural South and Appalachia. Housing shortages ensued, and some of the city's trademark row houses were hastily split up into apartments, changing neighborhood dynamics in the postwar years. The Bethlehem-Fairfield shipyard ceased operation in 1945, and little trace

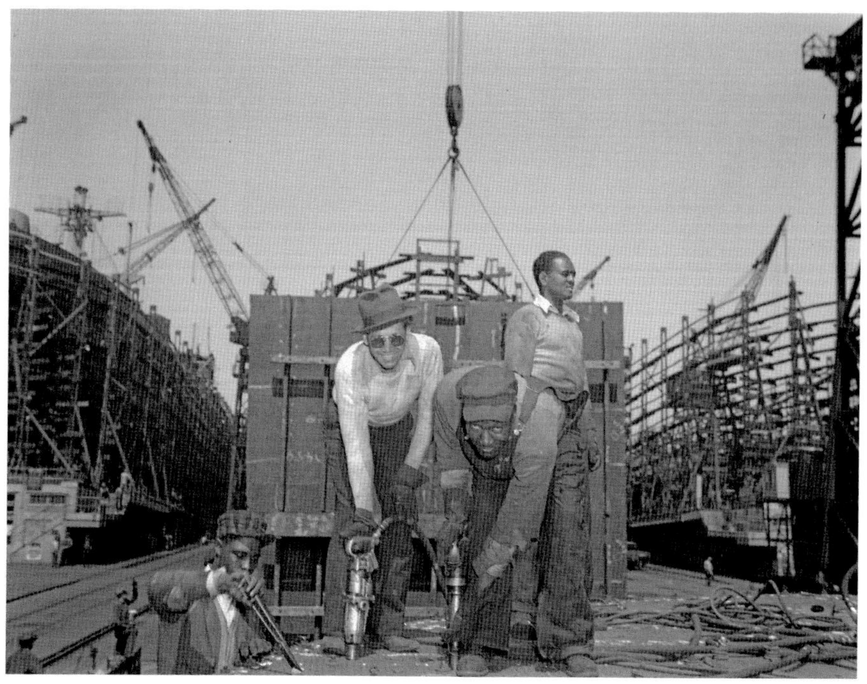

Arsenal of democracy: Baltimore built the most Liberty ships during World War II. *Courtesy of Library of Congress.*

of the 1,300-acre facility remains. Part of the site is now used for importing Mercedes-Benz vehicles.

Baltimore's wartime manufacturing prowess would have dwelled in the historical shadows if a pivotal event that almost happened here *had* happened: Winston Churchill's assassination. On June 25, 1942, the British prime minister—and plucky symbol of Allied resolve—was at Baltimore's original airport, Harbor Field, preparing to board a British seaplane to fly home after a weeklong visit with President Roosevelt. On the boarding pier, a pistol-wielding airfield employee shouted a desire to kill the cigar-chomping statesman and was wrestled to the ground by the Secret Service. The incident was never mentioned in the wartime press.

In 1967 came another response to war. Four peace activists—a priest, an air force vet, an artist and a writer—entered Baltimore's Selective Service office in the Custom House downtown and poured blood (their own, augmented with duck blood) on draft records. Thereafter known as the "Baltimore Four," their pioneering act of civil disobedience inspired many others throughout the Vietnam War era.

YOUR GUIDE TO HISTORY

Baltimore Civil War Museum at President Street Station
601 South President Street • Inner Harbor
(443) 220-0290 • https://presidentstreetstation.org • Admission Fee

Billed as the oldest surviving downtown train station in the United States, President Street Station is a handsome Greek Revival artifact from 1850. It was the southern terminus of the Philadelphia, Wilmington & Baltimore Railroad, where passenger services had ended by 1911. It's an appropriate location to chronicle the city's Civil War history since so much of it actually happened here as Union troops met deadly violence after detraining. Volunteers run the museum—opening hours can fluctuate, but their enthusiasm for the subject is resolute. If you have even a passing interest in understanding Baltimore and Maryland's tragic brother-versus-brother period, the guides, dioramas and photo exhibits here can help. Another historic happening at the station involved a fearful president-elect Lincoln, having received less than 2 percent of the state's vote, sneaking through the station incognito in 1861.

Star-Spangled Banner Flag House
844 East Pratt Street • Inner Harbor
(410) 837-1793 • www.flaghouse.org • Admission Fee

In 1813, anticipating an attack by the British navy, Fort McHenry commander Major George Armistead hired a local professional seamstress, Mary Pickersgill, to create "a flag so large the British will have no difficulty seeing it at a distance." Assisted by family members, an African American apprentice named Grace Wisher and several neighbors, Pickersgill actually made two flags, the larger of which, thirty feet tall and forty-two feet wide, was so huge it had to be assembled on the floor of a nearby brewery. The smaller flag, seventeen by twenty-five feet in size, was referred to as a "storm flag" and was probably the actual banner that flew over Fort McHenry during the heavy rain that began on the afternoon of September 13, 1814, and continued through the night—hence the smaller flag would have been the one that Francis Scott Key glimpsed in the "rocket's red glare." Early in the morning of September 14, as the British fleet gave up the attack and readied its ships to sail away, the Americans raised the gigantic woolen flag that is now known as the Star-Spangled Banner. Mary Pickersgill's shop, which specialized in making naval flags and pennants, was located in this modest Federal-style house, built in 1793 and typical of its era. It has been a museum, commemorating Pickersgill and her most famous accomplishment, since 1927. The huge flag itself—restored, preserved and displayed at the cost of more than $21 million—is on view at the Smithsonian Institution's National Museum of History in Washington, D.C. Pickersgill's original charge for the big flag was $405.90.

Battle Monument

North Calvert Street at East Fayette Street • Downtown

In 1815, just one year after the British attack on Baltimore, French architect Maximilian Godefroy started work on this monument honoring the thirty-nine soldiers and officers who died defending the city. (It is considered the first military monument in the country to honor rank-and-file soldiers rather than just the leaders.) It may be the city's most potent symbol, as depictions of the monument appear on both the city seal and flag. The nearly forty-foot-tall monument was not completed until 1822, with citizen contributions of

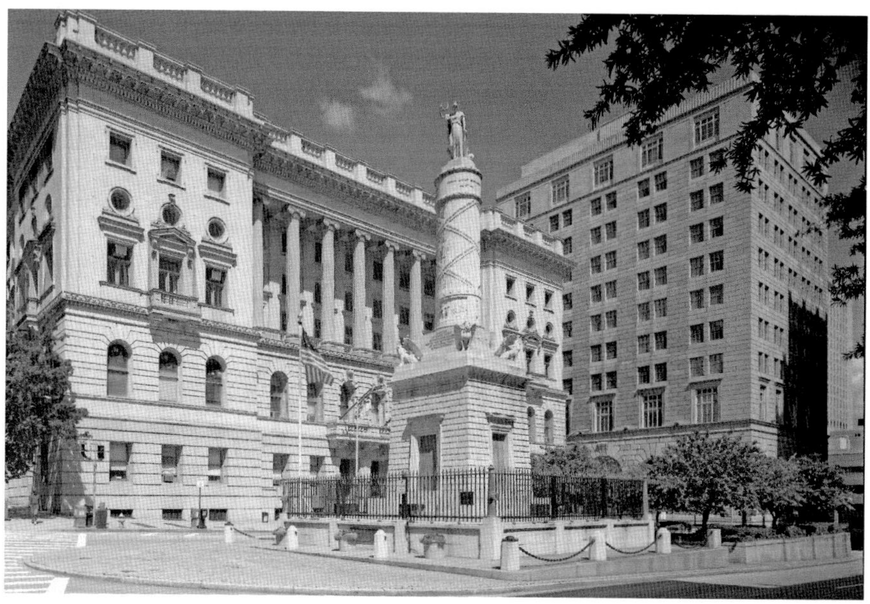

Their finest hour: the Battle Monument memorializes the fallen in the victorious Battle of Baltimore. *Courtesy of Library of Congress.*

five dollars each providing much of the funding. It is a complex assemblage of ancient military and funerary symbols, all carved in marble: an Egyptian-esque tomb-like structure topped with a shaft resembling a bundle of rods, or *fasces*, the ancient Roman symbol of strength and unity, topped in turn by a draped female figure representing Baltimore, holding the laurel wreath of victory in one hand and resting the other hand on a rudder. (A concrete copy of her stands here today, with the original marble version moved indoors at the Maryland Center for History and Culture in 2013 to prevent further weathering.) At the base of the *fasces* shaft are two shallow reliefs representing the defense of Fort McHenry and the Battle of North Point.

War Memorial Building

101 North Gay Street • Downtown
(410) 396-8013 • https://war-memorial.baltimorecity.gov • Free

This staid Neoclassical edifice, facing War Memorial Plaza across from City Hall, was dedicated in 1925 to honor the 1,752 Marylanders killed in World War I whose names are carved on its interior marble walls. As the so-called War to End All Wars proved anything but, the building was rededicated in 1977 to include the state's fallen in subsequent conflicts. The pair of carved aquatic horses flanking the façade is symbolic of America's might crossing the oceans to aid its allies. Civic and arts events are held in the main hall, which has room for some one thousand chairs. Filling the south wall behind a balcony is Baltimore artist R. McGill Mackall's 1927 mural *A Sacrifice to Patriotism*, featuring a stylized procession of nude Greco-Roman figures rendered with Art Deco flair. A miniature military museum rambles through the ground floor—cases of helmets, gas masks and weapons centered on a large, dramatic diorama of the Omaha Beach landings. War Memorial Plaza out front is home to *Negro Soldier*, Baltimore artist James Lewis's 1971 bronze statue honoring the sacrifice of Black service members in our nation's wars.

John Eager Howard Statue

Mount Vernon Place, North Square • Midtown

This bronze equestrian statue of the Revolutionary War leader enjoys pride of place on the north end of Mount Vernon Place, where the celebrated Continental Army colonel and statesman (congressman, senator and governor) is forever seen striding up Charles Street. (An equestrian statue of his French wartime compatriot the Marquis de Lafayette strides south down Charles from the opposite square.) The work of French sculptor Emmanuel Frémiet, the statue was erected in 1904. (Curiously, the 1925 Lafayette statue is by American sculptor Andrew O'Connor.) While memorialized here for wartime leadership, which included leading-from-the-front bayonet infantry charges, Howard also shaped Baltimore as a generous landowner and early urban planner. The statue is but a few blocks south of Howard's former estate, Belvidere, whose sprawling acreage included much of modern midtown. He donated land for various civic purposes, including the Washington Monument, and laid out early street grids and building lots, presaging how a growing city would eventually swallow his leafy estate, which was demolished in the 1870s. As with many members of the city's antebellum aristocracy, Howard was a slaveowner. Upon his death in 1827, five enslaved people resided at Belvidere. The historical record suggests that they were freed by his heirs.

Maryland Museum of Military History

219 West 29th Division Street • Midtown

(410) 576-1496 • www.marylandmilitaryhistory.org • Free

More than 380 years of Maryland military history rambles through multiple rooms within the Fifth Regiment Armory, a looming stone National Guard redoubt built in 1901 (and setting of the 1912 Democratic Convention where Woodrow Wilson was nominated for president). The first state militia was formed in 1634, represented here by a figure of Captain John Price holding a circa 1588 matchlock musket. You will also meet the "Maryland 400," a storied Revolutionary War regiment that suffered enormous casualties while engaging a much larger British force during the Battle of Long Island in August 1776, allowing George Washington to successfully evacuate the bulk of his forces to Manhattan. The 1814 Battle of Baltimore gets its own expansive exhibit. And then there's the Twenty-Ninth Army Infantry Division (now a National Guard formation), known as the "Blue and Gray" because its soldiers came from across Civil War battle lines, from Maryland down to South Carolina. It was first formed to go "Over There" in 1917 and subsequently stormed Omaha Beach on D-Day. Among the plethora of fascinating artifacts and full-size uniformed figures on display is the World War II jeep "Vixen Tor," which division commander General

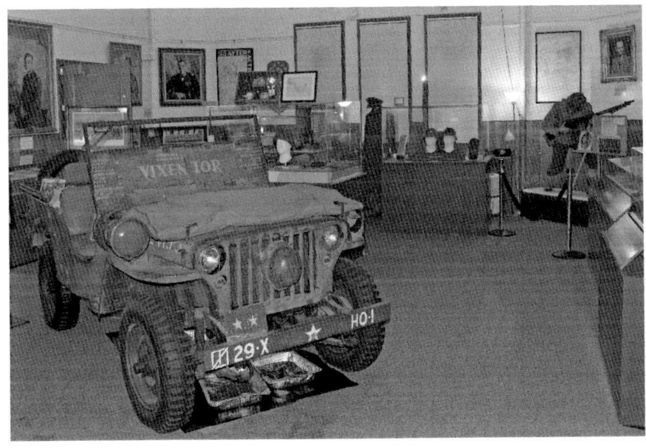

The little jeep that could. The Maryland Museum of Military History includes a vehicle that's been to the D-Day beaches twice. *Courtesy of Brennen Jensen.*

Charles Gerhardt used from D-Day until Germany's defeat. (The battle-hardy vehicle actually returned to Omaha Beach in 1994 as part of fiftieth-anniversary celebrations.) The museum resides within an active military installation; call to verify hours and have a photo ID ready for the guards.

Union Soldiers and Sailors Monument

Wyman Park, North Charles Street at West 29th Street • North

Since 2017, this has been Baltimore's only public monument to the Civil War. Dedicated in 1909 on the eastern end of Druid Hill Park, the bronze sculpture was moved to its present Wyman Park location in 1959 to make way for the construction of the Jones Falls Expressway. The sculpture, facing the intersection of North Charles and 29th Streets, represents a man who has left behind his peacetime work, symbolized by a plow and anvil, to take up arms for the Union cause. Behind him stand winged figures representing War and Victory. Situated on the southeast corner of Wyman Park Dell, this monument served until recently as a counterweight to the double equestrian statue of Confederate generals Robert E. Lee and Thomas "Stonewall" Jackson, which stood on the opposite side of the Dell. In the twenty-first century, Confederate monuments have sparked opposition as symbols of White supremacy, prompting a number of cities to pull them from their pedestals. On the night of August 14, 2017, Baltimore mayor Catherine Pugh ordered all of Baltimore's pro-Confederate and proslavery monuments—four, counting the statue of Supreme Court justice Roger Taney, author of the Dred Scott decision—taken down and placed in storage.

Wells and McComas Monument

East Monument Street at Aisquith Street • East

This simple obelisk commemorates two young Baltimore sharpshooters, Daniel Wells and Henry McComas, who were found dead on the North Point battlefield following the fateful, fatal shooting of the British general Robert Ross. For circumstantial and possibly emotional reasons, the dead youths were given credit for the shot that killed Ross, thereby stalling and greatly demoralizing the invading British. This legend gained popularity after the war. Wells and McComas came to be called "the Boy Martyrs," and a campaign was launched for a monument to commemorate them. In 1858, their caskets were moved from Green Mount Cemetery to the site where the unfinished monument was under construction. The two caskets lay in a temporary vault until 1872, when the obelisk was completed and the heroes were interred inside its base.

Hampstead Hill

South Patterson Park Avenue at Pratt Street • Southeast

Hampstead Hill on the western edge of Patterson Park, generally known today as "Pagoda Hill" after the whimsical observation tower erected atop it in 1890, is the scene of summer concerts and winter sledding. Seven cannons are about the only man-made reminders of how this strategic site figured in the defense of Baltimore in 1814. That summer, Baltimoreans were anticipating British attacks from the east, both by water and by land. Urged on by city leaders, thousands of people volunteered to build a line of defensive earthworks along the city's eastern edge. Hampstead Hill became the defenders' heavily fortified command center. On September 12, the British attacked exactly as expected. The following morning, after a day of skirmishes, the felling of General Robert Ross and a rainy night of battlefield camping, the British marched into sight of the city and were shocked and awed to see a defensive line extending north some two miles from the Canton waterfront to Belair Road. Half a mile up the line stood (to quote British officer George Cockburn) "an extensive hill on which was an entrenched camp and great quantities of artillery," as well as, in Cockburn's (perhaps inflated) estimation, "15 to 20,000 men." After failing in several attempts to circumvent the defenses, the outnumbered, outmaneuvered British marched back to North Point and rejoined their

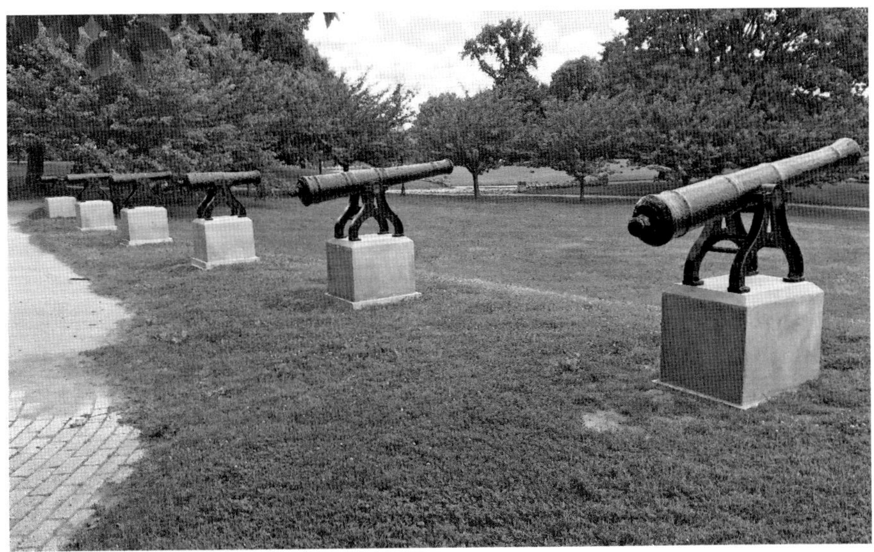

Only armies of picnickers storm Patterson Park's Hampstead Hill today, but 1814 defenses here rebuffed the invading British. *Courtesy of Baltimore Heritage/Eli Pousson.*

Louisiana-bound fleet. Union army officers set up camp on the hill during the Civil War, but ever since then, the green prominence has been dedicated to peaceful recreation.

Pulaski Monument

Patterson Park near intersection of Eastern Avenue and South Linwood Avenue • Southeast

This bronze relief statue of Casimir Pulaski by noted local sculptor Hans Schuler was dedicated in 1951 and restored and rededicated in 2001 by members of the city's Polish American community—obviously proud of the derring-do of the Polish-born hero of the Revolutionary War credited with helping save George Washington's life during battle. Pulaski formed his cavalry in Baltimore and rose to the rank of brigadier general. Pulaski is depicted here leading his final cavalry charge in October 1779 during the Siege of Savannah, where he was mortally wounded. He died two days later at age thirty-two. The horseman depicted immediately behind Pulaski is his loyal aide, French-born Captain Paul Bentalou, who has a West Baltimore street named after him. A final wrinkle in the Pulaski saga occurred in 2019, after his skeletal remains were discovered in an unmarked

Savannah, Georgia grave. Certain aspects of the skeletal structure appear female, leading many to conclude that the Father of American Cavalry, known to have been diminutive in stature but invariably depicted with a jaunty mustache (as here), might have been intersex—possessing physical attributes of both sexes.

SS *John W. Brown*

Pier 13, 4601 Newgate Avenue • Southeast
(410) 558-0146 • www.ssjohnwbrown.org • Admission Fee

One of only two surviving and operational Liberty ships rapidly built during World War II to supply Allied forces, SS *John W. Brown* was launched from the city's Bethlehem-Fairfield shipyard on September 7, 1942. It is named after a labor leader involved in organizing miners and the marine trades. *Brown* is now a museum ship run by Project Liberty Ship, a nonprofit that works to preserve and highlight the unheralded but utterly crucial contribution such ships made to winning the war. (We couldn't have successfully launched an invasion across the English Channel on D-Day without millions of tons of munitions and supplies first crossing the oceans.) Liberty ships (and their larger siblings, Victory ships) were armed merchant vessels operated by civilian seamen with guns manned by navy personnel. More than 2,700 were built (with some 200 lost at sea during the war). *John W. Brown* completed more than a dozen wartime voyages, spending much of its time in the Mediterranean. Today, it is available for tours and makes periodic living history day sailings of the Chesapeake Bay that feature live 1940s music and flyovers of World War II aircraft.

Fort Carroll

Patapsco River below Key Bridge • South • Exterior Only

A strange, hexagonal ruin squats in the middle of the Patapsco River, just downstream from the Key Bridge. This was once Fort Carroll, built by army engineers in 1848 with the aim of defending Baltimore Harbor from a naval attack. Within a few years, with the fort just one-third complete, engineers halted construction because the structure was sinking into the river bottom. The unfinished fort was nonetheless armed with thirty cannons throughout the Civil War and armed again during the Spanish-American War, circa

1900. No attack ever came. (Ironically, the fort's first supervising engineer was Brevet Colonel Robert E. Lee, who would, a dozen years later, opt to command Southern forces in armed rebellion against the United States.) In 1958, the abandoned artificial island was sold to a private investor, and it remains in private hands to this day. Landing and trespassing are prohibited. Trespassers report that there is beautiful masonry among the ruins.

Fort McHenry

2400 East Fort Avenue • South
(410) 962-4290 • www.nps.gov/fomc/index.htm • Admission Fee

Probably the most famous structure in Baltimore, Fort McHenry successfully defended the city against the British naval assault of September 13–14, 1814. As recounted in the lyrics of "The Star-Spangled Banner," the fort, with its enormous flag still flying, survived a twenty-seven-hour pounding with more than 1,500 bombs and Congreve rockets. Built in 1799 and continually improved over the following decades, Fort McHenry is built around a five-sided courtyard; each corner of the fortified pentagon extends into a diamond-shaped bastion. This star-like design would have allowed defenders to fire at land-based attackers from any angle, but the British attackers in 1814 mostly stayed in their ships, two miles from the American stronghold, wreaking long-distance destruction with superior artillery. One British bomb made a direct landing in the storeroom that held the fort's supply of gunpowder, but the bomb never exploded—its fuse was doused either by the constant rain or (per local legend) by the quick action of a brave soldier. The invaders made one attempt to sneak around American defenses in the dark, along the south side of the Patapsco, but the trick was discovered and routed. Eventually, the British naval command, re-estimating their odds, turned their fleet around and sailed to Louisiana to join the doomed attack on New Orleans.

During the Civil War, Fort McHenry was put to work as a military prison for Confederate soldiers and leading pro-Confederate Marylanders, including at times the mayor and city council members of Baltimore City, members of the Maryland General Assembly and several newspaper editors. In the twentieth century, the fort and its grounds served multiple purposes: a military hospital in World War I, a national park beginning in 1925 and a Coast Guard post during World War II. Designated today as a National Monument and Historic Shrine, it is operated by the National Park Service.

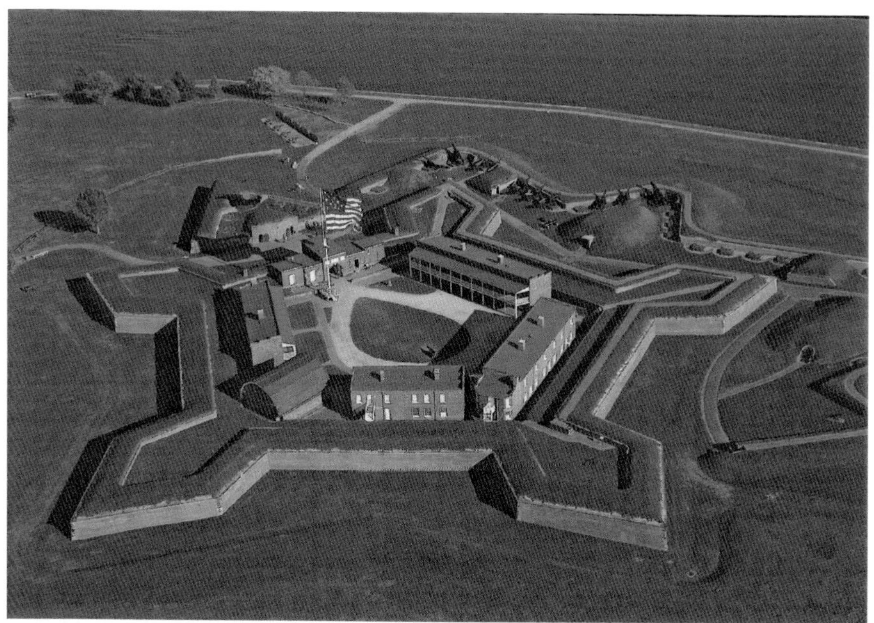

Our Star-Spangled Banner flies over storied Fort McHenry. *Courtesy of Maryland State Archives/Tom Darden.*

Every September, Baltimoreans gather at Fort McHenry to celebrate Defenders' Day, honoring the struggles of 1814. (It once was a state holiday.) Men in period uniforms march, beat drums and fire muskets, while dignitaries make speeches and patriotic songs are performed. Aside from the smell of gunpowder, it is usually a lighthearted event ideal for picnicking.

Francis Scott Key Monuments (Two Sites)

1700 block of Eutaw Street • West
Fort McHenry, 2400 East Fort Avenue • South

Not surprisingly, Baltimore has a number of structures, streets and institutions dedicated to the Maryland lawyer who, in 1814, composed the lyrics of "The Star-Spangled Banner" after witnessing the British assault on Fort McHenry. Among the city's many tributes to Francis Scott Key are two highly symbolic sculptures: the first, erected in 1911 on the median of Eutaw Street at West Lanvale Street in Bolton Hill, represents Key standing in a rowboat, saluting a gilded figure of Liberty. The goddess is perched on top of a four-pillared, temple-like structure, waving a sculpted American flag. The second Key monument, from 1922, is both more grandiose and more obscurely symbolic: a twenty-four-foot-tall bronze nude representing Orpheus, the lyre-playing Greek demigod of poetry, stands on a fifteen-foot pedestal bearing a bas-relief portrait of Key and a lineup of heroic figures in classical Greek attire. The monument stands on the grounds of Fort McHenry, to the west of the fort itself.

Loudon Park Cemetery
3620 Wilkens Avenue • West
(410) 644-1900 • www.loudonparkcemetery.net

Baltimore's biggest boneyard sprawls across nearly five hundred leafy and undulating acres on the city's west side and dates to 1853. Both blue and gray are interred here, the latter on Confederate Hill. More than two thousand Union dead rest in the adjacent, federally managed Loudon National Cemetery, along with five recipients of the Congressional Medal of Honor. Other notables in eternal slumber here include Mary Pickersgill, who sewed the Star-Spangled Banner hoisted proudly over post-bombardment Fort McHenry in 1814, and the Sage of Baltimore—consummate newspaperman and social critic H.L. Mencken. The Bonaparte family plot contains not only Jérôme Bonaparte (son of Napoleon's younger brother) but also Jérôme's son Charles Bonaparte, secretary of the navy and attorney general under Theodore Roosevelt, considered one of the fathers of the FBI. The tallest and most elaborate monument—a multi-tiered, carved-stone wedding cake of a thing—belongs to the Wiessners, a wealthy family of Baltimore brewers whose sudsy empire flourished until Prohibition. (Their ornate Victorian erstwhile brewhouse—known today as American Brewery—still looms over East Baltimore.) Samuel J. Seymour's grave marks a historical curiosity: he was the last surviving witness to Lincoln's assassination. Seymour was five when he attended Ford's Theatre that fateful night in 1865. He discussed the evening on a television program in 1956, shortly before his death at age ninety six.

Chapter 4

A HIGHER CALLING

CHURCHES AND TEMPLES REFLECTING FAITH IN THE CITY

While Charleston, South Carolina, is nicknamed the "Holy City," the moniker fits Baltimore just as well. The city is the birthplace of American Catholicism and is home to the mother churches of American Methodism and Unitarianism. Baltimore is where the nation's first ordained rabbi served an assembly and is also considered the birthplace of Reformed Judaism in America. Even the devoutly undevout can appreciate that many of the city's historic houses of worship are architectural gems.

When Baltimore Town began in 1729 as sixty building lots on the north shores of the Patapsco River, one of their number—the loftiest one, number nineteen—was acquired by the colonial-era legislative body, the Maryland Assembly, for the St. Paul's Episcopal Church. This shows how religion was woven into the city's fabric from the start.

Alas, that the government itself was establishing the church shows that Maryland had backslid from its earlier days of religious tolerance. Maryland was the only state founded by Catholics when it received a charter in 1632—by design, a refuge for Catholics fleeing persecution in Europe. In 1649, the Maryland Toleration Act became law, further cementing the freedom of Catholics to assemble and worship. (Okay, the act was only *so* tolerant—failure to proclaim the divinity of Jesus was punishable by death.) Forty years on, echoing the devolving religious atmosphere in Britain, where the Catholic monarchy was deposed, Maryland was swept by a Protestant Revolution ushering in laws banning Catholics from practicing their faith or holding

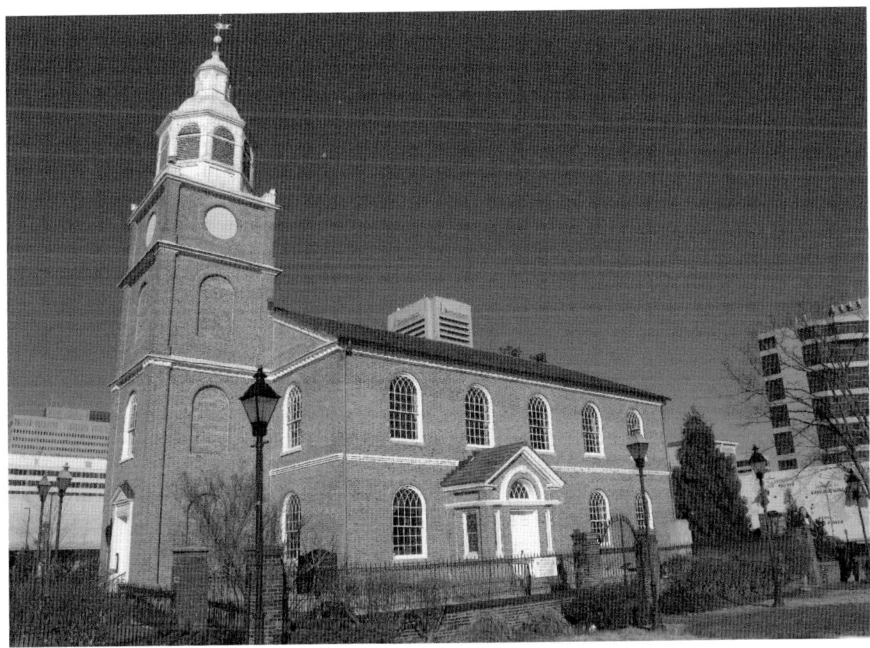

Built in 1785, Old Otterbein United Methodist Church is Baltimore's oldest still-active church. *Courtesy of Brennen Jensen.*

political office. And so, a city that would become home to the nation's first Catholic bishop, diocese and cathedral began as a solidly Protestant affair.

Brick structured St. Paul's Church was completed in 1739 (and replaced with the first of a series of larger edifices just fifty years later). Other denominations began appearing in tiny Baltimore Town. German Lutherans arrived in the 1750s, and Presbyterians were meeting in a log house by 1763. That same year saw Solomon Gabriel become the city's first Jewish resident, although it was an inauspicious start for a faith to play a major role in civic life: Gabriel was a British convict transported to America for a period of servitude from which he escaped after a year. Jewish merchants and traders began to trickle in during the ensuing decades, some of whom fought in the Revolutionary War, but it was well into the next century before there were sufficient numbers to truly plant their flag.

Quakers, or members of the Society of Friends, have been in Maryland since at least the 1670s. Their first Baltimore-area meetinghouse was erected north of town on the Harford Turnpike in 1713. While the building is gone, the site (off today's Harford Road near Clifton Park) is home to the city's oldest graveyard. What's now known as the Old Town

Meetinghouse was built in 1781, and the two-story brick building is the city's oldest religious building. Befitting a faith lacking conventional worship or clergy, the Quakers didn't leave behind grand buildings—meetinghouses are modest affairs—but the faith's progressive positions on social issues and promotion of philanthropy have had an outsized impact on Baltimore relative to the more popular mainline faiths. Johns Hopkins, Moses Sheppard and Elisha Tyson were just some of the philanthropists guided by this forward-thinking faith.

Meanwhile, the first Catholics began arriving, Irish as well as Acadians. The latter were descendants of the French settlers of maritime Canada expelled by the British between 1755 and 1764. (The Acadians ultimately ended up in Louisiana as what we now call Cajuns.) While religious freedom wasn't formally codified until the First Amendment of the Constitution in 1791, laws against Catholic worship were laxly enforced, as Catholic Baltimoreans had erected a simple brick church called St. Peters by 1770. Its priest was John Carroll, cousin of Maryland-born Founding Father Charles Carroll of Carrollton. He became the nation's first bishop in 1790, when all thirteen states constituted the diocese. In 1806, he laid the cornerstone of the nation's first cathedral, the Basilica of the Assumption. Carroll, who also founded Georgetown University, died an archbishop six years before the cathedral was consecrated in 1821.

Methodism began in 1730s England after John Wesley founded a breakaway movement within the Church of England dedicated to a more earnest and methodical approach to religious practice. It soon crossed the pond to these shores, with the first Methodist sermon in Baltimore delivered outside a blacksmith shop in 1765. Nine years later, Baltimore's first Methodist meetinghouse was erected on Lovely Lane (a street long since wiped out by downtown development). Here, in 1784, the church was formally organized in the United States with Francis Asbury—Wesley's chosen American emissary—as its first bishop. The church moved to a series of ever-larger church buildings until the 1884 debut of its stone edifice at St. Paul and 22nd Streets, called Lovely Lane United Methodist Church in honor of its birthplace.

Another religious splinter group that can be said to have formalized here is Unitarianism, an offshoot of the Congregationalist Church. In addition to other breaks from traditional Christianity, this group's adherents view god as a singular entity rather than a trinity—father, son and the Holy Spirit. The movement migrated southward from New England, and Unitarians were meeting privately here by 1816. Within two years, Baltimore adherents erected the nation's first Unitarian church. Designed by Maximilian M. Godefroy, it stands a block north of the Basilica. In 1819, William Ellery Channing delivered what's come to be known as "The Baltimore Sermon" outlining the faith's positions and formally embracing the name "Unitarianism."

Reverend Martin Luther King called Sunday mornings the most segregated time in America, and this state of affairs dates in large part to our nation's earliest days, when Black citizens were increasingly disenfranchised by White-dominated congregations. Some Black Methodists in early Baltimore, upset by their church's lax approach to abolition and a lack of Black clergy, began holding private prayer meetings in a cellar. By 1787, the Colored Methodist Society had been founded; ten years later, calling itself the Bethel Free African Church, it separated from Lovely Lane to erect a church on Sharp Street in 1802. One of the church's deacons, Daniel Coker, formerly an enslaved farmhand in Frederick County, broke with Sharp Street in 1811 and founded the African Methodist Bethel Church, which later became Bethel African Methodist Episcopal Church. Both institutions remain pillars of the African American community.

By the early nineteenth century, Jewish immigration was on the uptick. German-speaking Jews dominated until the 1880s, when surges of Poles and Russians arrived, fleeing eastern European pogroms. Authors Eric L. Goldstein and Deborah Weiner, in their history of the Jews of Baltimore, *On Middle Ground*, wrote that the dramas of immigration, acculturation and assimilation the city's Jews experienced were a microcosm of the American Jewish experience. Like Catholics before them, Jews had to contend with faith-based laws of disenfranchisement. A pair of prominent Jewish Baltimoreans, Solomon Etting and Jacob Cohen, helped pass the so-called Jew Bill in 1826 ending a requirement that Maryland elected officials take Christian oaths to hold office. (Both were elected to the city council that same year as the state's first Jews to hold elected office.)

The Baltimore Hebrew Congregation formed in 1830, meeting in rented space above a Fell's Point grocery store. Ten years later, it hired Bavarian-born Rabbi Abraham Rice and became the nation's first congregation led by an ordained rabbi. But earlier, in 1832, disagreements with what might be described as an old-school approach to Judaism led some congregants to form the splinter Har Sinai congregation, pioneering Reform Judaism on these shores with printed Bibles and, later, organ music during services. Maryland's first synagogue arrived in 1845 when the Baltimore Hebrew Congregation completed the Lloyd Street Synagogue in East Baltimore, now the third oldest in the country.

A good number of the newly arriving Jews entered the lower rungs of the economy as peddlers or small-scale dry goods merchants. A few—including Moses Hutzler, Max Hochschild, Samuel Hecht and Joel Gutman—would become household names by the twentieth century after their namesake department stores and chains came to dominate regional retailing. Jews also found success in the city's growing needle trades, especially in the burgeoning field of ready-to-wear clothing. German Jewish immigrant Henry Sonneborn arrived here penniless in 1849 and ultimately erected the world's largest menswear factory in 1905. In the late nineteenth century, East Lombard Street north of Little Italy became the center of Baltimore's Jewish commercial and community life; little remains of that commercial corridor—later dubbed "Corned Beef Row"—other than a few delis, including Attman's, stubbornly rooted there since 1915.

Prosperity did not bring Jews full access to Baltimore society, as many clubs, institutions and private schools closed ranks against them. Unwritten "gentlemen's agreements" (instead of the deed specifications that barred Black citizens) also kept many of the city's tonier neighborhoods, such as Guilford and Roland Park, "restricted." This term was openly used to denote that only White Christians were welcome. As late as the 1950s, at least one Baltimore swim club sported a "Gentiles Only" sign. By the second half of the last century, accumulating Jewish wealth begot general civic philanthropy, and names such as Meyerhoff, Krieger and Blaustein began to appear on buildings and institutions.

While the city does not have a sizable Islamic community, Muslims began organized worship here in the 1940s. The city's first designated mosque, Masjid ul-Haqq, opened in 1958, and Malcolm X came to the city to help with fundraising.

Finally, from tales of faith to no faith at all. In 1960, atheist activist Madalyn Murray filed a lawsuit against the Baltimore City public school system challenging its policy of beginning each school day with mandatory Bible readings. Murray, then a resident of the Northwood neighborhood, said that her son William J. Murray III was bullied for his desire not to participate. Madalyn Murray, later known by her married name Madalyn Murray O'Hair, didn't live in town long, and her case was consolidated with a similar one in Pennsylvania when it went before the Supreme Court in 1963. The high court decided, 8-1, that mandating religious practices in public schools violated the establishment clause and was unconstitutional. O'Hair went on to found American Atheists, an organization that continues to advocate for the rights of nonbelievers, while her son William later became an ordained Baptist minister and Christian activist.

YOUR GUIDE TO HISTORY

Jewish Museum of Maryland
15 and 27 Lloyd Street • Inner Harbor
(410) 732-6400 • www.jewishmuseummd.org • Admission Fee

This institution was founded in 1960 as the Jewish Historical Society of Maryland, with the purpose of rescuing the historic Lloyd Street Synagogue, which it acquired in 1962. The museum now incorporates both the Lloyd Street building and, two doors south, the B'nai Israel Synagogue, originally the home of the Chizuk Amuno congregation. Located in a modern structure between the old synagogues, the museum's display space offers an outstanding series of exhibits highlighting many aspects of Jewish life in Maryland and, more broadly, of Jewish contributions to American culture, business and society. Past and current exhibits have examined Jewish religious, social and military history and the Jewish role in various industries and occupations, from scrap metal and department stores to comic books and space exploration. The museum also features a gift shop and educational programs for both children and adults.

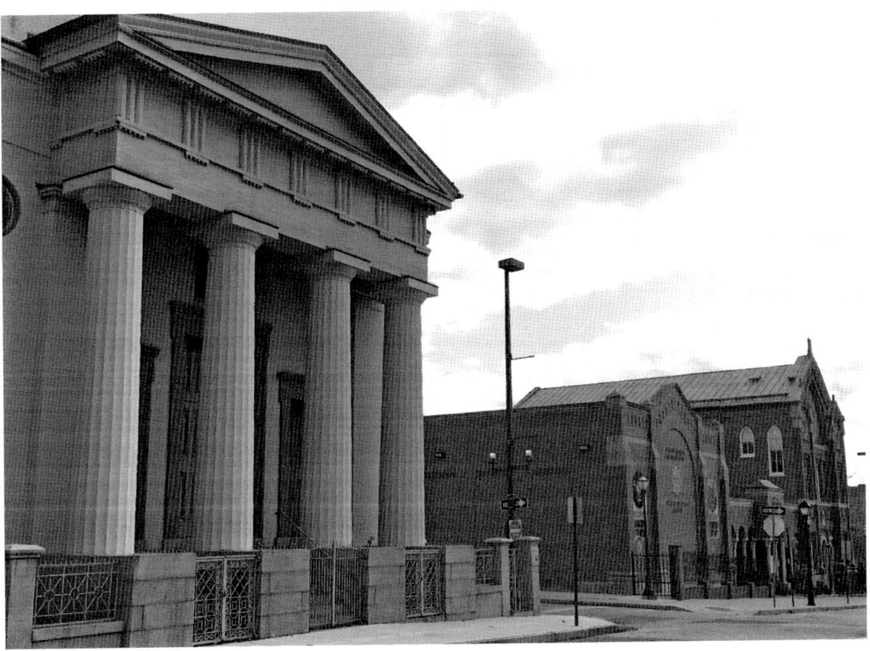

The 1845 Lloyd Street Synagogue, with the Jewish Museum of Maryland in the background. *Courtesy of Tom Chalkley.*

The Lloyd Street Synagogue, located at the corner of Lloyd and Watson Streets, is the oldest synagogue in Maryland and the third oldest in the United States. It was designed in 1845 by the prolific local architect Robert Cary Long Jr. The façade, a faithful reproduction of classic Greek temple architecture, is attached to a relatively simple brick sanctuary building. The stained-glass window at the far end of the sanctuary, featuring the Star of David, is said to be the first such window in America. In contrast to the stern-looking Lloyd Street building, the synagogue at 27 Lloyd Street was built in 1876 in an eclectic style that includes Middle Eastern decorative elements, alluding to the biblical origins of Judaism. Although attached to the museum, it is an active house of worship, home of the B'nai Israel congregation. The museum offers tours of both synagogues.

Old Otterbein United Methodist Church
112 West Conway Street • Inner Harbor
(410) 685-4703 • www.oldotterbeinumc.org

Baltimore's oldest still-active church was built in 1785, purportedly out of ballast bricks from visiting sailing ships. The beige behemoth of the Baltimore Convention Center almost swallows it up today, but the Georgian-style church, with its handsome tower housing bells cast in Bremen, Germany, holds its own. Its historic charms are enjoyed by summertime streams of Orioles fans heading to the ballpark a block west. The founding German Evangelical Reformed Church formed in 1771 and purchased land for its building from John Eager Howard. Its first and namesake pastor, German-born Philip William Otterbein, served until his death in 1813, when he was buried in the churchyard. He helped found the United Brethren in Christ in 1800, the country's first homegrown denomination (later merged with the United Methodist Church). The site also includes an 1811 parsonage and 1827 school building.

The Basilica of the Assumption
Cathedral and Mulberry Streets • Downtown
(410) 727-3565 • www.americasfirstcathedral.org

This Neoclassical masterwork, erected between 1806 and 1821, is the mother church of American Catholicism and the nation's first cathedral. Designed

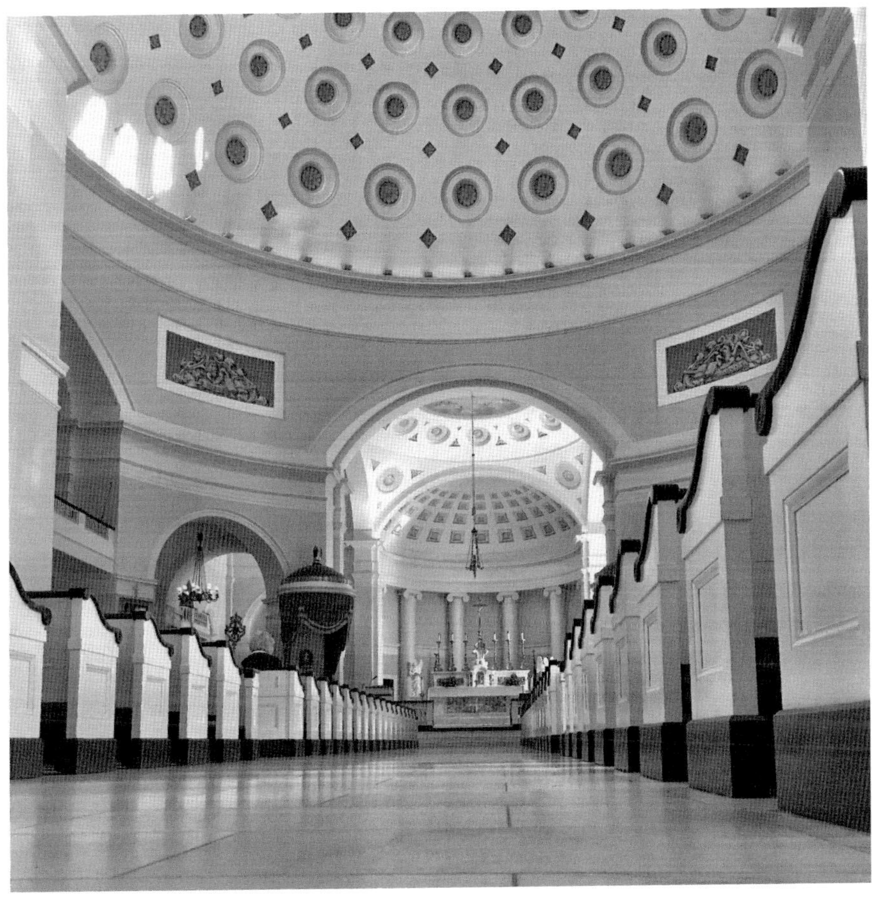

The Baltimore Basilica, America's first cathedral. *Courtesy of Brennen Jensen.*

by Benjamin Latrobe, architect for the U.S. Capitol, it's been hailed as no less than "Baltimore's greatest work of architecture" by critics John Dorsey and James Dilts in their *A Guide to Baltimore Architecture*. Its looming portico of Ionic columns, gray granite walls and twin towers topped with flattened onion domes are imposing and somewhat unecclesiastical, and they don't prepare you for the bright, airy interior lacking the brooding gloom of many European cathedrals. A $32 million restoration completed in 2006 helped banish the shadows by replacing 1940s stained-glass windows with original clear glass and reopening shuttered skylights. This allows the pastel color scheme—dominated by an ethereal hue that seems to fluctuate between peach, orange and yellow depending on viewpoint and time of day—to shine. Latrobe's soaring masonry dome incorporates twenty-four discreet windows whose indirect light gives it a mysterious glow. Underneath it all are the open-to-the-public crypt and undercroft, where numerous arches, inverted arches and barrel-vaulted ceilings present a masterclass in brickwork. Also uncovered and restored during the renovations was some darkness: a slender gallery tucked above the entrance where slaves, free Blacks and indentured servants sat before the Civil War.

The Greek Revival Archbishop's Residence (408 North Charles Street), built in 1829, connects with the rear of the cathedral. It was covered with a cement veneer in the 1950s designed to mimic the cathedral's limestone façade.

St. Paul's Protestant Episcopal Church
233 North Charles Street • Downtown
(443) 682-9587 • www.stpaulsbaltimore.org

St. Paul's Protestant Episcopal Church is known as Old St. Paul's and rightfully so. The congregation was founded in 1692, predating Baltimore itself. However, its brick Italian Romanesque church, designed by prominent architect Richard Upjohn, dates only to 1854. It's the fourth St. Paul's on this site—the only parcel from Baltimore's 1729 founding still in the same hands. Its immediate predecessor burned.

Zion Lutheran Church
400 East Lexington Street • Downtown
(410) 727-3939 • www.zionbaltimore.org

Baltimore Town was but six years old when German Lutherans united to form a congregation in 1755, and the resulting church has been a center of the German American community ever since. To this day, Zion holds Sunday services in both English and German. The brick neo-Gothic sanctuary dates to 1808, while the Hanseatic-styled parish house, parsonage and tower were built between 1912 and 1913. Some of the stained-glass windows honor famous German Americans or their accomplishments in Baltimore, including the Knabe Piano works, Ottmar Mergenthaler's linotype machine and artist Hans Schuler. Zion's walled garden and cloister provide a lovely retreat from the commotion of the urban environs and feature a symbolic Schuler carving of a German eagle within an American eagle. The church's sour beef dinner is a popular annual event.

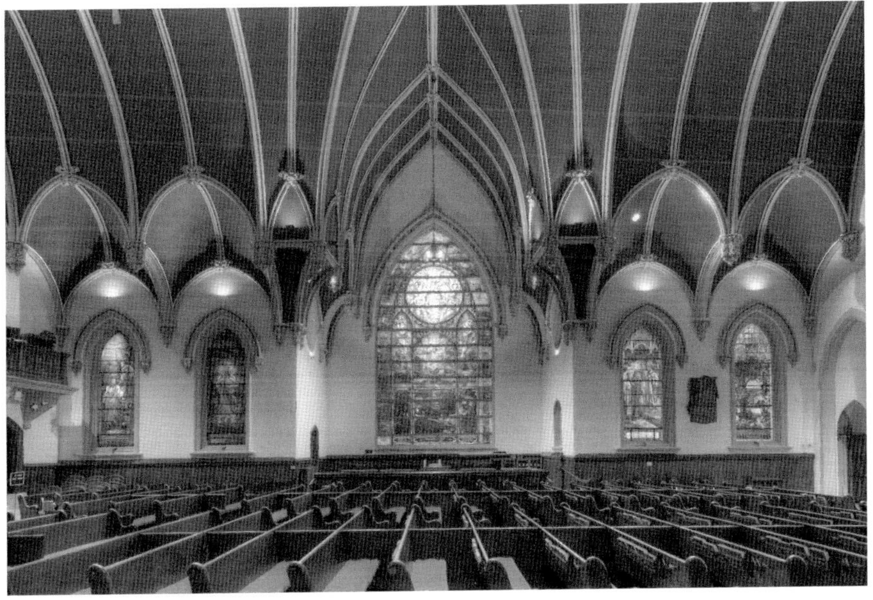

Numerous Tiffany glass windows adorn Brown Memorial Park Avenue Presbyterian Church. *Courtesy of Brian Kutner.*

Brown Memorial Park Avenue Presbyterian Church
1316 Park Avenue • Midtown
(410) 523-1542 • www.browndowntown.org

This Gothic Revival church of local limestone was completed in 1870 as a memorial to George Brown, son of storied investment banker Alexander Brown. It is known for its stunning interior featuring a twilight-blue vaulted ceiling and seventeen stained-glass windows, eleven by the renowned Tiffany Studios at the peak of its artistic power. The windows were installed between 1905 and 1910 and, along with the rest of the interior, underwent a $1.8 million restoration in 2003.

Eutaw Street Temple
1307 Eutaw Place • Midtown
(410) 669-4966 • www.mwphglmd.org

This imposing Byzantine-style structure, built in 1893, was the second home of Baltimore's Oheb Shalom ("Lover of Peace") Jewish congregation.

Its three rust-colored domes are visible from many directions. The Oheb Shalom congregation was founded in 1853 by German Jewish immigrants who did not feel at home with either the more orthodox Baltimore Hebrew Congregation, founded in 1830, or the "radical" Reform temple, Har Sinai, founded in 1842. The building now belongs to the Prince Hall Masons, an African American branch of the Masons fraternal organization, but its Jewish legacy is carved on the façade in the form of the Star of David and a pair of Hebrew-inscribed tablets. The arched shape of the tablets is echoed by ranks of arched windows and openings in the rough stone façade. In 1960, the Oheb Shalom congregation moved to its present-day location at 7310 Park Heights Avenue (claimed, incidentally, to be the highest point of land in Baltimore City). The old temple's tablet motif lives on in German master-modernist architect Walter Gropius's design of the newer building: the four tall tablet shapes visible from the road continue as vaulted spaces crossing the sanctuary within.

First and Franklin Presbyterian Church
210 West Madison Street • Midtown
(410) 728-5545 • www.firstfranklin.org

Gothic architecture—with towers, spires and pointed arches that seem to reach toward heaven—has long been favored for American churches. On the exterior, this Mount Vernon church, built between 1855 and 1875, looks like a straightforward urban adaptation of the medieval Gothic vocabulary. The 273-foot spire is the tallest church tower in the city. Inside, architect Norris Starkweather stuck to Gothic forms but took the style's gravity-defying spatial effects even further, dramatically widening the large sanctuary by eliminating the customary side pillars and replacing them with dangling ornaments called pendants. The elaborate plaster ceiling is composed of ribbed vaults that balloon upward like the undersides of parachutes. The secret of this airy space is hidden above the plaster: solid cast-iron trusses manufactured by the Patapsco Bridge and Iron Works in Canton. A $1.5 million renovation of the interior was completed in 2010. The slender spire, purely Gothic on the outside, has an interior of iron I-beams and brick. The building belongs to the oldest Presbyterian congregation in the city, founded in 1761. Its first minister, Reverend Patrick Allison, served as chaplain to the Continental Congress and was a confidant of George Washington. In 1973, the First Presbyterian

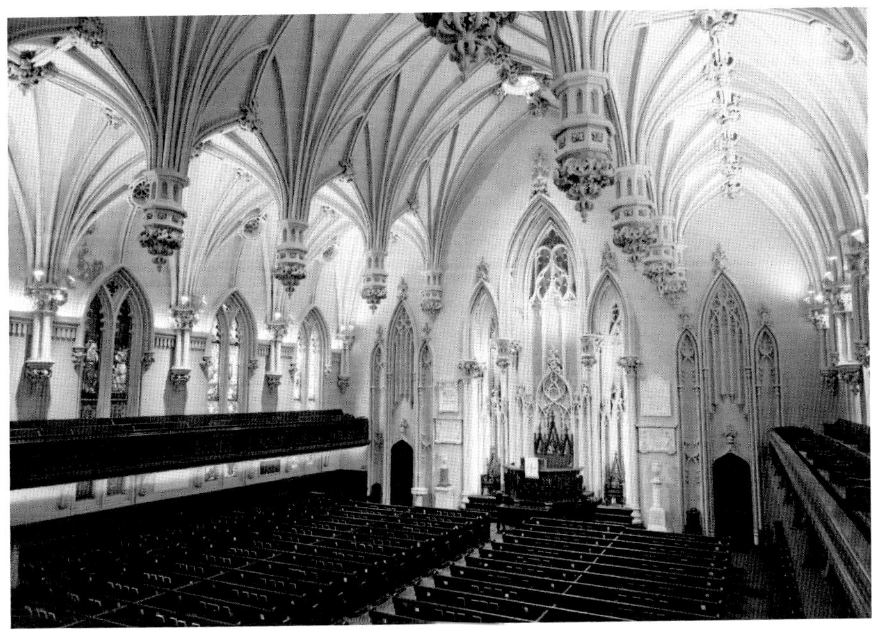

The First and Franklin Presbyterian Church and its gravity-defying Gothic interior. *Courtesy of Library of Congress.*

congregation merged with that of the nearby Franklin Street Presbyterian Church, hence the "First and Franklin" name.

First Unitarian Church
10 West Franklin Street • Midtown
(410) 685-2330 • www.firstunitarian.net

For non-Unitarians, this handsome domed building completed in 1818 is most notable for its simple but elegant Neoclassical architecture. Designed by Maximilian Godefroy (who also designed the Battle Monument), its exterior walls are faced with plain white stucco. The entrance on Franklin Street features three graceful arches and, above, a terra-cotta sculpture of "the angel of truth." This was the first church built for the Unitarian Church in America. A sermon given here in 1819 by the Boston-based preacher William Ellery Channing is regarded as one of the founding documents of the American Unitarian movement. Channing's speech stressed the values of freedom, reason and tolerance. The Franklin Street church, true to its roots, has served as a platform for progressive ideas and actions, both spiritual and secular, ever since.

Mount Vernon Place United Methodist Church
10 East Mount Vernon Place • Midtown
https://mvp-umc.org

To many passersby, this striking latter-day Gothic building is known simply as "the green church" for its naturally greenish walls of serpentine metabasalt mined in Baltimore County. The elaborate trim and medieval ornamentation, by contrast, are composed of reddish sandstone. Inside, unlike a traditional Gothic church, it has strikingly plain, pale walls setting off dark wooden balconies, slim cast-iron columns and wrought-iron ornamentation. The church was built in 1872. Previously, this prime location had been occupied by the home of Charles Howard and Elizabeth Phoebe Key Howard. Both wife and husband were the offspring of local heroes: her father was lawyer Francis Scott Key, author of the national anthem, and his father was John Eager Howard, a former governor of Maryland who served for eight years in the Revolutionary War. A bronze plaque on the side of the church notes that Key, the anthem writer, died on the site of the church.

Like many mainstream Protestant churches in Baltimore, this historic house of worship has lost most of its worshipers. In 2020, a New Jersey developer expressed interest in buying the church, raising concerns in the community.

Orchard Street United Methodist Church
512 Orchard Street • Midtown
(410) 523-8150 • www.gbul.org

This handsome brick church is the oldest existent building built for and by Black Baltimoreans. Erected in 1837 and subject to subsequent expansions through 1882, the façade presents a mix of revival styles. Its origins date to 1825 and a formerly enslaved West Indian Black man named Truman Le Pratt, who began holding services in his Orchard Street home. Over the years, many prominent citizens worshiped within, including Harry S. Cummings, elected as the first Black city councilperson in 1890. Teddy Roosevelt spoke at the church in 1912. The congregation relocated in the early 1970s, and the church entered a protracted period of abandonment and decay. Fortunately, the Baltimore Urban League, a social service organization, made it its headquarters in 1992, undertaking sweeping and ongoing renovations.

St. Mary's Seminary Chapel and Mother Seton House
600 North Paca Street • Midtown
(410) 728-6464 • www.stmaryspacast.org

In 1791, priests of the Roman Catholic Sulpician order established a French-speaking church and seminary to serve the west-side immigrant community called Frenchtown, today's Seton Hill. The Sulpician priests hired the French-born architect Maximilian Godefroy (like them an exile from turmoil in France) to design their two-story double chapel, with its second floor reserved for priestly trainees and its downstairs open to the local congregation. Godefroy later won fame as the creator of Baltimore's Battle Monument. The chapel has a delicately detailed Gothic façade and is said to be the oldest neo-Gothic building in America.

The same year that the chapel was dedicated, a formerly wealthy widow came with her two daughters to stay at a house nearby on Seminary property. This was Elizabeth Ann Seton, a convert to Catholicism who, after her husband's death, had tried to support herself by running a small school for young women in New York City. The Sulpicians of Baltimore invited her to found a school for young Catholic women. She lived in the house at 600 Paca Street, now known as Mother Seton House, for just a year before relocating to Emmitsburg, Maryland. There, with a donation of $8,000 from a wealthy seminarian, she founded St. Joseph's Academy, a Catholic girls' school, and started a community of religious sisters devoted to helping the poor. She died in Emmitsburg in 1821. In 1975, Pope Paul VI canonized her, making her the first American-born Catholic saint. Mother Seton House, built around 1805, is a well-restored example of the two-and-a-half-story Federal houses that could be found all over the city at the beginning of the nineteenth century. The St. Mary's Seminary Chapel is now known as the St. Mary's Spiritual Center. Tours are available at no charge, but visitors should call ahead.

Lovely Lane United Methodist Church
2200 St. Paul Street • North
(410) 889-1512 • Museum, (410) 889-4458 • www.lovelylane.net

Topped by a distinctive conical roof, the 186-foot bell tower of Lovely Lane Methodist is the most visible landmark in the north-central neighborhoods that lie between North Avenue and 25th Street. The Lovely Lane

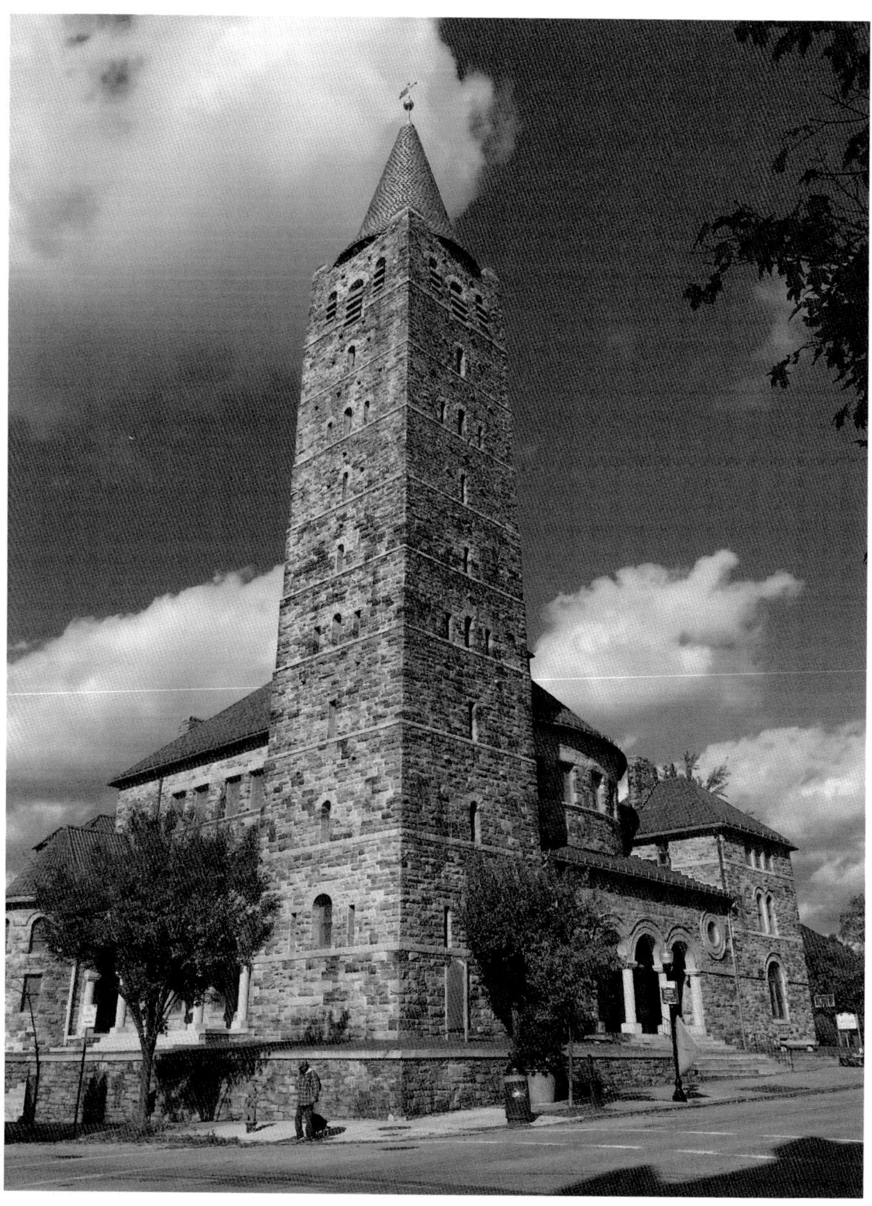

Lovely Lane United Methodist Church. *Courtesy of Tom Chalkley.*

congregation traces its origins to the first Methodist Episcopal church in America, founded in 1784 in a meetinghouse near today's Redwood Street; hence the church's curious name and its claim to be the "Mother Church of American Methodism." The building was opened for worship in 1887. It was designed by Stanford White, star of the famous firm McKim, Mead and White, as an extension of the adjoining original campus of Goucher College (since relocated to the suburbs), which White also had a hand in. Like the former campus buildings, the church is built of rough-faced stone. White, invoking early Christian history as well as the Methodist taste for simplicity, borrowed ideas from the solidly built Romanesque churches of Italy, with a dramatic oval sanctuary, round exterior arches and fortress-like walls. The domed sanctuary ceiling is decorated with a beautifully restored painting of the night sky, with a ring of clouds parting to show the stars and planets as they appeared on the date of the church's dedication. The church features a museum, and tours of the building are available.

Old Town Meetinghouse

Fayette Street at Aisquith Street • East • Exterior Only
(410) 276-5519 • www.mckimcenter.org

This simple brick structure, dating to 1781, is the oldest religious building in Baltimore. It was once the home of Baltimore's small but highly influential Religious Society of Friends, better known as Quakers. Quaker meetinghouses, then as now, are deliberately simple in design so that worshipers are not distracted from their practice of silent meditation. A curious feature of this building is the huge moveable wood-paneled partition that was used to separate male from female worshipers—again, to avoid distraction. Johns Hopkins worshiped here, even after he was "read out" of the Friends' meeting for merchandising alcohol. In later years, the city's Quakers split into two factions that went separate ways. The Aisquith Street congregation withered away in the 1820s, leaving the old meetinghouse and its graveyard behind. Most of the buried Quakers were relocated to a small cemetery on the 2700 block of Harford Road, but at least one casket, that of the Quaker philanthropist Elisha Tyson, was reinterred at Green Mount Cemetery. The Old Town Meetinghouse now belongs to the City of Baltimore and is administered by the nearby (and also historic) McKim Community Center.

St. Vincent de Paul Church
120 North Front Street • East
(410) 962-5078 • www.stvchurch.org

Built in 1841, this Roman Catholic church has served a variety of congregations and has undergone several thorough remodelings to adapt to changing times and tastes. The core church building is of white-painted brick with a three-tiered, 150-foot spire that overlooks the bottom end of the Jones Falls Expressway at East Fayette Street. The original interior included a balcony—still in place—that was intended for people enslaved by White congregants. After the Civil War, the simple Neoclassical sanctuary was ornately made-over to Victorian tastes, then "re-simplified" in 1941 and then reconfigured again in the 1990s to go along with the congregation's increasingly progressive and anti-hierarchical ethos. At one point in the decades around 1900, this church was almost entirely peopled by Italian immigrants. Today, it draws a citywide congregation of Catholics who have a tradition of social activism.

Bethel AME Church
1300 Druid Hill Avenue • West
(410) 523-4273 • bethel1.org

This large, socially active church began with a split in the Sharp Street Methodist Church. Daniel Coker—an antislavery activist, educator and ordained Methodist Episcopal deacon—had joined the congregation in 1801 and in 1807 started a school for Black children attached to the Sharp Street meetinghouse. Four years later, frustrated with the Methodist Episcopal hierarchy's insistence on putting White clergy in charge of Black congregations—including Sharp Street—Coker and his followers formed the African Methodist Bethel Church, with Coker as its first minister. In 1815, Coker's group moved to a building on Fish Street (now Saratoga Street) near Gay Street, where it remained for the next ninety-four years. In 1816, at a conference in Philadelphia, Coker joined with other like-minded Black pastors and lay leaders in founding the African Methodist Episcopal (AME) denomination, a new movement entirely separate from the White-led Methodist Episcopal Church. The Baltimore flock took on the name of Bethel AME Church. But Coker, who had become a supporter of the movement to "return" Black Americans to Africa, immigrated to Sierra

Leone as a missionary in 1820, accompanied by eighty-five other Black Americans, the first of such colonists to settle in what would become Liberia.

After Coker's time, Bethel AME grew to become one of the leading African American churches in the city. The congregation moved to its present location in 1910. Its pastors took leading roles in the civil rights movement of the 1950s and '60s, as well as in the anti-apartheid campaigns of the 1980s.

Hebrew Orphan Asylum

2700 Rayner Avenue • West • Exterior Only

Sporting ornate turrets and crenellations and perched assertively on a hilltop overlooking the Rosemont neighborhood, the red brick edifice looks like a fortress. But this hunk of Romanesque Victoriana has carved lettering reading "Hebrew Orphans Asylum" and is the oldest purpose-built Jewish orphanage in the country. It was erected in 1875 by the Hebrew Benevolent Society. At its peak, some 150 Jewish youngsters dwelled within. Not all were orphans in the strictest sense, as many were "half" orphans—placed there by either a mother or father who was having difficulty caring for them. The young charges actually had it pretty good by the standards of the day: along with schooling, they enjoyed modern conveniences that many in the city lacked, such as indoor plumbing and central heating. The orphanage downsized to a new facility in 1923, and the faux fort was incorporated into a hospital complex before falling into vacancy in the late 1980s. Decades of decay ensued until pretty much all that was left was the dramatic outer walls. Fortunately, these have been preserved, and a new community health center was created within them.

Sharp Street Memorial United Methodist Church

1206 Etting Street • West

(410) 523-7200 • www.sharpstreet.org

Baltimore's oldest Black congregation, dating to 1787, is named for the address where its first church was built in 1801. The original Sharp Street church took a leading role in the antislavery movement. As a young man, still enslaved, Frederick Douglass sang in its choir and found affirmation in his quest for freedom. In 1867, the church helped found (and was the first home of) the Centenary Biblical Institute, the forerunner of today's Morgan State University. The present-day Gothic Revival sanctuary, built in 1898, was the spiritual home of civil rights leader Lillie Carroll Jackson, who is said to have grown comfortable in front of crowds by singing in the choir on Sundays. During Jackson's decades-long term as president of Baltimore's chapter of the NAACP, the church became a center for civil rights organizing. Supreme Court justice Thurgood Marshall also worshiped here as a young man.

Chapter 5
SMOKESTACKS AND LOCOMOTIVES

BALTIMORE MADE THE RAILROAD...AND VICE VERSA

From the 1840s to the 1960s, Baltimore's economy stood solidly on three pillars: shipping, manufacturing and railroads. In the 1970s and '80s, thanks in large part to globalization, that solid base crumbled, displacing thousands of workers and undercutting the city's tax revenue. The city's post-industrial economy—dominated by healthcare, education and services—has changed the face of the city. Vestiges of the old, working Baltimore are getting harder to find, but Baltimoreans are still fond of evoking the past worlds of sailing ships and smokestacks—if only in the names and décor of bars and condominium towers.

Tellingly for a city that loves its beer, a brewery was perhaps Baltimore's first manufacturer back in 1748. By the late 1700s, land-based manufacturing centers had sprung up along the city's three stream valleys of Gwynns Falls, Jones Falls and Herring Run. The first water-powered mills were flour mills, processing grain that poured in from local farms. Then, beginning in 1810 along Jones Falls, millers turned to cotton shipped in from southern states. New mills drove looms and other machines that produced a variety of textiles, most importantly the heavy-duty sailcloth known as cotton duck that made shipping possible. Shipbuilding and related maritime trades flourished in Fell's Point.

By the early 1800s, Baltimore was in heated competition with other port cities for both manufacturing and Atlantic trade. But as the nation expanded, the next direction cities looked for trade opportunities was the inland frontier. Goods needed to reach the growing Midwest, and that burgeoning region's commodities needed to reach eastern—if not global—markets.

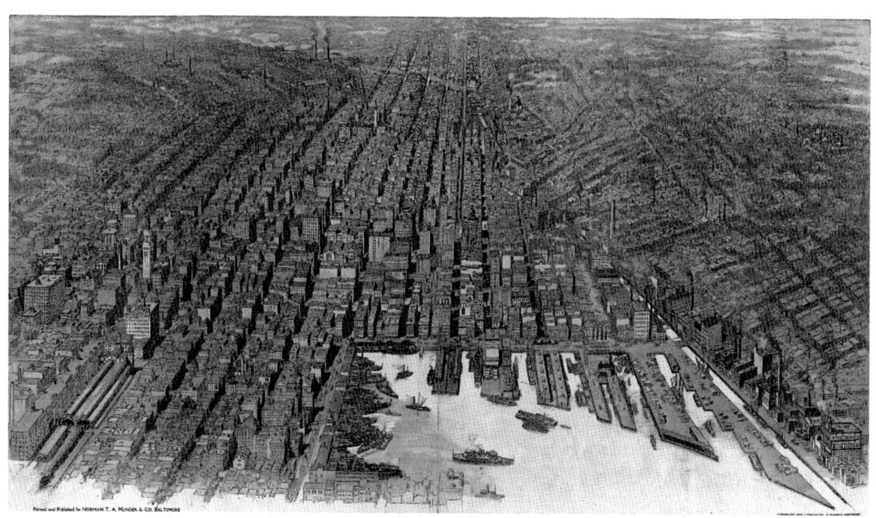

Smokestacks, ships and rail lines abound in this bird's-eye view of 1911 Baltimore. *Courtesy of Library of Congress.*

Baltimore enjoyed an early connection to the east–west National Road (begun in 1811), which gradually saw rutted, muddy trails paved with macadam. But moving bulk goods overland by wagon was slow and inefficient. The best inland transportation systems of the era involved water, and barring navigable rivers (such as New Orleans enjoyed at the mouth of the Mississippi) or lakes, that meant canals—purpose-dug waterways employing locks to deal with gradients and draft animals for propulsion. New York City got a huge boost in 1825 when, after eight years of construction, the 363-mile-long Erie Canal opened connecting the Hudson River near Albany with Lake Erie. Overnight, the city gained a water connection straight to the heart of the booming west. The following year, Pennsylvania began work on an ambitious canal and river project to connect Philadelphia with Pittsburgh. And by 1828, work was underway on the long-planned Chesapeake & Ohio Canal connecting Washington, D.C., to Cumberland, Maryland (and eventually beyond), along the Potomac River.

Baltimore boosters were terrified of being lapped by civic competitors and rendered irrelevant. (Or, as historian Sherry H. Olson put it, "Baltimoreans had visions of grass growing in the streets.") Lacking ready waterways to assist in its own canal scheme, Baltimore had to think outside the lock. The insightful duo of Philip Evan Thomas (one-time commissioner for the C&O Canal) and George Brown (Irish-born son of Baltimore banker Alexander Brown) looked across the Atlantic to England, where the steam locomotive was invented in 1797 and a public railroad running by 1825. The pair, in turn, convinced two dozen municipal movers and shakers (and investors) that the future of inland transportation involved railcars rather than canalboats. The Baltimore & Ohio Railroad (B&O) was chartered in 1828 with nonagenarian Declaration of Independence signer Charles Carroll of Carrollton turning over the first ceremonial spade of dirt.

They were right, of course. The C&O Canal—today a lovely bike trail—was largely a money-losing boondoggle after it opened in 1850. But it can't be overstated how bold the B&O was. The longest English railroad at this time stretched a mere twenty-five miles, was plagued with engineering problems (multiple deadly boiler explosions) and still relied on horses for stretches. To reach the Ohio River, Baltimore's pioneering railroad had to traverse more than three hundred miles of rugged terrain, including the Allegheny Mountains. The project invented modern railroading.

After the B&O broke ground, additional railroads sprouted immediately, notably the northbound Baltimore & Susquehanna Railroad in 1830 and the eastbound Baltimore & Port Deposit in 1832, both of which were later absorbed by larger and larger rail networks. Meanwhile, the nation's first chartered commercial railroad had horse-drawn wagons traversing thirteen miles of track to Ellicott Mills (today's Ellicott City) and back in 1830. The B&O's progress literally picked up steam after engineer/investor Peter Cooper demonstrated a tiny steam engine nicknamed "Tom Thumb" as the first American-built locomotive. Tracks reached Cumberland in 1842 and the Ohio River at today's Wheeling, West Virginia, less than a decade later. One new engineering marvel followed another in 1844 when Samuel Morse sent the Old Testament message "What hath god wrought?" via telegraph from the U.S. Capitol to the B&O's Mount Clare Station using thirty-eight miles of telegraph line strung alongside the rail line.

The railroad saved the city's bacon—protecting trade and manufacturing prospects while changing them as well. Coal railed in from Appalachia helped usher in the steam age. Old mills retired their waterwheels, and industry was increasingly liberated from the stream valleys. (Coal also became another commodity for export.) Manufacturers, distributors, breweries, distilleries, canneries and warehouses surrounded the harbor at the nexus of rail yards and waterfront. The influx of raw materials by sea and rail gave rise to oil refineries, copper- and steelworks and chemical plants—all industries that employed thousands of workers and, to a great degree, defined the city at the peak of its industrial power. Before the globalization of the manufacturing economy, Baltimore boasted major factories that built cars,

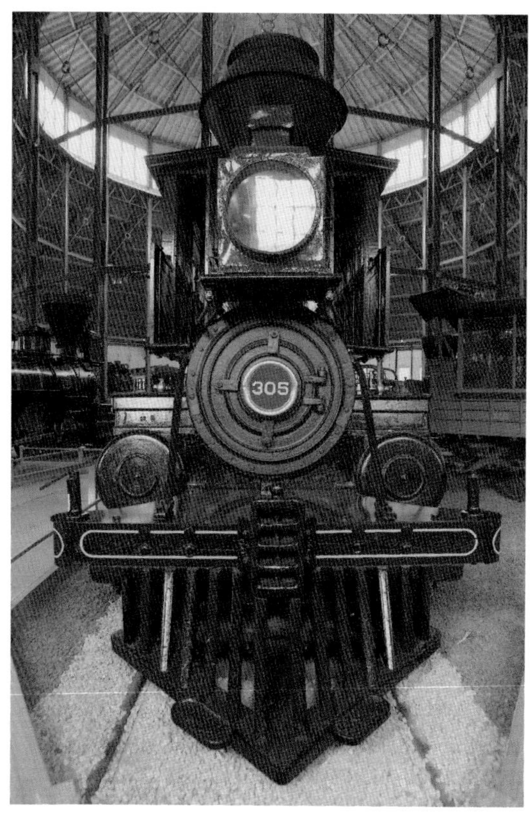

Early train at the B&O Railroad Museum. *Courtesy of Visit Baltimore.*

telephone equipment, pianos and scores of smaller plants that produced everything from toilets to patent medicine. The city's Canton neighborhood began in 1828 when the Canton Company bought some two thousand acres, essentially birthing the nation's first industrial park. (The city's shipbuilding history is discussed in Chapter 2.)

While big-shoulder, smoke-belching industries involving hot iron and towering cranes might symbolize the Industrial Revolution, from the Civil War until the 1920s, the needle trades—the manufacture of clothing, hats and shoes—constituted the city's largest industry, employing nearly one-third of the city's industrial workforce. Baltimore was second only to New York City in menswear production and so dominated in straw hats (which men wore in warmer months) that Straw Hat Day (May 15, when men switched their chapeaus) was tantamount to a civic holiday. The city's location played a big part in this success, as one-third or more of all stitched goods were sold to southern states. Canning was another industry taking advantage of the city's location—in this case the Chesapeake region's ready bounty of oysters and produce that turned the city into a global center of those industries. (The demand for preserved food burgeoned as the settlement of the West accelerated and as the Civil War banished thousands of men from the comforts of home cooking.) And there were more beery developments: the city's Crown Cork and Seal Company invented the modern bottle cap in 1892, making a fortune off the humble device. Willoughby McCormick probably didn't have a fortune in mind when he began peddling root beer extract door to door in Baltimore in 1889, but he birthed the Fortune 1000 McCormick & Company, now the world's largest spice maker. Until its operations entirely decamped to the city's suburbs in the 1980s, its massive Inner Harbor plant often made downtown smell of cinnamon.

Decades into the digital age, it is easy to overlook the Linotype machine German immigrant Ottmar Mergenthaler patented here in 1884, although it was probably the biggest boost to printing since Gutenberg's day. True to its name, Linotypes allowed typesetters to create whole lines of hot metal-cast type at once, ending the hand-setting of individual letters. Newspaper publication exploded nationwide after this time-saving device took off, and some of the contraptions were clattering away until the 1980s.

Baltimore's industrial might climaxed between 1940 and 1960, spurred by the demands of war and the postwar explosion of middle-class consumerism. Rail yards spilled across acres of land on both sides of the harbor channel. The city's population surged accordingly, peaking in 1960 just shy of 1 million. From the 1930s onward, the sheer scale of production forced major manufacturers to move down the harbor, to deeper waters and cheaper, less developed bottomlands on, and beyond, the boundary of Baltimore City. General Motors established a big Chevrolet plant in 1935, and Western Electric (the company that built all the equipment for the Bell Telephone monopoly) took over the grounds of a former amusement park in 1929. The biggest plant of all lay six miles southeast of the city line: Bethlehem Steel's facility at Sparrow's Point employed thirty thousand workers at its late 1950s peak, including thousands of city residents, Black and White. By the 1970s, this mammoth plant, like much of America's manufacturing economy, had fallen prey to international competition and its own complacent corporate management. The company failed to invest and innovate, while Japan, in particular, developed more efficient technologies. Unionized workers who had fought over two generations for safer jobs and better pay saw industrial jobs whisked away to union-free zones in the United States and overseas factories whose workers were paid poverty wages. At the same time, Baltimore's manufacturers began to be held accountable for the pollution they had discharged into water, seabed, soil and air. Citizens organized against incinerators, chemical plants and industrial dumps. Belching smokestacks, once icons of prosperity and progress, came to symbolize the degradation of the environment.

The 1970s and '80s are remembered as an era of deindustrialization, with a massive turnover of the city's real estate and its employment base. The mighty B&O, after nearly 160 years of operation, was absorbed into the Florida-based CSX Corporation in 1987. The industrial traditions of the Baltimore Harbor are preserved by such survivors as the Domino Sugars plant, the working wharves of Canton and the surviving "tank farms" of Curtis Bay. Under Armour is an example of a modern-day industry: the sports apparel giant has been headquartered in Baltimore since 1998, although its goods are largely manufactured overseas, mostly in Asia. Meanwhile, the vast acreage formerly occupied by GM's Broening Highway plant has been taken over by Amazon, which pays thousands of low-scale, nonunion workers to deliver things manufactured elsewhere.

Throughout the city, scores of former industrial buildings have been repurposed as residential blocks and retail complexes; many others have been subdivided and redesigned for such urban neo-industries as artisanal bakeries, craft breweries, small-batch coffee roasters, gyms and yoga studios. In the city's Station North Arts District, factories and warehouses have been occupied by artists since the end of the 1970s. For the old industrial communities of Hampden, Canton and Locust Point, an influx of "creatives" and professionals has been a harbinger of gentrification. At the same time, the inventors and innovators who occupy the old mills and warehouses are creating new jobs and attracting consumers to what could have been post-industrial dead zones. It remains to be seen whether the new urbanites can revitalize the old neighborhoods without displacing the old neighbors.

Baltimore's industrial past is celebrated at the Baltimore Museum of Industry, the B&O Railroad Museum, the Irish Railroad Workers Museum… and in one small blacksmith shop that has been open since 1810.

YOUR GUIDE TO HISTORY

Rye Whiskey Distilling

More than a century ago, Maryland was a major distilling state—third in booze production behind Kentucky and Pennsylvania. Rye whiskey was

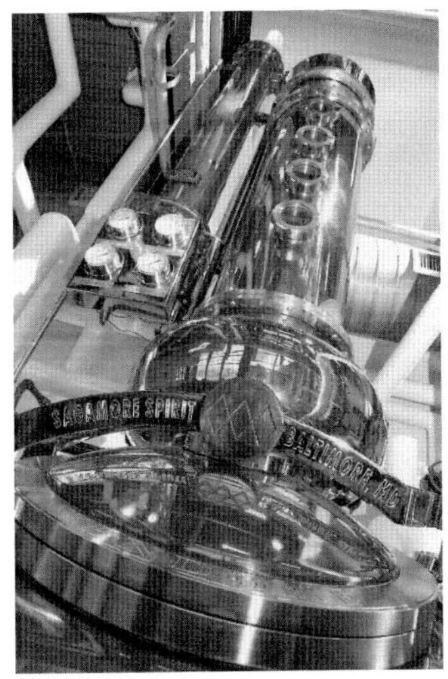

Once a distilling powerhouse, Baltimore is back to whiskey-making thanks to Sagamore Spirit Distillery and others. *Courtesy of Jim Burger.*

the most celebrated tipple, and Baltimore had scores of distilleries and bottlers turning out this flavorful whiskey (where rye is the principal grain used, as opposed to corn-based bourbon). Alas, local distillers struggled to recover after Prohibition, and the last Baltimore whiskey-maker closed shop in the 1970s. However, the craft distilling movement has rye barrels rolling again. Sagamore Spirit Distillery (301 East Cromwell Street • South) opened a capacious state-of-the-art facility with a forty-foot still in 2017. Tours and tastings are available, and its visitor center includes an interactive map highlighting the historic rye makers of yore. The more craft-scale Baltimore Spirits Company (1700 West 41st Street, no. 430 • North) was actually the first to bring Baltimore-made rye whiskey back when its award-winning Epoch Rye debuted in 2018. Visit its distillery and tasting room to also sample its Shot Tower Gin, named after the city's Phoenix Shot Tower.

Baltimore Museum of Industry
1415 Key Highway • Inner Harbor
(410) 727-4808 • www.thebmi.org • Admission Fee

Located in a former cannery on the south side of the harbor, this museum not only exhibits artifacts of Baltimore's industrial past, but it also re-creates entire Baltimore workplaces: permanent displays include a nineteenth-century oyster canning area, a garment-making shop, a machine shop and a print shop using century-old equipment. Other standing exhibits focus on local broadcast media and Baltimore-based petroleum companies. Rotating exhibits have focused on a very wide variety of related themes: work clothes, the art of sign painting, local banjo manufacturing and the world of small retail shops. Throughout, the museum strives to examine not just products and processes but also the lives of the people who did the work. The central exhibition gallery, with window-walls facing the harbor, is a popular site for social events, featuring colorful, beautifully designed displays relating to

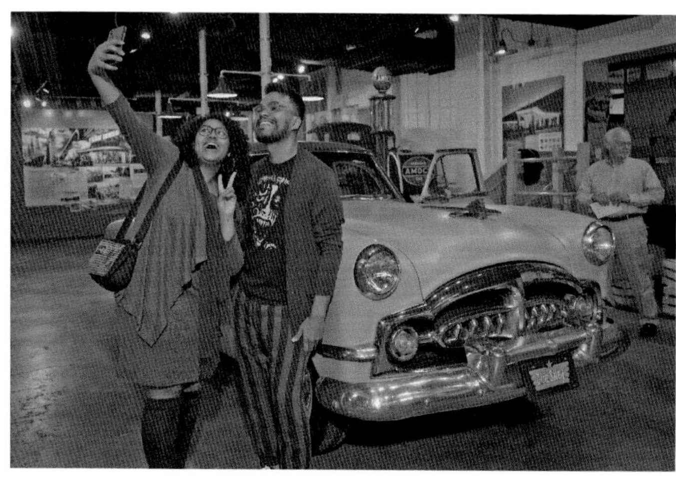

Selfie time at the Baltimore Museum of Industry. *Courtesy of Visit Baltimore.*

Maryland industrial firsts. The museum's five-acre waterfront campus boasts a one-hundred-foot-tall Clyde Ironworks whirley crane, once used to build Liberty and Victory ships at Bethlehem Steel's Fairfield shipyards, as well as numerous industrial objects.

G. Krug and Son Iron Works and Museum

415 West Saratoga Street • Downtown
(410) 752-3166 • www.gkrugandson.com • Admission Fee (group tours only)

This business identifies itself as "the oldest continuously operating blacksmith's shop in the United States." It is certainly one of the oldest continuously operating businesses of any kind in Baltimore. The original ironworking shop on this site was set up in 1810 by a German immigrant, Augustus Schwatka, who produced nails, hinges and other small fittings. In 1830, Schwatka sold the shop to a local ironworker, Andrew Merker. Gustav Krug, who emigrated from Germany in 1850, joined Merker's shop as an employee and later became a partner in the firm. The shop has been owned and operated by members of the Krug family for five generations.

The Krugs specialize in wrought iron, both functional and decorative, mostly for homes and historic institutions, including Johns Hopkins Hospital and Green Mount Cemetery. Two centuries of Krug products are visible along Baltimore streets, from grills and railings in Mount Vernon to gates and fences in Homeland and Guilford. A significant part of the firm's present-day work is the production of authentic replacements for original Krug-wrought products that have worn out after a century or more of constant use.

Proud of their shop's historic character, the owners offer tours Monday through Friday (call ahead to schedule). Part of their shop is set aside as a company museum that preserves historical documents and masterpieces of ironwork, such as their collection of delicate screens woven from thick black wires and rotini-like twists of metal. Tours of the workshop and museum are limited to groups of ten or more and must be arranged two weeks in advance.

The Loft Districts

Downtown

As the needle trades evolved, the industry moved from piecework done domestically to cramped sweatshops and, ultimately, to so-called Skyscraper Factories—looming loft buildings where thousands toiled turning bolts of fabric into ready-to-wear garments. Baltimore's needle trades coalesced around several blocks south of downtown beginning in the 1870s, now recognized by a pair of National Historic Districts: North Loft District (roughly the blocks around the intersection of South Paca Street and Cider Alley) and South Loft District (500 block of West Pratt). Of the nineteen former vertical factories here, the grandest is the looming nine-story Paca-Pratt building on the northeast corner of South Paca and West Pratt Streets built by Henry Sonneborn & Company in 1905. At its peak, this world's largest menswear factory housed an army of four thousand workers turning out three thousand suits per day. Most of the lofts have successfully been converted into residential and office use.

Old Shopping District

The blocks around the intersection of North Howard and West Lexington Streets • Downtown

Some of the goods the city turned out in its manufacturing heyday never left town. And retailing was an industry in itself. Alas, Baltimore's tatterdemalion downtown shopping district was done in decades ago by parking-encircled shopping malls (themselves now in decline). But Baltimoreans of a certain age fondly recall the homegrown department stores—Hutzler's, Hochschild Kohn's, Stewart's and others—whose grand flagships were anchors in a bustling sea of shoppers and trundling streetcars. A few small outlets keep the lights on along a once-busy corridor that presents an eclectic architectural mix, from ornate Victorian to Moderne.

German-born Moses Hutzler helped his son Abram open a dry goods store at the corner of Howard and Clay Streets in 1858. Business was good, as evidenced by the Romanesque "Palace Building" that replaced it in 1888 and the sleek adjacent Art Deco annex added in 1931. (Hutzler's Department Store closed in 1990, and the hulk buzzes now, not with shoppers but with internet traffic as a major web hub.) Across Howard Street from Hutzler's, the ivory Renaissance Revival building was home to Stewart's department store and is office space today. The four-story building on the southwest corner of Howard and West Lexington Streets was built as the flagship of the local Read's drugstore chain. In 1955, a group of Black college students staged a sit-in here to protest the chain's segregation policies. The event—five years before the more famous Woolworth's sit-in in Greensboro, North Carolina—got Read's to desegregate two days later. (However, Black residents weren't able to freely shop in the district's tonier stores until 1960.) Entertainment was part of the business mix here as well, and the terra-cotta ornamented structure at 115 North Howard (a sneaker store at last check) is actually one of the city's oldest surviving movie theaters, opened as the Pickwick nickelodeon back in 1908.

Mount Royal Station

1400 Mount Royal Avenue • Midtown
(410) 669-9200 • www.mica.edu/buildings/mt-royal-station

Mount Royal Station was built in 1896 and served the B&O's first electric-powered passenger line—a shrine to travel at its most civilized. It closed in the early 1960s, unable to compete with newer modes of travel. The nearby Maryland Institute College of Art bought the grand structure in 1964 and converted its lofty interior into two stories of studio and gallery space. The architects left the exterior of the building almost intact and preserved much of the interior's original craftsmanship. It's easy to see how the building appealed to the art school, not only because of its large, well-lit spaces but also because the building itself is a bold architectural statement. Its details evoke the Renaissance, but the exterior walls are solid, almost unadorned granite with wide, low-rise hipped roofs that are echoed by the long train sheds. This very horizontal structure is set off by its 150-foot clock tower. Since the 1980s, the station's bowl-like setting has served as an amphitheater for concerts at the city's annual Artscape festival. CSX freight trains still use the adjoining tracks, rattling MICA's metalwork and fabric arts studios.

Pennsylvania Station

1500 North Charles Street • Midtown

Baltimore's principal passenger rail station and only city-limits Amtrak stop dates to 1912. The granite and terra-cotta building in restrained Beaux-Arts style is the third station built on this site, beginning with a wooden structure opened in 1873. Originally known as Union Station, the name was changed in 1928 by its owner the Pennsylvania Railroad, by then the only railroad it served. Now owned by Amtrak, it is among the top-ten busiest rail stations in the country. An interior, balcony-wrapped atrium is topped with a stunning leaded-glass skylight that was blacked out during World War II and largely forgotten about until it was uncovered in the 1980s. The towering humanoid artwork out front is sculptor Jonathan Borofsky's stainless steel *Male/Female*, erected in 2004 to decidedly mixed reviews. As of this writing, plans are underway to renovate and expand the station.

Baltimore Streetcar Museum

1901 Falls Road • North

(410) 547-0264 • www.baltimorestreetcarmuseum.org • Admission Fee

A shrinking number of Baltimoreans remember the days when electric trolleys, powered by overhead cables, shuttled up and down the major thoroughfares of Baltimore. Horse-drawn streetcars began running between Fell's Point and downtown in 1859. The city made history in 1885 when the nation's first electric streetcar entered service, running between midtown and Hampden. The city's streetcar system had more than four hundred miles of track at its 1920s peak and came to an end in 1963, a victim of economic forces, including public funding for road construction and a society that favored the private automobile. Just a few years after the end of the trolley era, streetcar enthusiasts started this museum. Presently, it has two dozen antique streetcars in its collection, including one example of a trackless trolley, powered by an overhead electric line but riding on rubber

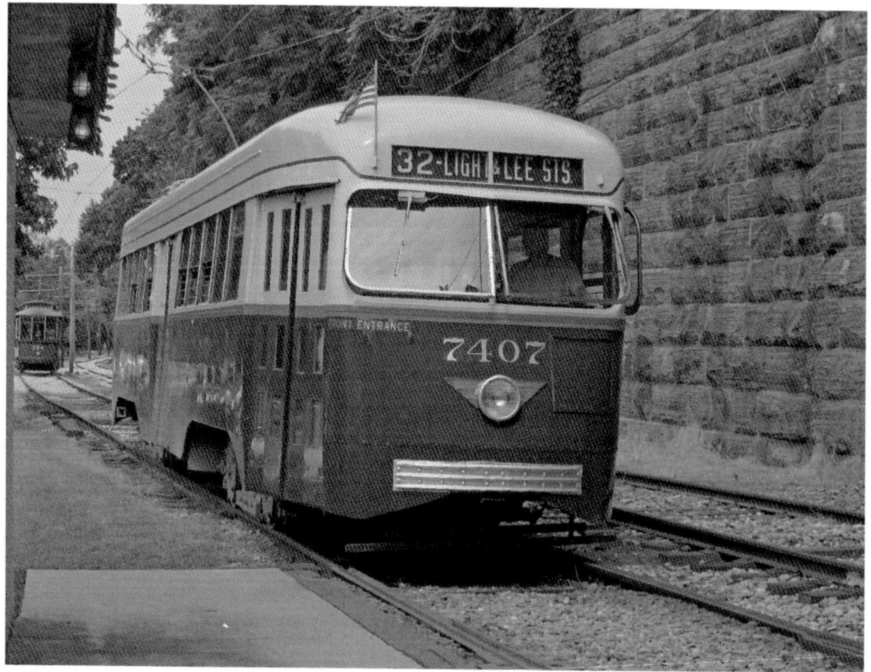

The Baltimore Streetcar Museum celebrates the city's lost but beloved transit system. *Courtesy of Leonard Adler.*

tires, as well as a few cars from pre-electric days, when horses pulled trams on various rail loops around downtown. The museum offers rides on some of its operational cars, running them on a looped track.

Hampden

Baltimore neighborhood roughly occupying the triangle within 40th Street to the north, the Jones Falls to the west and Keswick Road to the east • North
www.hampdenmerchants.com

First settled in 1802, Hampden is the largest of the nineteenth-century mill communities originally catering to textile workers along the Jones Falls. Though incorporated into Baltimore City with the border expansion of 1888, this community of largely two-story brick row houses and modest frame houses has always had an independent spirit—a village within a city. This go-its-own-way streak continues in the current century, as the community's commercial heart, a roughly five-block stretch on and around 36th Street, is now chockablock with an eclectic mix of non-chain businesses. Known locally as "The Avenue," it's a walkable assortment of indie bookstores, antique shops, clothing boutiques, coffee shops, craft beer bars and dining options ranging from Nepalese to New Mexican.

Briefly known as Slabtown in its earliest days, Hampden was ultimately named after English Parliamentarian and anti-tax crusader John Hampden. Hampden Hall looms over the intersection of 36th and Roland Avenue. Now housing apartments, it was built in 1882 as a meeting place for Civil War vets. It sports a mural honoring a pair of neighborhood Congressional Medal of Honor recipients from World War II and also depicts the Baltimore–Hampden line, the nation's first electric railway, which had a terminus here in 1885.

Jones Falls Valley: A Post-Industrial Windshield Tour

Intersection of Falls Road and East Lafayette Street and where Clipper Mill Road ends at Union Avenue • North

Once among the largest employment centers in the nation, the mills and manufacturers along the Jones Falls Valley played a pivotal role in Baltimore's growth and development. And yet some woodsy stretches alongside the rippling waterway evoke a secluded Appalachian back road. It's a curious and fascinating valley, and this two-mile tour offers a good mix of history and greenery between midtown and Hampden. (You could walk or bike it with the caveat that some stretches of road lack sidewalks or even decent shoulders.)

Touring from the south, turn right onto Falls Road from East Lafayette Street (near where the Jones Falls goes underground to continue its journey to the Inner Harbor). You pass beneath the colorfully painted Howard Street Bridge and then the masonry North Avenue Bridge, with its graceful, brick-ribbed vaulting dating to 1895. A tone is set for this journey: it feels like a twenty-first-century city going about its businesses overhead, while the valley remains reclusive and of another time. The Streetcar Museum's facilities (described earlier) are soon on your right, and the Jones Falls Trail (see Chapter 12) crosses Falls Road to run alongside it on the left. The massive curving train bridge passing overhead carries the old B&O Railroad Belt Line, which opened in the 1890s. It's still a busy line for CSX, and about a third of a mile south of here, the rails enter the 1.7-mile Howard Tunnel to pass beneath much of West Baltimore. (It was the scene of a disastrous subterranean train fire in 2001 and is slated for a massive multimillion-dollar overhaul to enlarge the nineteenth-century tunnel to accommodate double-stacked shipping containers.)

The dilapidated and graffitied freight pavilion for the Maryland & Pennsylvania Railroad—or the Ma & Pa, as it was affectionately known—is up next, close by the road on the right. This short-line railroad connected Baltimore to southern Pennsylvania and made milk, mail and passenger runs until 1958. Among the railroad detritus, note the large rusty eight-spoked wheel south of the pavilion. It's a relic of the city's short-lived cablecar system similar to the system still employed in San Francisco; this is one of the giant grooved wheels that helped propel the city's system of underground cable. The cable system ran from 1891 to 1896, when the line was electrified. The road then sweeps gently to the right, and the valley opens up. On the right, at 2601 Falls, sits the Ma & Pa's stone roundhouse, in serious disrepair after being used for years to store road salt (discussions on repurposing the unique curvilinear structure have begun). Falls Road soon passes under the 28th Street Bridge and then the soaring stone arches of the 29th Street Bridge, built amid the Depression as an employment/infrastructure project of the Works Progress Administration (WPA).

A bit farther on, down and off to the left near where the Jones Falls Trail crosses back over the road to zigzag up a hill to detour into Druid Hill Park, the streambed is interrupted by Round Falls. This semicircular ten-foot waterfall is a vestige of an early nineteenth-century flour mill. (If you go down for a closer look, tread lightly on the steps and waterside viewing platform, both needing repair as of this writing.) While everything from airplane tires to ice cream cones has been made in the valley, flour milling was its first industry and textile milling its largest—especially manufacturing a sturdy canvas known as cotton duck used for sails, tents and other purposes. At its 1890s peak, the Mount Vernon–Woodberry Cotton Duck Company operated nine mills, employing some four thousand. Working conditions were often brutal. There were twelve-hour shifts, and children as young as eight tended machinery. The textile industry declined after World War II, eventually relocating south to avoid unionization and then overseas.

After a leafy stretch, the sprawling Mount Vernon Mill No. 1 complex comes into view. Most of it was built in 1873 to replace an earlier mill that burned (and earlier still, a flour mill run by industrialist/philanthropist/abolitionist Elisha Tyson). It is unique among the mills in that it straddles the Jones Falls, with a pedestrian bridge leading to a building on the stream's western shore. Its 2013 renovation into residences, office space

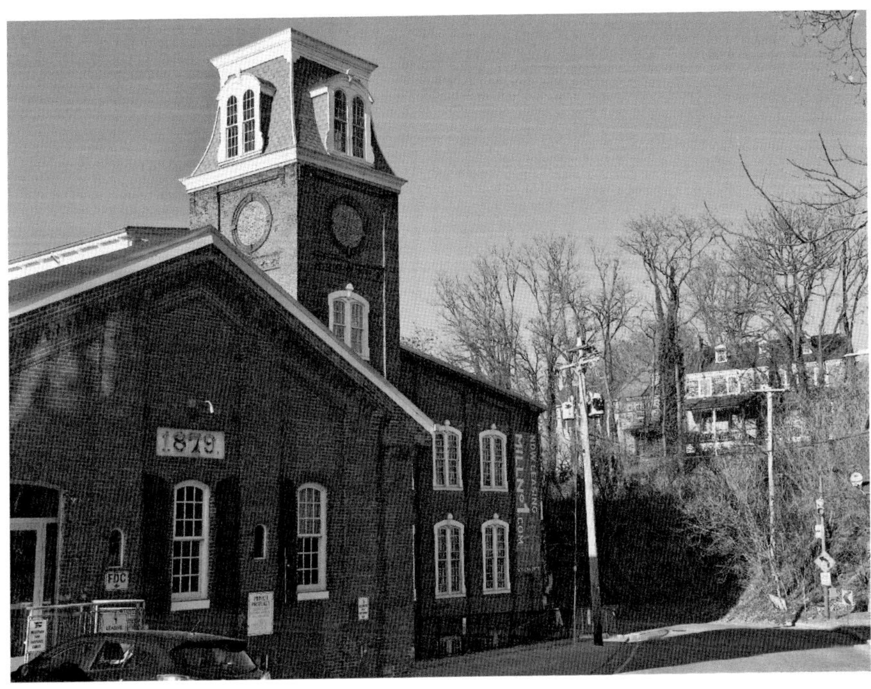

A repurposed Jones Falls Valley textile mill, with industrialist and abolitionist Elisha Tyson's stone summer house visible through the trees. *Courtesy of Brennen Jensen.*

and a restaurant required millions of dollars for all the looming, multi-pane windows that had been bricked up. Industrial pioneer Tyson chose a bluff directly overlooking the mill as the site for the summer house he built in 1811. The house is still up there, best seen from the southeast corner of the mill complex when the leaves are off the trees. At the stop sign intersection with Chestnut Avenue, to the right you can see Mount Vernon Mills Nos. 2 and 3, former cotton duck mills converted into office space and artists' studios in 1987. (Periodically, the artists here hold "open studio" days when you can tour the building and buy artwork and wares.)

Leaving the mill cluster, the road takes a bucolic turn and you can briefly forget you are motoring through a city. At the next stop sign, Falls Road continues to the right, but you head straight on under the bridge to continue on Clipper Mill Road. If you look off to the right in the intersection, you can just see the light-gray, mixed-use Fox Building on a hillside. It was built in 1926 as a Noxzema plant. The skin cream was invented in Baltimore in 1914, and its first "factory" was a row house back on East Lafayette near where the tour began. (The cream was later made out in Baltimore

County, a product of the Noxell Corporation perhaps better known for its CoverGirl line of makeup.) Another leafy stretch ensues before the Whitehall Mill complex appears on the left, with buildings erected between 1865 and 1875 and replacing an early eighteenth-century gristmill. Renovation into a mixed-use complex was completed in 2016, and its Whitehall Market offers a wealth of food and drink options. Up and off to the right are a collection of 1840s millworker houses of the sort sprinkled throughout the valley made from locally quarried stone. Past Whitehall, an elevated section of the Jones Falls Expressway (JFX) appears on the left. The highway was completed in 1961. On the right, Hampden houses appear to tumble down a steep hill. Clipper Mill Road ends at Union Avenue. Across Union and up to the right, the large stone building with an Italianate clock tower is the former Druid Mill, opened in 1877 as the state's largest cotton mill. Now called Union Mill after a 2012 renovation, it houses offices for nonprofits and residences for city schoolteachers, as well as a popular café. Turn right to go up the hill to rejoin Falls Road and explore Hampden or turn left to cross over the Jones Falls (and beneath the JFX) and enter Woodberry.

Woodberry

Neighborhood bounded by the Jones Falls to the east, Druid Hill Park to the south, Greenspring Avenue on the west and Cold Spring Lane to the north • North

This historic mill village and industrial area on the west side of the Jones Falls opposite Hampden saw its first mills arrive in the late eighteenth century, with development taking off after 1840. The handsome brick Meadow Mill (3600 Clipper Mill Road) close to the Jones Falls sports a belfry tower bearing the words "WM. E. Hooper & Sons" and the year 1877. Three generations of the Hooper family were major players in the textile industry. In the latter half of the twentieth century, Meadow Mill was acquired by the makers of London Fog brand raincoats and got Baltimore branded "raincoat capital of the world" (a nice soggy-day follow-up to the city's previous moniker, "umbrella capital of the world," earned in the 1800s after the nation's first umbrella factory opened downtown). The mill is now a mixed-use facility with offices and a bakery, a music school, a gym and a restaurant. A non-textile outlier, Woodberry's largest employer was the Poole & Hunt Foundry and Machine Works, which began in 1853. As many as seven hundred employees turned out all manner of machines and machine parts (including textile machinery), as well as iron columns used in the expanded Capitol dome in Washington. A deadly 1994 fire destroyed a chunk of the complex, and it was subsequently reborn as Clipper Mill, a mixed-use residential and commercial campus centered on Clipper Park Road that includes the city's coolest swimming pool dramatically set amid mill ruins. Clipper Road, parallel to the train tracks, is lined with 1840s stone millworker homes.

American Brewery Building

1701 North Gay Street • East • Exterior Only (outside of public events)

This looming example of High Victorian architectural exuberance is the most fanciful edifice from Baltimore's nineteenth-century brewing heyday. Its ornate rooflines and eclectic variety of windows have led it to be playfully dubbed the "Bavarian Pagoda." It was erected in 1887 by German-born John Frederick Wiessner as the centerpiece of his bustling Wiessner Brewery, which turned out more than 100,000 barrels of beer per year in 1901. The rangy Wiessner family row house across the street included rooms for newly arrived German immigrants brought over to work the malt and hops. A larger-than-life zinc statue of a beer-wielding King Gambrinus, folkloric

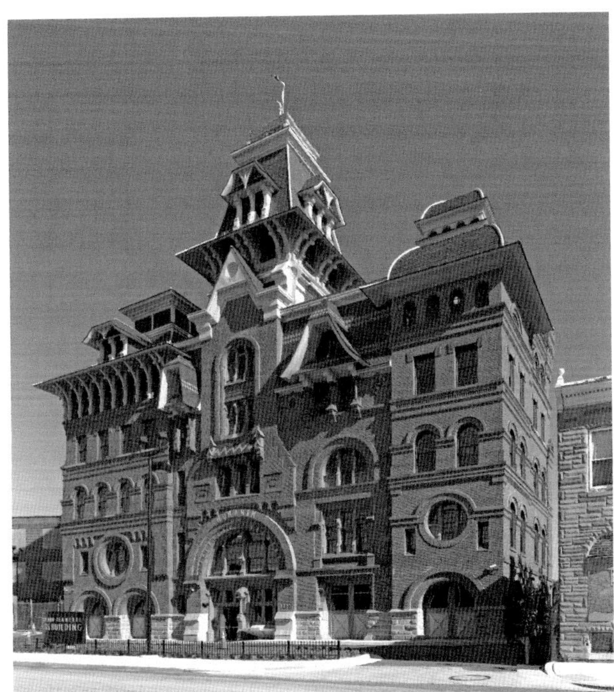

Known as the American Brewery Building, this 1887 edifice has been dubbed the "Bavarian Pagoda." *Courtesy of Library of Congress/Carol M. Highsmith.*

patron saint of beer, once perched on a façade niche and is now at the Maryland Center for History and Culture. The namesake American Brewery occupied the facility from 1950 to 1973, and then it was left to decay—like much of the neighborhood in its shadow. The building was rescued from years of abandonment in 2009 when the social services charity Humanim moved in after an award-winning restoration.

Canton: A Post-Industrial Windshield Tour

Multiple sites along Boston Street • Southeast

Present-day Canton, on the east side of Baltimore, is known as an upscale residential neighborhood featuring condo towers and low-rise modern townhouses mixed with renovated nineteenth-century row houses. The community's early maritime history, dating to the late 1700s, is literally buried. Harris Creek, the wide stream where some of America's first naval ships were built, now occupies a jumbo culvert under Lakewood Avenue. In 1786, wealthy sea trader Captain John O'Donnell bought the Harris Creek area and hundreds of acres of coastal plain and marshland to the east. He named his vast property after Canton, the Chinese port city (today's Guangzhou) that made him wealthy. In 1830, a group of investors bought the estate from O'Donnell's heirs. Visionary capitalists, they laid out plans for an entire industrial community that would link Baltimore's outer harbor to the brand-new world of railroads and steam-powered manufacturing. The Canton Company built wharves, laid out roads and short-haul railroads and created housing for thousands of industrial workers. Over the course of 150 years, the company bought, improved, sold and leased a total of almost four thousand acres of East Baltimore. By the early twentieth century, Canton was the heart of industrial Baltimore. America's canning industry burgeoned here; metal foundries rubbed shoulders with distilleries and furniture factories. Stockpiles of imported bird guano gave rise to Canton's long-running fertilizer industry. Acres of rail yards served the district's wharves and factories. Industrial Canton surged to its peak after the Second World War, as did Baltimore City. General Motors, Western Electric and Standard Oil occupied huge campuses, employing thousands of workers. By the 1970s, the Canton Company had essentially worked itself out of a job, having sold off all its land, buildings and rail lines. The industrial district had already begun to hollow out as machinery aged and manufacturers moved south or abroad or simply closed down in the face of competition.

Since 1980, clubs, shops and restaurants have filled in old storefronts along Boston Street and O'Donnell Square, while new shopping centers and massive Amazon warehouses have moved in where refineries and "tank farms" once stood. Former factories have turned into condominiums and office buildings. The area's southernmost section, south of Boston Street, is still an industrial waterfront, with silos full of cement and mountains of coal and salt that are visible from the interstate highways near the harbor tunnels.

One way to get a sense of old, industrial Canton is to drive east along Boston Street from Fell's Point, taking note of the older buildings that have been converted from industrial to residential and retail purposes. The Can Company, 2400 Boston Street, now a retail and office center, was part of the American Can Company's factory complex, itself the last stand of Boston Street's erstwhile "Cannery Row." The Shipyard condominium, 2639 Boston Street, was the factory of the Edward Renneburg Company, which manufactured specialized machinery for other manufacturers—prior to Renneburg, it was a chair factory, and in the 1850s, the site was actually a shipyard at the mouth of Harris Creek, dating back to the 1780s. The Tindeco Wharf apartment building, 2809 Boston Street, was the factory of the Tin Decorating Company, which made colorful metal containers of all shapes and purposes. The next building, no. 2901, started as a storage building for Tindeco. It's now a condominium complex called Canton Cove. At 3500 Boston Street, a former broom factory is now a trendy retail-and-office complex called the Broom Factory. In the water, off the shore of today's Canton Waterfront Park, stands a peculiar rectangular steel structure that is the remnant of a ferry-to-rail transfer bridge, part of a system by which loaded railroad cars were carried on barges across the harbor between terminals in Canton and Locust Point. The curious orphaned relic has not been repurposed, but it has been adopted as an icon of the modern Canton community.

To see what remains of the old Canton industrial zone, take a right on Clinton Street south toward Lazaretto Point. After a few blocks, waterfront industries and industrial piers, some vacant, will appear on your right; warehouses and port services will be on your left. At the far end of Clinton, near the Lehigh Cement silos, the road makes a sharp left turn and becomes Keith Avenue. On the right appears the black mountains of the Canton Coal Pier—on the left, Interstate Highways 95 and 895 plunge into their respective tunnels under the harbor.

National Brewing Company/Brewers Hill

O'Donnell Street at Conkling Street • Southeast

Founded in 1881, the National Brewing Company grew into Baltimore's largest beermaker before competition from the likes of Budweiser, Miller and other out-of-state giants bludgeoned it out of business. Its original East Baltimore brewery shuttered in 1980 and has been repurposed as a mixed-use development called Brewers Hill, which also includes the adjacent Gunther's Brewery, another local brand. But perhaps the most lasting vestige of the old brewery is Mr. Boh, the mustachioed, one-eyed cartoon mascot for its former flagship beer, National Bohemian. Natty Boh, as the beer is commonly called, has long been made out of state by Pabst and is marketed almost exclusively in Maryland as a nostalgia-driven bargain brand. Mr. Boh imagery pops up all over town, and somewhat of a kitschy cottage industry has grown up around the figure. (No, there is no clear answer as to why he has but one eye; some say he is winking.) In its middle-of-last-century glory days, National beers were ubiquitous on Baltimore bar rails, and charismatic company president Jerold Hoffberger owned the Baltimore Orioles, maintaining a long-standing Baltimore connection between baseball and beer. Older Baltimoreans will remember the slogan that National Brewing bestowed on the state of Maryland: the "Land of Pleasant Living." Along with Mr. Boh, that catchphrase sold a lot of beer.

O'Donnell Square

2900 Block of O'Donnell Street • Southeast

This commercial district dates back to the early nineteenth century. The "square" is actually a long rectangular park between the east- and westbound sides of O'Donnell Street, surrounded by bars, restaurants and shops that draw visitors from around the city. In the center of the park stands a statue of Captain John O'Donnell, master of the original Canton estate, created by Baltimore artist Tylden Streett. Today, O'Donnell's memory is tarnished by the community's growing awareness of his history as a slave owner, and many neighborhood residents want the statue gone.

The old neighborhood's core extends along O'Donnell Street, beyond the commercial square, to St. Casimir's Church on the west and, on the east, the Canton branch of the Enoch Pratt Library, the oldest continuously operating branch of the city's library system.

B&O Railroad Museum
901 West Pratt Street • South
(410) 752-2490 • www.borail.org • Admission Fee

This world-famous, must-see museum stands just a few yards away from the spot where American railroading began in 1828. Its exhibit of 1800s steam locomotives and railroad cars occupies the former B&O passenger-car repair shop, a roundhouse 235 feet in diameter, built in 1883. The museum's indoor collection of rail cars and engines spans the first eighty or so years of railroading. Among the exhibits is a reconstruction of the "Tom Thumb," the tiny steam engine that was built by the inventor and B&O investor Peter Cooper to demonstrate the practicality of steam power for railroading. Visitors are allowed to climb aboard some of the cars, while others are for eyes only. Adjoining the roundhouse is an 1851 station building, which now houses a gift shop, a variety of historic exhibits and the museum's entrance. Outside, in a rail yard parallel to Pratt Street, massive mid-twentieth-century engines and cars are displayed.

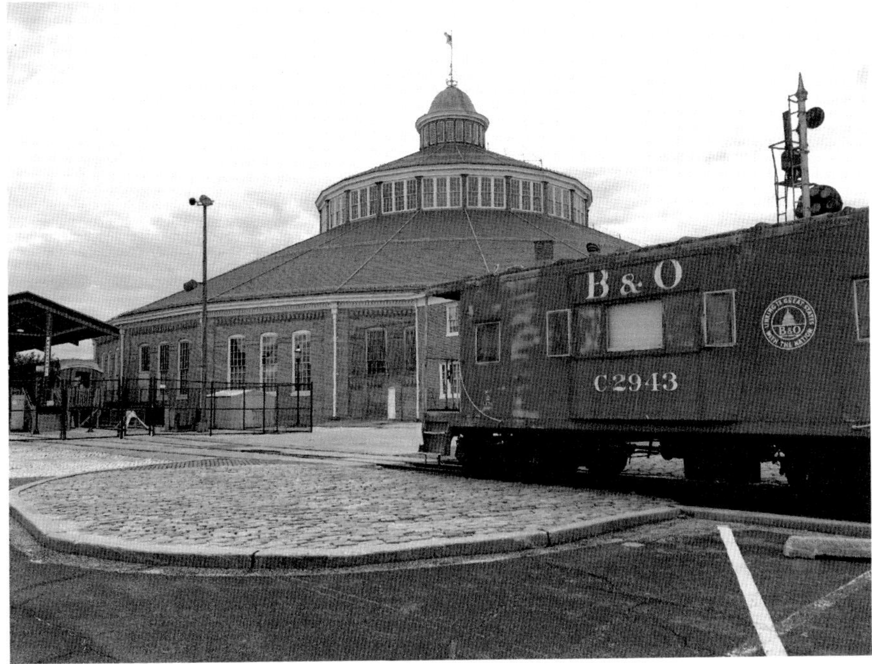

The B&O Railroad Museum honors the birthplace of American rail; the roundhouse dates to 1884. *Courtesy of Tom Chalkley.*

Camden Station

301 West Camden Street • South • Exterior Only

A B&O Railroad terminus since 1853, with the present building erected in 1857 (and enlarged in 1865), this brick Italianate structure featuring a trio of cupola-topped towers had been in continuous use longer than any other train station in the country when it ceased rail operations in 1988. Five years later, it was painstakingly restored by the Maryland Stadium Authority to its 1860s appearance and today is largely seen as an elegant component of the adjacent Oriole Park at Camden Yards ballpark complex. This was the station Union soldiers were marching toward when mobs of Confederate sympathizers attacked them during the Pratt Street riots of 1861. President Lincoln passed through Camden on multiple occasions, including while en route to speak at Gettysburg and, seventeen months later, in his coffin heading back to Illinois for burial. As many as twenty or more people were killed in these environs in 1877 during the bloody Baltimore Railroad Strike, a component of the national Great Railroad Strike of that year. Troops and police in the station were repeatedly attacked by thousands-strong mobs angered by marked reductions in railroad worker pay. As of this writing, the building is largely vacant. A small modern train depot south of the historic station, also called Camden Station, serves as terminus for commuter trains serving Washington, D.C.

Carrollton Viaduct

Gwynns Falls, a half mile upstream from Washington Boulevard • South

This simple but handsome single-span stone bridge crosses Gwynns Falls 1.5 miles southwest of the B&O Railroad Museum. Built in 1829, it is America's first and oldest railroad bridge; the first trains to cross it were hauled by horses, not steam engines. The bridge is still in regular use by trains far heavier than it was built for. While it's visible from Interstate 95, the viaduct is hard to spot from ground level. By far the easiest way to reach it is by following the Gwynns Falls Trail on foot or bicycle. North of Washington Boulevard, near Mount Clare Park, the trail passes through a small arched tunnel that was originally built into the bridge to permit horse and wagon traffic along the river.

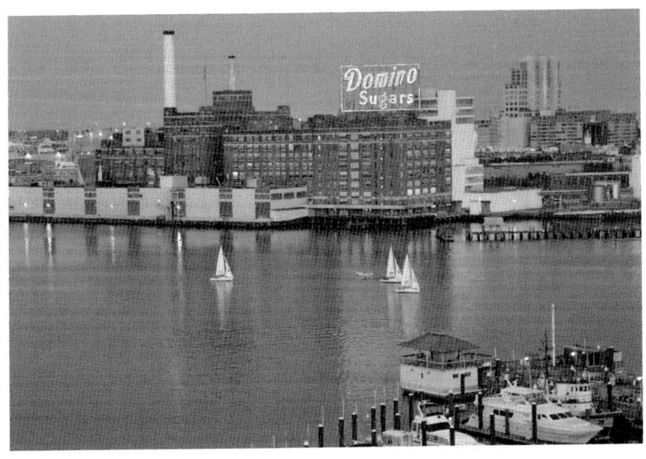

The Domino Sugars sign is an Inner Harbor icon. The plant has refined the sweet stuff since 1921. *Courtesy of Brennen Jensen.*

Domino Sugars

1100 Key Highway • South • Exterior Only

The last active industrial site in the Inner Harbor is hard to miss. Perched atop its nine-story plant is a massive neon-red sign reading "Domino Sugars" that is larger than a basketball court (the dot in the *i* is six feet across). The landmark sign dates to 1951, while the refinery beneath it began operation in 1921. The six hundred or so workers in the "sugar house" process more than 6 million tons of raw sugar a day and annually produce about 14 percent of the nation's refined sugar, in bags, boxes and some 350 billion individual single-serve packets. At this writing, the iconic sign is being retrofitted with energy-efficient LED lighting designed to faithfully mimic the original neon.

Irish Railroad Workers Museum

918 and 920 Lemmon Street • West

(410) 347-4747 • www.irishshrine.org • Free

Just a short walk from the B&O Railroad Museum, this small shrine tells another side to America's railroading story. In 1848, a local carpenter named Charles Shipley built this strip of modest brick alley houses to sell to railroad workers. Every one of these houses went to a buyer with an Irish surname, some if not all of them immigrants who had fled their homeland to escape the catastrophic potato famine. Irish workers like these became part of the bedrock of Baltimore's growing industrial economy. They and their children also battled the B&O during the Railroad Strike of 1877, and they got involved in politics, contending with anti-immigrant natives. The museum occupies two houses: no. 918 is a house museum, presenting a facsimile of how these people lived, with humble mid-1800s furnishings and fixtures, and no. 920 offers changing exhibits of documents, photographs, relics and mementos relating to the Irish immigrant community.

Chapter 6

THE AFRICAN AMERICAN EXPERIENCE

EYES ON THE PRIZE IN THE ONE-TIME BLACK CAPITAL

Situated well south of the Mason-Dixon line, old Baltimore was very much a southern city in a southern state. Baltimore had been a slaveholding town since its founding, and Maryland was the home state of Roger B. Taney, the chief justice of the U.S. Supreme Court who wrote the infamous Dred Scott decision of 1857, ruling that Black Americans did not merit equal rights with Whites. Yet Baltimore owed its existence to the enslaved workforce: prior to the Civil War, captive labor was used in building nearly all of the city's infrastructure, its churches and public buildings and the ships in its harbor. Organized antislavery activism began 1789 with the founding of the Maryland Society for the Abolition of Slavery, spearheaded by civic leaders and religious congregations, particularly in the Society of Friends (Quakers) and the Methodist Church. The Sharp Street Methodist Church, located near Pratt and Hanover Streets downtown, was the leading Black church involved in antislavery work.

By 1830, almost a quarter of Baltimore's population was of African descent—some 18,500 people, three-quarters of whom were free people. In fact, Baltimore in the 1830s had the largest free Black population of any American city, one of the factors that has prompted later writers to call the city "the nineteenth-century Black capital." Many of the free African Americans had previously been enslaved but bargained their way to emancipation; others had been set free when their captors no longer needed them. As the rural economy shifted from labor-intensive tobacco to grain farming, thousands of African Americans, cut loose with little more than the clothes they wore, came to Baltimore on foot, searching for work and community. At the same time, Baltimore became a center of slave export: many Maryland slaveholders, instead of freeing their captives, sold them to dealers whose auction houses hovered around the city's harbor. Free Black people protected only by their "free papers" ran the constant risk of being kidnapped, held in a "slave jail" and sold south. One of the chief activities of early antislavery organizations in Baltimore was rescuing kidnap victims.

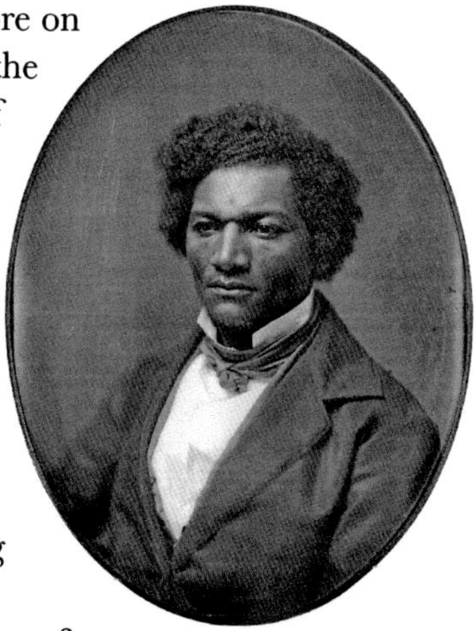

Frederick Douglass as a young man. *Courtesy of Onondaga History Association.*

Despite poverty and the intractable racism of the White majority, free Blacks organized their own schools, churches, small businesses and volunteer organizations. In 1811, when the Methodist Church insisted on putting White clergy in charge of Black congregations, a group of African American pastors and lay people broke away and started the Bethel Church Society. Now called Bethel African Methodist Episcopal (AME) Church, it has been a leading Black institution in Greater Baltimore for two hundred years. By the 1850s, there were fifteen Black Protestant churches in Baltimore, counting more than six thousand members.

In the nineteenth century, there were very few educational opportunities for Black children or adults. Most Black Baltimoreans had to educate themselves and one another. Again, religious organizations took the lead; the government did nothing to educate Black children until after the Civil War. In the 1820s, Mary Elizabeth Lange, an immigrant from Cuba, started a school for African American children in Fell's Point and later founded America's first Black Roman Catholic religious order to expand the mission. Free Black men and women formed "self-improvement" groups that met in homes and churches to discuss religion, philosophy, politics and abolition. Although he was still enslaved, young Frederick Bailey—later known as Frederick Douglass—joined such a group in Fell's Point, finding the free Black friends who would help him escape from slavery, launching his career as the preeminent Black leader of the century. Into the same Fell's Point community, in 1835, Isaac Myers was born, a ship caulker and a natural leader who organized his embattled Black coworkers to open their own cooperative shipyard.

With its large community of free African Americans, its proximity to free Pennsylvania and its sprawling network of roads, rails and water routes, Baltimore was inevitably involved in the secret northward movement of refugees from slavery. Among the White population, Methodists and Quakers were especially active in smuggling "runaways" toward freedom. The Quaker industrialist Elisha Tyson (1758–1824) is credited with freeing hundreds of people from slavery by legal means and was probably involved in a secret network that assisted fugitives in escaping to the Philadelphia area.

Ironically, Maryland's enslaved population was not freed by Lincoln's 1863 Emancipation Proclamation, which was aimed only at "states in rebellion"; Maryland was excused because the state legislature, in 1861, had decided unanimously not to rebel against the Union. Nevertheless, the Lincoln administration put the state under martial law to suppress pro-Confederate uprisings. Slavery was not abolished in Maryland until 1864, when, by a narrow margin, state legislators adopted a new antislavery constitution.

After the Civil War and the defeat of Reconstruction, Baltimore's White establishment quickly created new mechanisms to keep Black citizens at the bottom rungs of society. Throughout Maryland, professional organizations, public schools and colleges, swimming pools, tennis courts, movie theaters and amusement parks were restricted to White people. Some privately owned businesses were still posting "Whites Only" signs until the early 1960s. In the early twentieth century, the Roland Park Company pioneered the use of legal compacts to prevent African Americans from moving in or buying property. Baltimore banks innovated the practice of "redlining" Black neighborhoods, branding them as bad financial risks and unworthy of loans—a practice later adopted by federal housing agencies. Rendered unable to move at will while simultaneously denied the ability to secure loans to acquire or improve existing housing stock, Black Baltimoreans were trapped in conditions that would lead to concentrated, intergenerational poverty. When the dam burst in the 1960s, the real estate industry found a way to profit off Black aspirations and White prejudices via "blockbusting"—unscrupulous agents introducing a token Black family into a White block and then buying houses on the cheap from panicked Whites to turn around and sell at a profit to incoming Blacks. Whole neighborhoods changed hands with dizzying speed: Lower Park Heights was 92 percent White in 1960 and 95 percent Black by 1970.

Meanwhile, pro-Confederate monuments were erected, silently broadcasting the sentiments of the city's White authorities. The last of these, honoring Confederate generals Robert E. Lee and "Stonewall" Jackson, was put up in 1948, just as thousands of Black veterans were resettling in Baltimore. In

2017, following the lead of other cities, Mayor Catherine Pugh ordered the removal of the city's Confederate monuments, plus the statue of Supreme Court Justice Taney, of "Dred Scott" infamy. The removal crews did their work after dark to avoid controversy. Once accomplished, Pugh's action was generally accepted.

Locally, nationally and on the state level, Baltimore's Black leaders were on the front lines of the fight for political and social equality. After the Civil War, John Murphy, formerly enslaved, founded the *Afro-American* newspaper. Through the next one hundred years and several generations of Murphys, the Baltimore-based paper was a leading national voice on racial justice. In the 1930s, the *Afro*'s activist editor Carl Murphy recruited a friend, Lillie Carroll Jackson, to lead the Baltimore chapter of the National Association for the Advancement of Colored People (NAACP). "Ma" Jackson became a formidable leader, staging nonviolent protests in Baltimore when Martin Luther King Jr. was a toddler, as well as personally pressing Maryland's governors to desegregate schools and public facilities. Jackson's daughter, Juanita Jackson Mitchell, became a leading civil rights lawyer in Maryland, while her husband, Clarence Mitchell Jr., was the NAACP's lobbyist in Washington, D.C.; his brother, Parren Mitchell, became Maryland's first Black congressman. Another man from "Ma" Jackson's Marble Hill neighborhood, Thurgood Marshall, led the NAACP's legal effort in Washington. In 1967, President Lyndon Johnson appointed Marshall as the first African American justice of the U.S. Supreme Court.

In the face of institutional racism, Black Baltimoreans continued to build religious congregations, businesses and cultural institutions. Pennsylvania Avenue, on the west side, became a center of Black cultural life, centered on the Royal and Regent Theaters. The Royal was a stop on the so-called chitlin' circuit, where nationally known Black bands and performers attracted thousands of fans. Still, Baltimore was no place for a homegrown Black performer to build a career. Eubie Blake, Billie Holiday, Chick Webb, Cab Calloway and other stars of twentieth-century music grew up in the city but moved north to find a more welcoming culture (see Chapter 10). Some handsome residential stretches near what was called "The Avenue" became home to the city's small Black middle class and were dubbed "Sugar Hill" after a similar enclave in Harlem. Alas, some lower parts of Black West Baltimore had concentrations of squalid, substandard housing where tuberculosis was so rampant they were collectively called the "Lung Block."

The 1968 assassination of Martin Luther King Jr. sparked massive civil unrest in Baltimore, as in major cities around the country. Along several corridors, including Pennsylvania Avenue and Gay Street, fires and looting ravaged old commercial districts that have never fully recovered. By 1980, Baltimore was a majority-Black city. Kurt Schmoke became the first elected Black mayor in 1987, amid a crack cocaine epidemic and corresponding spike in crime. The Rhodes Scholar and former state's attorney for Baltimore was a voice in the wilderness when he spoke of decriminalizing drugs and reframing the drug crisis as less of a "war" and more of a public health issue, positions that are more mainstream today. In the decades since, Black leadership has swelled throughout government, civic and cultural life—less so in the worlds of business and finance.

Although the symbols of White supremacy have been torn from their pedestals, the entire Baltimore area contends with the legacies of slavery and institutionalized racism, particularly the de facto segregation of public schools; patterns of discriminatory marketing, lending and investment; and in racially motivated police practices. The social scars of slavery and the Jim Crow era persist despite the city's long history of political and social struggles. Led by a rising generation of activists, today's protests against police violence are the latest manifestation of a centuries-old battle for justice.

YOUR GUIDE TO HISTORY

Reginald F. Lewis Museum of Maryland African American History and Culture

830 East Pratt Street • Inner Harbor
(443) 263-1800 • https://lewismuseum.org • Admission Fee

Opened in 2005, the museum's permanent collections include an excellent trove of traditional African art and artifacts and extensive archives of documents and photographs relating to African American life and culture, particularly in Maryland. Of special interest to historical researchers is a collection of original documents from the eras of slavery, Reconstruction and Jim Crow, including periodicals, sheet music and advertisements. A hoard of political buttons represents Black engagement in electoral politics. Over the years, the museum's rotating exhibits have been a major attraction, including unforgettable displays of the works of artists Romare Bearden, Jacob Lawrence and Elizabeth Catlett and the classic Baltimore photography of Roland Freeman. The museum is named for the Baltimore-born businessman who, as CEO of TLC Beatrice International Holdings,

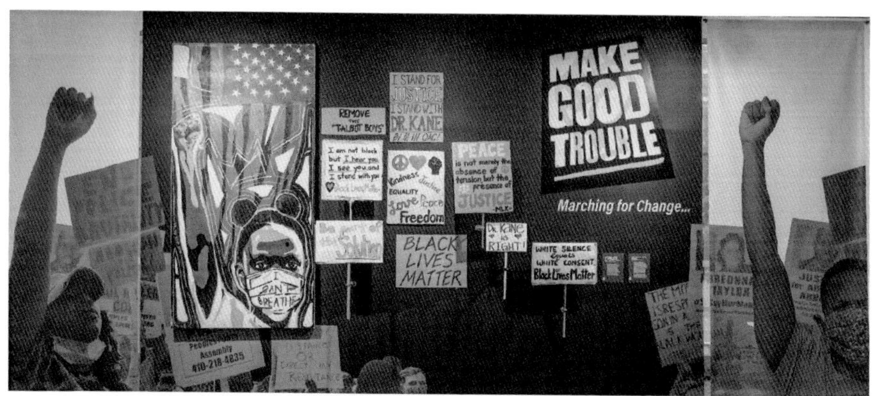

Exhibit at the Reginald F. Lewis Museum of Maryland African American History and Culture. *Courtesy of Reginald Lewis Museum.*

became one of the wealthiest Black men in America before dying at the age of fifty in 1993. After his death, the Reginald F. Lewis Foundation gave $5 million to create the Baltimore museum.

Thurgood Marshall Statue

Corner of West Pratt Street and Sharp Street • Inner Harbor

This tribute to one of Baltimore's greatest citizens is somewhat "hidden in plain sight" near the drab south entrance of the Garmatz U.S. Courthouse. It seems an inadequate setting for this son of Baltimore who became the first African American justice of the Supreme Court. Marshall, who grew up in West Baltimore's Marble Hill neighborhood, was denied entrance to the University of Maryland Law School. After earning his law degree from Howard University, one of his first cases was a successful anti-discrimination suit against the school that had excluded him. As chief legal counsel to the NAACP, Marshall argued and won key racial discrimination cases before the U.S. Supreme Court, including the important *Brown v. Board of Education*, which opened the door to the desegregation of public schools nationwide. In 1967, President Lyndon Johnson nominated him as a Supreme Court justice. He served until 1991 as a powerful advocate of civil rights and equal justice for all. The statue is the work of Reuben Kramer, one of Maryland's best-known twentieth-century sculptors.

Frederick Douglass Sites in Fell's Point

Frederick Douglass—the great antislavery activist, orator and publisher—was born into bondage in Talbot County, Maryland, in 1818. His original name was Frederick Bailey. At the age of eight, he was sent to Fell's Point to work as a babysitter for the family of Hugh Auld, a shipbuilder. The gifted boy taught himself to read and write and grew up observing society's complex divisions—the maritime neighborhood included prosperous sea captains, a White middle class, poor Irish immigrants and African Americans, both free people and enslaved. In his teens, Frederick was sent back to Talbot County, where he experienced the brutal conditions of plantation slavery. After a foiled escape attempt, he was sent back to Baltimore. In Fell's Point, while still enslaved, he became a shipyard worker. While his wages were surrendered to his enslaver, Hugh Auld, he got a tantalizing taste of freedom and made friends with many free Black Baltimoreans. On September 3, 1838, aided by friends and disguised as a free Black sailor, he boarded a train toward Philadelphia and began his historic campaign to abolish slavery. He did not revisit Baltimore until 1864, after Maryland lawmakers, by a narrow vote, passed a state constitution that banned slaveholding.

Although none of the houses where Douglass lived is known to have survived to the present, a number of local tour guides offer walking tours around the streets and waterfronts where Douglass lived and worked in his youth. "Urban Ranger Tours" of Fell's Point, available through the Baltimore National Heritage Area, include stops at Douglass-related locations.

Frederick Douglass/Isaac Myers Maritime Park

1417 Thames Street • Fell's Point
(410) 685-0295 • https://livingclassrooms.org/programs/frederick-douglass-isaac-myers-maritime-park • Admission Fee

Frederick Douglass lived under slavery with the Auld household in at least three known Fell's Point locations—on Happy Alley (now Durham Street), Philpot Street and Fell Street—but none of the buildings has survived to the present. Instead, the great antislavery leader is commemorated at the Frederick Douglass/Isaac Myers Maritime Park, which also celebrates the founder of Baltimore's first Black-owned shipyard and incorporates a museum that documents both men's stories. The Maritime Park, developed by Baltimore's Living Classrooms Foundation, occupies two buildings,

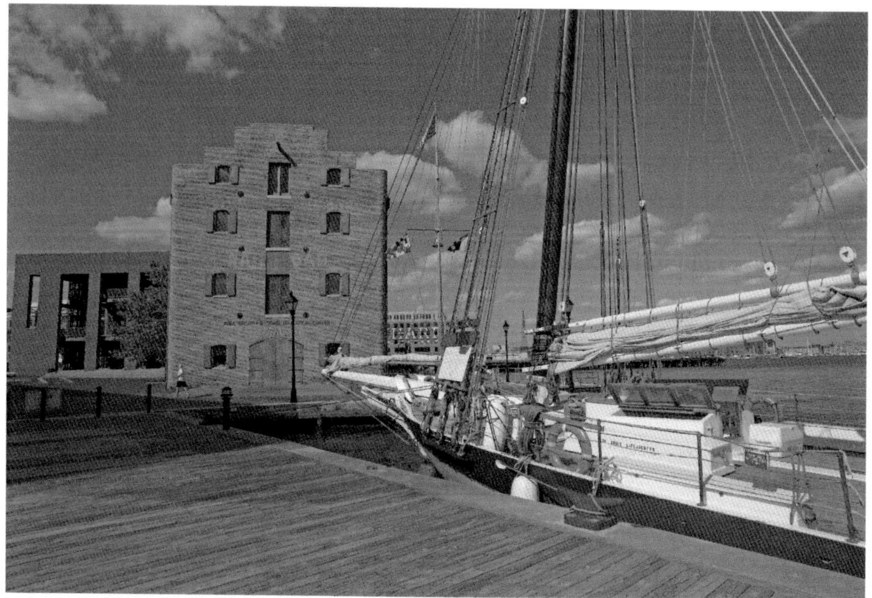

The Frederick Douglass-Isaac Myers Maritime Park incorporates an 1840s coffee warehouse. *Courtesy of Visit Baltimore.*

including an 1840s coffee warehouse three blocks east of the now-vanished Philpot Street, where the Aulds lived during Frederick's adolescence. In addition to its historic exhibits, the Maritime Park offers a gallery displaying local artists' work and event space with views to the harbor, available for rental. The grounds of the Maritime Park feature a monumental portrait sculpture of Douglass.

Douglass Place

500 block of South Dallas Street • Fell's Point • Exterior Only

In 1864, sixteen days after the abolition of slavery in Maryland, Douglass came to Fell's Point to celebrate emancipation at the Methodist Episcopal church on Strawberry Alley (now Dallas Street), where he had worshiped in his youth. Later, while living in Washington, D.C., Douglass returned to Baltimore to speak on many occasions. In 1892, he found that the old Strawberry Alley church had been vacated. Douglass bought the old church, paid to have it demolished and, in its place, built five simple row houses. He intended the project to provide rental housing for Black families. For many decades, the marble plaque on the façade of 520 Dallas Street reading "Douglass Place" was hidden under Formstone siding. When the plaque was re-exposed in the 1980s, it was Fell's Point's sole memorial to its greatest resident. A more recent plaque provides more detail on the history of the site. None of the Douglass Place homes is open to the general public, although the owner of 524 South Dallas Street has filled the much-renovated house with African American art and memorabilia and rents the house to visitors through online rental services.

St. Frances Academy

501 East Chase Street • East
www.sfacademy.org

This building dates to 1871, but its story goes back to 1828, when Mary Elizabeth Lange, a Cuban-born schoolteacher, was commissioned by Baltimore's Catholic archbishop to begin a school for African American children. Lange, who had previously taught Black students in Fell's Point, became a Catholic nun and recruited other educated Black Catholic women to join her in founding the Oblate Sisters of Providence, the first order of African American nuns. Despite their own poverty and the constant oppression of racism both within and outside the church, the Sisters carried on with their mission. St. Frances now stands as the oldest school in America dedicated to teaching Black children; today, the school has about three hundred students. The Oblate Sisters have mounted an ongoing campaign to honor "Mother Lange" as a Catholic saint. The tiny room where she died in 1882 is preserved at the school. A simple bed, a washstand and a crucifix are the only furnishings. Visitors should contact the school through its website.

Lillie Carroll Jackson Civil Rights Museum

1320 Eutaw Street • West
(443) 885-5300 • www.lilliecarrolljacksonmuseum.org • Admission Fee

"Ma" Jackson, as she was called, was literally the mother of the modern civil rights movement in Maryland. Along with her daughter, Juanita Jackson Mitchell, and son-in-law, Clarence Mitchell Jr., she was a nationally influential figure in the legal and legislative battle for racial equality; several of her Mitchell grandchildren and great-grandchildren have been elected to city and state government. She served thirty-five years as president of Baltimore's influential chapter of the NAACP, playing a very personal role as a lobbyist. Republican governor Theodore McKeldin is quoted as saying, "I'd rather have the devil after me than Mrs. Jackson. Give her what she wants." She didn't get everything she wanted, but Maryland desegregated its schools and public facilities years ahead of other Jim Crow states. Jackson's house in the Marble Hill neighborhood, much restored after decades of neglect, is now a museum operated by Morgan State University, dedicated to Jackson and to Baltimore's role in the civil rights movement. Visiting hours are limited; see the website for details.

Mount Auburn Cemetery

Waterview Avenue and Annapolis Road • South

The Mount Auburn Cemetery sprawls down a broad, fifty-five-acre slope near Cherry Hill in the city's south end. Here lie the remains of some seventy-nine thousand African Americans, including a number of major figures in Baltimore history. Lillie Carroll Jackson, matriarch of Baltimore's civil rights movement, is buried here. So is John Murphy, founder of the *Afro-American* newspapers, as are many others less famous who, like Murphy, started their lives in slavery. Joe Gans, whose monument bears only his last name, was the world's lightweight boxing champion from 1902 to 1908, the first Black man to hold that title. Mount Auburn Cemetery was begun in 1872 by Sharp Street Church, one of the first and, in its day, foremost Black congregations in the city. Today, families and volunteers mow the site when they can; otherwise, these peaceful slopes have largely become a de facto nature sanctuary.

Arch Social Club

2426 Pennsylvania Avenue • West
(410) 669-9856 • www.archsocialclub.com

This venerable social institution, facing the intersection of Pennsylvania Avenue and West North Avenue, is the only entertainment venue remaining on a commercial corridor that pulsed with music in the mid-twentieth century. The club itself was founded in 1905 and incorporated in 1912, serving as a means to raise funds for members' widows, orphans and funeral expenses—a homegrown self-insurance group for people who were excluded from White institutions. In 1972, the organization moved to its present location, a former vaudeville and movie theater built in 1912, with an appropriately arched façade. Today, the club continues to raise money, as it has done for many decades, by hosting concerts and dances featuring music styles ranging from straight-ahead jazz to hip-hop.

National Great Blacks in Wax Museum

1601 East North Avenue • East
(410) 563-3404 • www.greatblacksinwax.org • Admission Fee

This singular attraction, employing more than one hundred wax figures to show and tell more than a millennium of Black history, began humbly in the 1980s. That's when founders Joanne Martin and her late husband, Elmer Martin, fearing that so much of Black history was "faceless," commissioned the creation of a quartet of wax figures: educator Mary McLeod Bethune, abolitionist and author Frederick Douglass, abolitionist Harriet Tubman and revolt leader Nat Turner. They drove the waxen group around in their hatchback to set up and discuss wherever anyone would have them. Today's sprawling, multi-level museum in a former firehouse attracts more than 150,000 visitors annually to an otherwise untouristed corner of the city to see how a medium, often associated with boardwalks and celebrity-focused outfits, effectively presents a full-body history lesson. The museum pulls no punches: the lynching display is so graphic that signage warns against

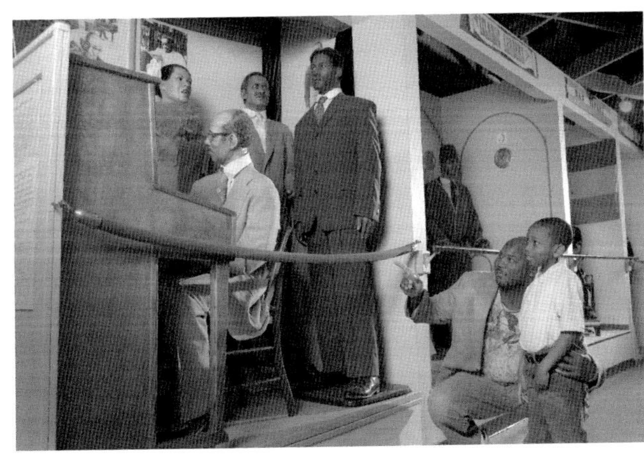

The Great Blacks in Wax Museum offers life-size history lessons. *Courtesy of Visit Baltimore.*

children under twelve viewing it. Visitors also walk through a creaking slave ship making the Middle Passage. But there really is no way to sugarcoat some of this history, which also includes the life-size likenesses of civil rights leaders, clergy, artists, athletes and, of course, a certain president.

"Arabbers"
At large in West Baltimore
(443) 683-7218 • https://www.facebook.com/baltimorearabbers

Baltimore is the last American city to preserve the age-old tradition of street vendors selling produce from horse-drawn wagons. The local name for these itinerant Black merchants is "arabbers," a term with an obscure history, long separated from its ancestral ethnic meaning. According to the Arabber Preservation Society, only three or four men, members of long-standing arabber families, still ply the streets, drawing attention with their distinctive cries and jingling harnesses. The wagons, traditionally built

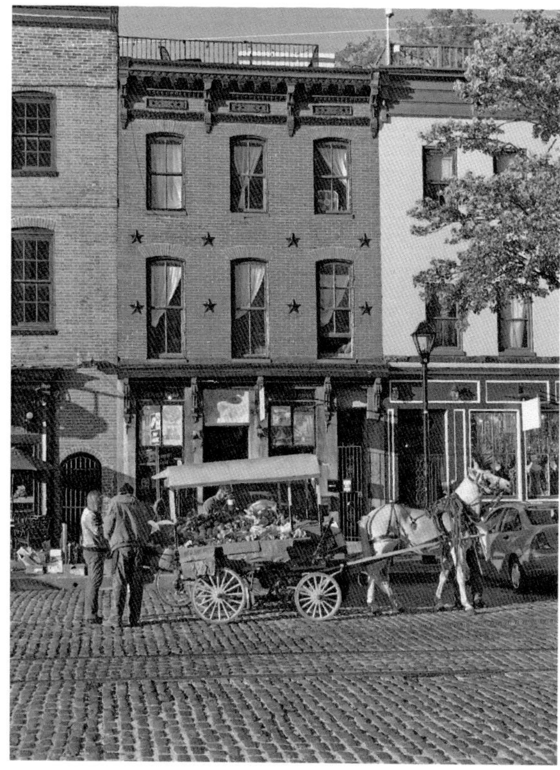

A few peddlers known as "arabbers" still sell produce from horse-drawn carts. *Courtesy of Klaus Philipsen.*

by Amish craftsmen in Pennsylvania, are of nineteenth-century design, painted bright red with yellow spoked wheels. Three West Baltimore stables house the small, docile cart horses. The vendors and their culture constitute a living history museum. The Preservation Society recently hired several arabbers to be part of the city's much-needed food distribution network, delivering free fruits and vegetables in Baltimore's lowest-income urban "food deserts."

Chapter 7

THE LEGACY OF WEALTH

PHILANTHROPISTS AND PLUTOCRATS WHO LEFT THEIR MARK

While Baltimore is named after an English nobleman who died before the city existed, it could be said that a flinty bachelor merchant with an oft-misspelled first name has done as much as any to put the city on the map. Johns Hopkins (1795–1873) made his fortune here and left behind a namesake university, hospital and medical school that enjoy a global reputation. (No, it's not John; his parents turned his great-grandmother's surname into a first name.)

Hopkins is one of a quintet of nineteenth-century men whose names now grace edifices and institutions as part of the city's fabric. Our homegrown Carnegies and Rockefellers include philanthropic pioneer George Peabody (1795–1869), whose legacy includes a music school; Enoch Pratt (1808–1896), whose largesse led to a library system; and William Walters (1820–1894) and son Henry (1848–1931), the art collectors who created a museum. Other plutocratic surnames celebrated for their giving and good deeds include Garrett, Sheppard and Tyson. (All but Peabody are buried at the city's storied Green Mount Cemetery.)

George Peabody is dubbed the Father of Modern Philanthropy, and his largesse—more than $10 million worth—is celebrated by communities on both sides of the Atlantic, and perhaps nowhere more than in his 1795 birthplace of Danvers, Massachusetts, which renamed itself Peabody in 1855. One of eight children in a cash-strapped clan, his formal schooling ended after four years. At age eleven, he was working as a grocery clerk. Family fortunes worsened after his father died, and sixteen-year-old Peabody

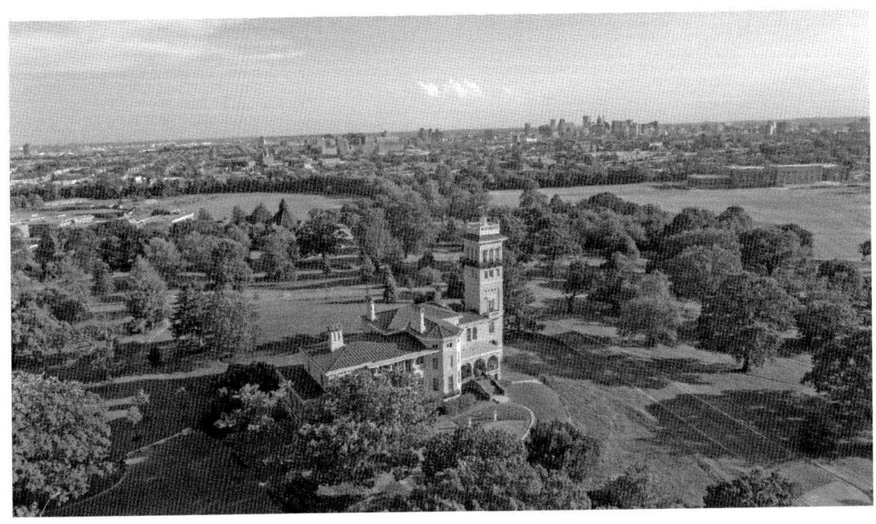

Johns Hopkins fashioned his Clifton estate to be "a paradise on earth." *Courtesy of Friends of Clifton Mansion.*

went to work at an uncle's store in Washington, D.C. (During this time, Peabody served as a volunteer artilleryman in the War of 1812.) He moved to Baltimore in 1815 at age nineteen. Here, in just over twenty years, he grew a fledgling dry goods business into multi-state success before moving into the heady world of finance. Banking led Peabody to move permanently to what was then the world's financial capital, London, England, in 1836. There, he channeled pivotal capital to U.S. ventures and helped save the State of Maryland from bankruptcy during a steep depression.

A millionaire by age fifty, the bachelor business tycoon didn't wait to bequeath his wealth and launched into philanthropy—his giving driven by memories of youthful privation. Moving in powerful, learned circles, he was also frequently reminded of his lack of formal education. ("I am well qualified to estimate its value by the disadvantages I labor under," Peabody wrote in 1831.) He set up the Peabody Trust with $2.5 million to provide housing for poor Londoners (and it's still in operation to this day), and another $2 million went to an education fund to help southern schools rebuild after the Civil War. To Baltimore, where his fortunes began, went the third-biggest gift: a total of $1.4 million to create the Peabody Institute, which has been described as the first major intellectual and arts center in an American city. As it happened, two Baltimore philanthropists became conjoined in 1986 when the Peabody Institute became a division of the Johns Hopkins University.

Johns Hopkins, the only Marylander among the initial four, was born on his family's five-hundred-acre Anne Arundel County tobacco plantation, the second of eleven children. His formal education ended at age twelve. The long-established explanation for the curtailed schooling was that his father, yielding to his Quaker faith's teachings, had freed his enslaved workers and young Hopkins was needed in the fields. Recent research by his namesake university casts this in doubt, showing the Hopkins family with a longer involvement with slavery. But whether to escape farm life or for other reasons, a teenage Hopkins left for Baltimore in 1812 to work for a merchant uncle.

One wonders what Hopkins's life and legacy would have been if he had a family of his own with children to inherit. But that path shut for him early when Quaker restrictions against such familial unions forbade him to marry the love of his life, his sixteen-year-old first cousin Elizabeth Hopkins. (Neither ever married—perhaps, it's said, because of a lovers' pact not to do so.) With no one waiting for him at home, Hopkins just focused on making money. And he excelled at it. After learning the mercantile ropes, he struck out on his own, chasing down myriad ways to amass wealth: selling everything from whiskey to guano, investing in manufacturing and shipping and moving into banking and finance. At age fifty-two, he largely retired from such activities to serve as director of the Baltimore & Ohio (B&O) Railroad, where he was a large investor. He was one of the country's richest men.

As North/South conflict intensified leading up to the Civil War, Hopkins was initially neutral—loyal to the railroad and its profitability above all. He eventually took a pro-Union position, putting him at odds with the bulk of the city's monied elite. Hopkins provided some financial support to abolitionists, although recent research shows he utilized enslaved domestics himself until at least 1850. For unknown reasons, he destroyed his personal papers, and historians are hamstrung to discern his private thoughts on social issues or much else. It's thought that a near-fatal bout of cholera in 1832 spawned an interest in improving medicine. (People of that era survived illness and injury not because of medical treatment, but despite it.) George Peabody likely encouraged his philanthropy as well. Hopkins's will left $7 million—among the largest philanthropic bequests up to that time, much of it in B&O Railroad stock—to create a hospital, a university with an affiliated medical school and an orphanage for Black children.

After he died in 1873, the Johns Hopkins Colored Children's Orphan Asylum was up and running by 1875. (Alas, the founder's noble vision for providing housing and education for as many as four hundred boys and girls was severely diluted by trustees; it never held more than a few dozen girls, who trained as domestics, and it closed in 1927.) The university—minus a medical school—arrived in 1873 (although the present campus wasn't acquired until 1902). The hospital had a problematic birthing before finally opening in 1889. But it was the medical school that hit a real snag: a funding shortfall due to a devaluation of its supporting railroad stock. It might have never opened in 1893 if not for the generosity of Mary Elizabeth Garrett, daughter of Baltimore-born railroad mogul John Work Garrett. She launched a Women's Fund for the school and ponied up more than $400,000 herself with the strings-attached stipulation that women be admitted on equal footing with men. And so the Johns Hopkins School of Medicine had three women in its first graduating class of 1897. (Writer Gertrude Stein later attended for three years.) The Johns Hopkins University, meanwhile, didn't admit female undergraduates until 1969.

Curiously, the first public building erected in Baltimore bearing the name Walters was a bathhouse in 1900, one of a handful of such philanthropically funded neighborhood facilities bolstering hygiene for citizenry lacking modern sanitary conveniences. (The last public bathhouses closed in 1959; one Walters facility still stands, converted into a residence.) But it is beauty, not bathing, for which the family is known.

William Thompson Walters was born in the Susquehanna River town of Liverpool, Pennsylvania. After some level of private education in Philadelphia, he arrived in Baltimore in 1841 armed with little more than ambition. He ultimately founded the financially lucrative wine and liquor business W.T. Walters & Company. Period engravings depict its bustling five-story home and boast that the firm possessed the largest stock of rye whiskey in the country. Walters was fond of saying that he bought a painting with the first five dollars he earned, but this was likely an apocryphal line. His mother gets the credit for his artistic inclinations, with her stated belief that "accumulating and appreciating the noble works of literature and art" was the worthiest way to spend spare time and money.

An outspoken Southern sympathizer, during the Civil War Walters exiled himself and his family (wife Ellen, son Henry and daughter Jennie) to Europe. As the horrors unfolded back home (where he likely would have faced imprisonment had the family stayed), he rubbed shoulders with artists in Paris and Rome, buying and learning. Walters returned to Baltimore a widower, as Ellen died of pneumonia during a visit to England. He never remarried.

Merging and modernizing a series of southern railroad lines added to his fortune, fueling more art buying. In addition to the nineteenth-century paintings from the likes of Millet, Alma-Tadema and Decamps, Asian art

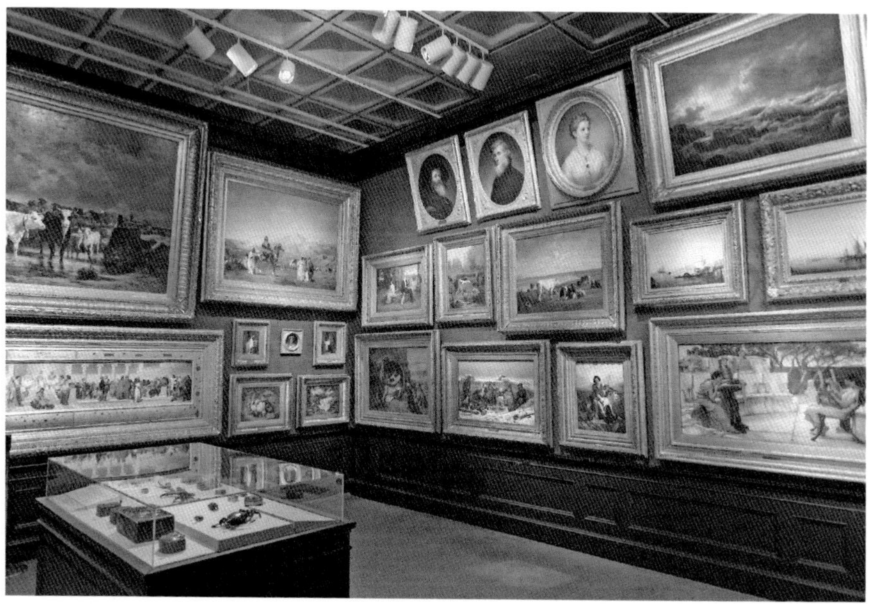

The Salon Room at the Walters Art Museum re-creates the picture gallery William Walters created at his Mount Vernon home. *Courtesy of Walters Art Museum.*

became a passion as well—porcelains, lacquerware, carvings and prints. The family's home at 5 Mount Vernon Place resembled an art gallery—and essentially became one in the 1880s when he began opening it to the public on certain days, charging fifty cents per head. The money went to a charity assisting the city's poor.

Upon William's death in 1894, Henry Walters assumed his father's business and art endeavors. The younger Walters shared his father's penchant for walrus mustaches but was more attuned to the Gilded Age good life, indulging himself with a two-hundred-foot steam yacht. The buying continued, everything from a Raphael painting to Fabergé eggs to the entire contents of an Italian collector's Tuscan villa. His catholic interests led him into buying incunabula, Egyptian antiquities, Renaissance bronzes, arms and armor, manuscripts, Islamic metalwork, pre-Columbian artifacts and more—a vast range of things. Crated objects were arriving in Baltimore by the steamer load. But there remained omissions. Henry Walters was "obdurately unreceptive" to contemporary art movements, wrote biographer William Johnson, adding that Walters bought his first impressionist work in 1900, an Alfred Sisley, "out of recognition of its historical significance rather than any appreciation of it." The de facto gallery at the Walters residence became a standalone public one after the Walters Art Gallery opened in 1909; it was given to the city upon Henry's death in 1931.

Like Peabody, Enoch Pratt was a transplanted New Englander, born in eastern Massachusetts, where his father was a farmer turned hardware-wholesaler. Leaving school at fifteen, he moved to Boston and then Baltimore, arriving in 1831 at age twenty-two with $150 in his pocket. He started a successful business selling nails and horseshoes and became an active member of the recently organized First Unitarian Church, where he met his wife, Maria Louisa Hyde. As he was a staunch supporter of the Union during the Civil War, his business flourished during the conflict. The postwar years saw him move into finance, railroads and manufacturing of his own wares in the burgeoning industrial community of Canton. Money poured in, but Pratt's frugality was legendary—it's said that he cut up used envelopes for his stationery.

Wealthy, childless and getting on in years, Pratt began to ponder his legacy. He'd already given much to his church and served as a trustee at the Peabody Institute. Concluding that it would largely serve the well-off, he nixed the idea of founding a college. A Unitarian pastor is credited with convincing him that the city needed a lending library. Pratt studied the concept for several years before offering the city just over $1 million in 1882 to construct a central library and four branches. Flying in the face of a highly segregated city, Pratt mandated that the libraries must be open to all, regardless of class, race or religion. All five buildings were completed, and the Enoch Pratt Free Library system was lending books by 1886. (Of the four original branches, only the one in Canton is still in use by the library system.) Pratt's library largess later inspired his friend, industrialist Andrew Carnegie (perhaps the wealthiest American ever), to fund the construction of more than 2,500 libraries around the world (including fourteen Pratt branches in Baltimore).

Pratt's name is also philanthropically twinned with that of Moses Sheppard (1771–1857), a wealthy Baltimore Quaker merchant with an interest in improving the treatment of the mentally ill. (While serving as commissioner of the Baltimore City Jail, Sheppard saw how many so-called lunatics were simply thrown behind bars.) Sheppard's will bequeathed more than $500,000 to construct the Sheppard Asylum just north of the city in Towson. Construction began in 1862, but the Civil War and financial shortfalls delayed completion until 1892. Pratt's own will gave the asylum a $2 million endowment in 1896, providing for additional construction and financial stability. It became the Sheppard and Enoch Pratt Hospital and is still providing mental health and addiction services to this day.

YOUR GUIDE TO HISTORY

The Engineers Club of Baltimore (Garrett-Jacobs Mansion)
7–11 West Mount Vernon Place • Midtown
(410) 539-6914 • www.esb.org

This building's stately, almost somber exterior offers no hint of the impressive interior, which is, above all, a monument to the woodworker's craft. The visitor steps into a series of rooms lined with dark, lustrous wooden panels, moldings, balustrades, parquet floors and curving stairways that evoke a golden age of handcraft. Tiffany windows, mosaics, metalwork, tapestries and a grand marble staircase continue the theme of hand-tooled opulence, announcing the wealth of its owners. The core structure was built in 1853, but the rich interior dates to a costly 1884–93 renovation by the famed architectural firm of McKim, Mead and White.

This was the home of one of Maryland's richest and most powerful couples, Robert and Mary Frick Garrett. He was the president of the B&O Railroad Company, inheriting the job from his father, John Work Garrett, in 1884; Mary Garrett, in her own right, was the undisputed queen of Baltimore's high society and the driving force behind the mansion's design,

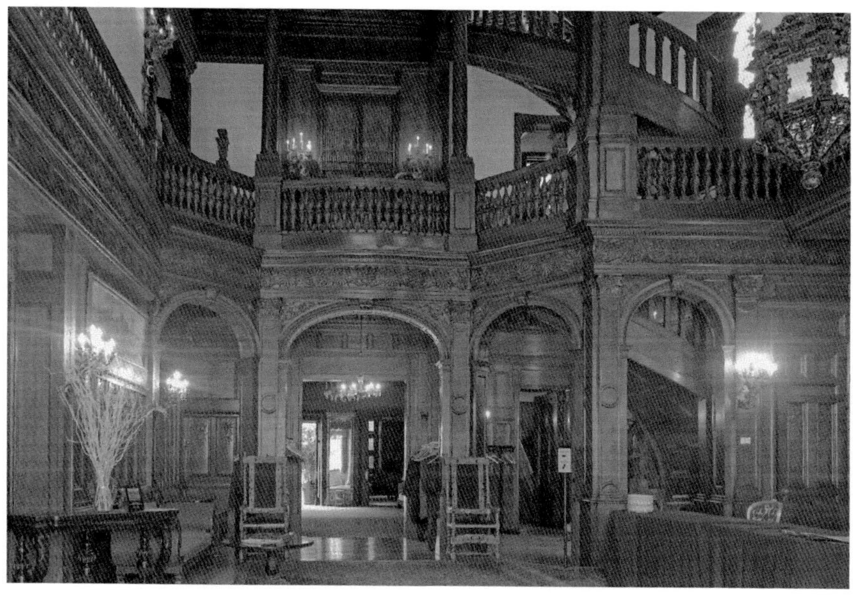

The Engineers Club of Baltimore at the Garrett-Jacobs Mansion. *Courtesy of Wikimedia Commons/Smash the Iron Cage.*

decoration and (after getting widowed and then remarried to Dr. Henry Jacobs) its expansion. Not one to scrimp, Mary Frick Jacobs hired John Russell Pope, the original architect of both the Baltimore Museum of Art and the National Gallery of Art in Washington, D.C., to extend the house to the east. The Engineers Club purchased the building in 1961. The mansion schedules public tours and special educational programs, and the club can be rented for weddings and other events. If you visit, ask (on your way out) about ghosts. Legends linger, and a few employees whisper, off the record, about uncanny experiences in the stairways and cellar.

Enoch Pratt Central Library

400 Cathedral Street • Midtown

(410) 396-5430 • www.prattlibrary.org • Free

With a design inspired by the all-are-welcome vision of its namesake benefactor, merchant philanthropist Enoch Pratt, the central library of the Enoch Pratt Free Library system is everything the New York Public Library's main building is not. The latter institution presents an imposing façade—its lofty entrance reached via a grand staircase flanked by marble lions. By contrast, you enter Baltimore's main library at street level after passing plate glass windows with ever-changing biblio-related displays. This 1933 building replaced the original and outgrown central library erected in 1886. Baltimore architect Clyde N. Friz was directed by library leadership to avoid a "fortress" look and strive for "friendliness rather than aloofness." The limestone exterior mingles Renaissance and Grecian design, while ornamental metal grillwork around doors and windows nod to Art Deco. Inside, coffered ceilings grace some rooms, and there's an airy central atrium flanked by marble columns and paintings of various Lords of Baltimore.

A 50,000-square-foot annex opened in 2003, now home to the African American Department and the Maryland Department, the latter an important repository of books and ephemera relating to the city and state. In 2014, the longtime head of the Enoch Pratt library system, Carla Hayden, left for a new position as librarian of Congress. Most recently, a three-year, $115 million renovation of the 300,000-square-foot main building was completed, modernizing infrastructure while restoring ornate plasterwork and hand-painted detailing—readying the building for a second century of service while maintaining its slot on the shortlist of the most beautiful public libraries in the country.

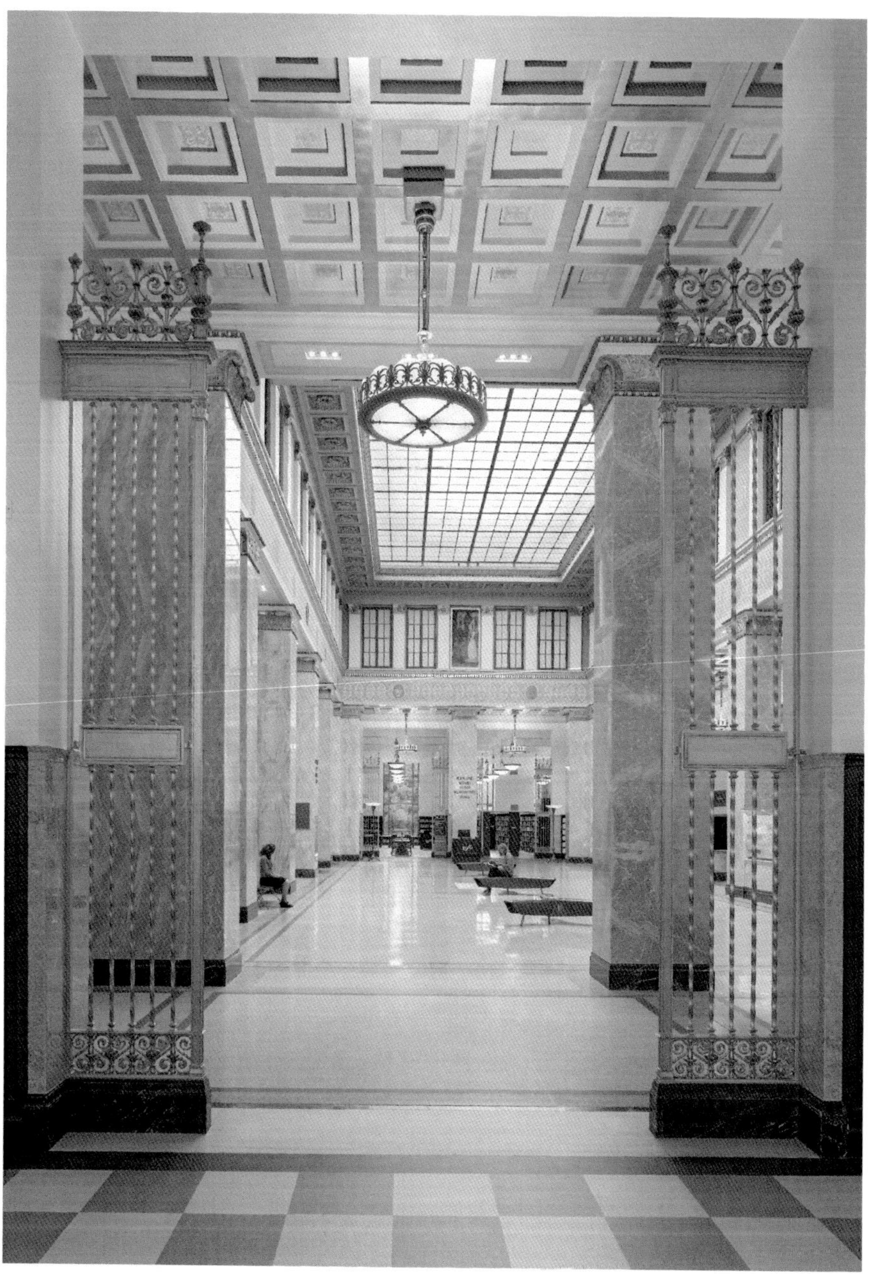

The City that Reads. The Central Library of the Enoch Pratt Free Library System is handsome and inviting. *Courtesy of Joseph Romeo Photography.*

Enoch Pratt House

201 West Monument Street • Midtown • Exterior Only

Erected in 1847 and enlarged in 1868 to incorporate a fourth floor beneath a mansard roof, this grand, five-bay Greek Revival house on two building lots was merchant-philanthropist Enoch Pratt's home until he died in 1896 (with his widow remaining in residence until her death in 1911). It is part of the Center for Maryland History and Culture's campus, though as of this writing, plans call for selling the underutilized property, perhaps returning it to residential use.

Peabody Institute of the Johns Hopkins University

1 East Mount Vernon Place • Midtown
(410) 516-8000 • www.peabody.jhu.edu

Founded in 1856 as an urban arts center, Peabody Institute's Italianate marble home sits proudly on the southeast corner of Mount Vernon Place. Designed by English-born architect Edmund George Lind, it was completed in 1861, but the Civil War delayed the formal opening until 1866, when financier philanthropist George Peabody himself was on hand from London to attend the ribbon-cutting. Today largely known as a music conservatory (as such, the nation's second oldest), it opened with a reference library, art gallery and lecture space. The institute also has one of the oldest continuously operating dance programs in the country. The Neoclassical Miriam A. Friedberg Concert Hall seats more than six hundred as the largest of the numerous onsite performance venues and recital halls where student, faculty and ensemble performances are held, many open to the public. Peabody Institute began its affiliation with Johns Hopkins University in 1977, becoming a full-fledged university division in 1986.

Peabody Library

17 East Mount Vernon Place • Midtown
(667) 208-6715 • www.peabodyevents.library.jhu.edu • Free

One of the world's great libraries and perhaps the city's most dramatic interior space, this "Cathedral of Books" opened as an addition to the adjacent Peabody Institute in 1868. The Peabody Stack Room features a

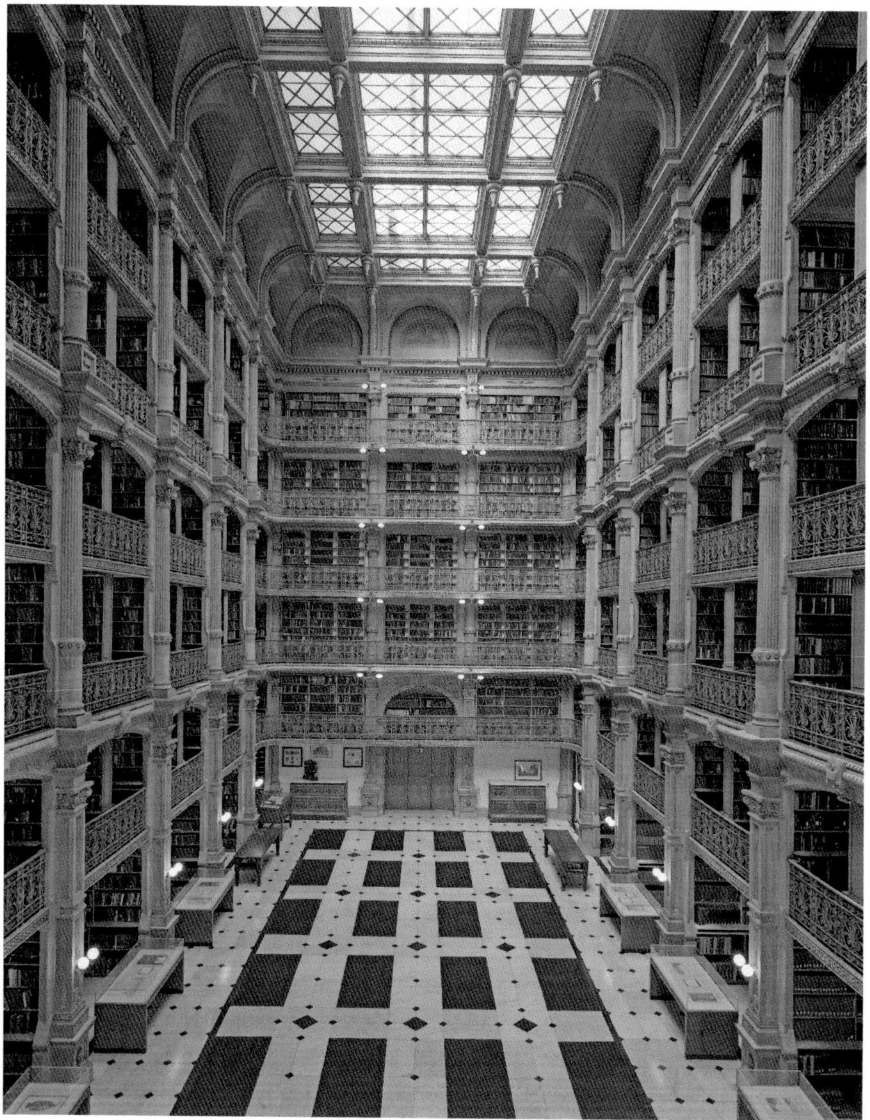

The Peabody Library is a veritable "Cathedral of Books." *Courtesy of Jim Burger.*

soaring sky-lit atrium surrounded by five tiers of bookshelf-laden balconies. Though appearing to be fashioned from carved stone, this dramatic home to some 300,000 books, most dating to the nineteenth century, is an exceptional example of cast-iron architecture. It can be rented for private events and is a popular wedding venue.

The Walters Art Museum
600 North Charles Street • Midtown
(410) 547-9000 • www.thewalters.org • Free

The Walters opened in 1909 as home to the encyclopedic, globe-spanning assortment of art and antiquities amassed by father-and-son collectors William and Henry Walters. It was bequeathed to the city following Henry's death in 1931, and its initial collection of twenty-two thousand objects has swelled to thirty-six thousand via ongoing acquisitions. The main building's Renaissance Revival exterior was modeled after a Parisian hotel, and the airy interior atrium was inspired by a palazzo in Genoa, Italy. A 1974 expansion in the Brutalist style nearly doubled exhibition space, and (thankfully) a 2001 retrofit brightened some of the grimness inherent in that architectural form.

A singular experience is the Salon Room, a re-creation of the picture gallery that William built behind the family home in 1884. Gilt-framed works are hung chockablock, in the nineteenth-century fashion, so images whimsical, horrific and tranquil combine to present a unique sensory experience. Also not to be missed is the Chamber of Wonders, which re-creates how an eclectic seventeenth-century Flemish nobleman might have displayed curiosities from man and nature. Here, painter Pieter Huys's sixteenth-century, Bosch-inspired hellscape of tortured sinners hangs alongside a desiccated puffer fish and a stuffed flying squirrel. The Hackerman House, an opulent 1850s mansion, is part of the museum as well, with its sweeping stairwell beneath a dazzling skylight of Tiffany glass and world-class hoard of Asian art.

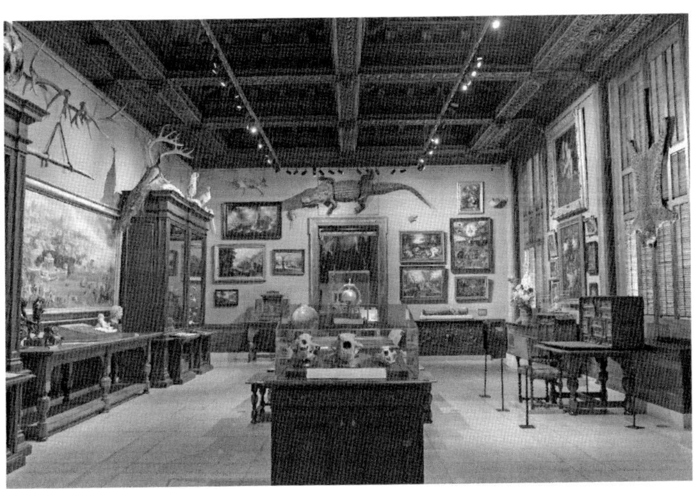

The eclectic and curious Chamber of Wonders at the Walters Art Museum. *Courtesy of Walters Art Museum.*

Elisha Tyson's House

732 Pacific Street • North • Exterior Only

This substantial Federal-style stone house, built in the early 1800s, was the summer home of one of Maryland's most important early philanthropists and a fierce champion of the antislavery cause. Elisha Tyson (1750–1824) was a Pennsylvania Quaker who came to Baltimore in 1781 to develop flour mills along the Jones Falls near the present-day Hampden neighborhood. He became a millionaire through his enterprises and investments and put much of his wealth into charitable work, particularly antislavery activism. In 1800, he retired from business and devoted the rest of his life to the abolitionist movement. A tireless organizer, Tyson lobbied in Annapolis to make it easier for owners to legally set their enslaved workers free; he personally intervened to free hundreds of Black people who had been kidnapped into slavery. He also helped found the first antislavery organization in Maryland.

As a highly public person, Tyson was strict about following the laws that governed slavery, but it's possible and even probable that he was involved in the illegal and secretive smuggling of fugitives from slavery. Quaker histories allege that, circa 1800, Tyson collaborated with Jacob Lindley, a Quaker minister in Avondale, Pennsylvania, to establish one of the earliest known routes of what would later be called the "Underground Railroad," following today's Route 1. A few years later, Tyson was one of the partners in the building of Falls Road, which today travels north from Hampden to within three miles of the Pennsylvania line. Circumstantially, it seems likely that Tyson, in his Falls Road project, had the secret agenda of providing a route north for refugees from slavery. (During the 1814 Battle of Baltimore, panicked city bankers brought their gold up Falls Road to hide in Tyson's basement.) When Tyson died, his funeral procession was joined by thousands of Black Baltimoreans who honored his work, but the city's White establishment, rife with slaveholders, did its best to ignore his legacy and forget his name. He was originally buried at the Old Town Meetinghouse, but his grave was later moved to Green Mount Cemetery. Tyson's house is now in private hands; as of this writing, a section of it is available as rental accommodations through Airbnb. It sits among twenty stone duplexes built in the 1840s for millworkers, constituting the tiny neighborhood called Stone Hill.

Evergreen Museum and Library

4545 North Charles Street • North
(410) 516-0341 • https://museums.jhu.edu • Admission Fee

Commanding a high wooded lot just north of Loyola University on Charles Street, this forty-eight-room mansion houses a motherlode of art, furniture and literature, as well as a history with an overlay of tragedy. Open to the public in its own right as a house museum, Evergreen hosts frequent tours, rotating art exhibits and musical and theatrical performances as well as private events. Among the mansion's unique treasures is its library of rare books, prints and manuscripts, as well as the charming, eccentric theater designed in 1922 by the Russian artist Léon Bakst.

Evergreen's opulence is dazzling, but its darker historical context is generally overlooked. Built in 1858, the original quasi-classical Evergreen House changed hands several times before it was purchased in 1878 by B&O Railroad president John Work Garrett as a gift for his son, T. Harrison Garrett. Just one year before this extravagance, the elder Garrett had taken the leading role in both provoking and, with the help of Maryland's National Guard and the U.S. Marines, crushing the Great Railroad Strike of 1877.

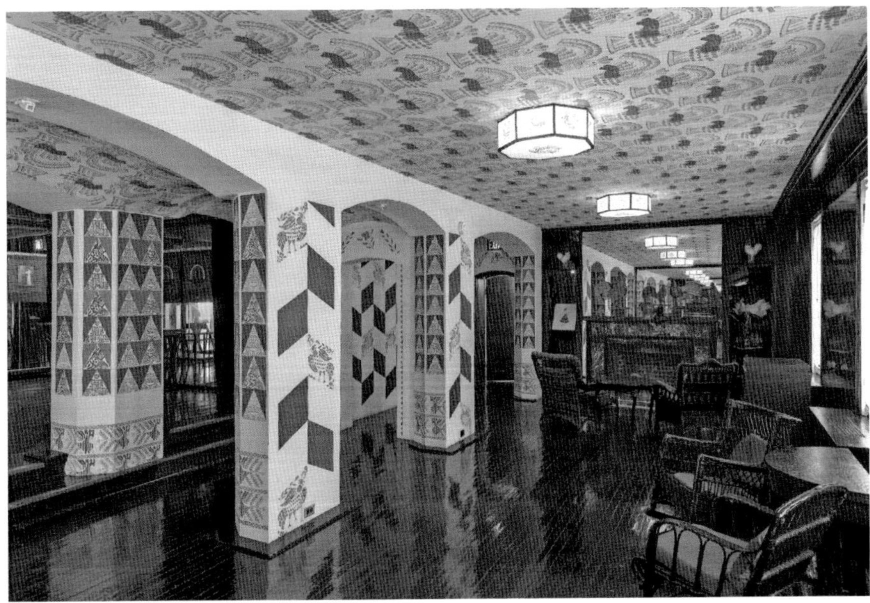

Evergreen includes a colorful theater designed in 1922 by Russian artist Léon Bakst. *Courtesy of Evergreen Museum and Library/JHU.*

All told, some one hundred civilians were killed in the course of the strike, and more than one thousand were jailed.

The following year, Garrett bestowed the Evergreen House on his son; two years after that, Garrett (whose brutal suppression of the strike met with wide disapproval) established the B&O Employees' Relief Association to provide workers with benefits in cases of sickness, injury and death. J.W. Garrett died in 1884, with a net worth of $15 million (around $4.2 billion in 2021 dollars). Just four years later, T. Harrison Garrett died in a yachting accident. The property was eventually inherited by T. Harrison's son, the second John Work Garrett, who built the mansion's collections of books and art. After expanding the house in the 1920s and '40s, the latter Garrett died in 1942. He willed Evergreen and its collections to its present-day owner, Johns Hopkins University.

Johns Hopkins University Homewood Campus

3400 North Charles Street • North
(410) 516-8000 • www.jhu.edu/life/campuses/homewood

Maryland's most famous university, founded in 1876, owns many properties in Baltimore and is by far the city's largest private employer. Among its many scholarly credits are the thirty-nine (and counting) Nobel Prizes awarded to Hopkins affiliates. After many years in a haphazard collection of downtown buildings, the university acquired 140 acres along North Charles Street between 29th Street and University Parkway to create Homewood Campus in 1902. The architectural firm of Parker and Thomas designed the original core campus using the 1801 Homewood mansion, on the east side of campus, as its stylistic model. The heart of the campus is Gilman Hall, opened in 1915, which enlarges many of Homewood's features—the pale panels above the windows, the rounded dormers, the shield-shaped design on the classical pediment—with the addition of a multi-staged clock tower and cupola. Lesser campus buildings, old and new, echo the same architectural style to varying degrees. More modern buildings include the Muller Building, on San Martin Drive, headquarters of the Space Telescope Science Institute, which operates the world-famous Hubble Space Telescope.

Johns Hopkins University Archaeology Museum

Gilman Hall, Johns Hopkins Homewood Campus • 3400 North Charles Street • North

(410) 516-0383 • https://archaeologicalmuseum.jhu.edu • Free

Tucked into the bottom level of Gilman Hall, the small Archaeological Museum is a treasure chest of antiquities, with an especially fine collection of classical Greek pottery, decorated with lively paintings based on Greek mythology, drama and domestic scenes. Other artifacts represent the ancient cultures of Rome, Egypt and the Americas. Hours are limited, so a call ahead is recommended.

Clifton Mansion

2701 St. Lo Drive, Clifton Park • East

(410) 366-8533 • www.friendsofcliftonmansion.org • Admission Fee

Sprawling Clifton Park includes a public golf course, tennis courts and playing fields, all overlooked by its namesake: the towered, Italianate mansion that merchant philanthropist Johns Hopkins created as his country estate. The original structure on this site was a circa 1803 Federal-style house built by Henry Thompson, a wealthy merchant who led a horse brigade during the Battle of Baltimore. The present Clifton Mansion was built around this core, but with an enlarged exterior, stucco walls and arcaded porches added after Johns Hopkins bought the house in 1841. Another addition is the eighty-foot observation tower from which, using a spyglass, Hopkins could watch his ships sail up the harbor. As redesigned by the prominent firm of Niernsee and Neilson, the mansion and its grounds were intended to impress visitors with the owner's wealth and worldly tastes; Hopkins said that he wanted the landscaped grounds to look like "a paradise on earth." The interior featured intricate decorative painting, panels of faux wood grain and marble, gorgeous black walnut trim and murals, including a ten-by-fifteen-foot depiction of the Bay of Naples. Hopkins, always too busy to travel abroad, created his own Italian fantasy.

Hopkins envisioned the estate becoming the site of the namesake university that his will set out to create, but after his death, the trustees chose the site of today's Homewood Campus and the city acquired Clifton. It eventually became a public golf course with the mansion as its clubhouse.

The elaborately decorated walls—murals and all—were unceremoniously painted over, and countless golfers clomped through the interior in spiked shoes. Alarmed by the edifice's abuse and decay, the late Sam Hopkins Sr., a great-grandnephew of Johns Hopkins, helped form the nonprofit Friends of Clifton Mansion in 1996 to oversee renovations. Civic Works, a youth employment-training program, leases Clifton for its headquarters. Call for information about tours.

Green Mount Cemetery

1501 Greenmount Avenue • East
(410) 539-0641 www.greenmountcemetery.com • Free

Opened in 1838, this verdant sixty-eight-acre cemetery is the nation's fourth-oldest example of the era's rural or garden cemetery movement, wherein sprawling park-like settings replaced crowded and confined urban churchyards—such as the eighteenth-century Westminster Burial Ground—as preferred places of burial. Not only does its more than sixty-five thousand interments present a who's who of the famous and infamous of yore—from philanthropist Johns Hopkins to Lincoln assassin John Wilkes Booth—but its leafy, undulating beauty and stunning funerary art are draws in themselves as well. Even birdwatchers are attracted to this midtown oasis.

Johns Hopkins's modest tomb (he was a Quaker after all) is joined here by those of fellow philanthropists Mary Elizabeth Garrett, Enoch Pratt, Moses Sheppard, Elisha Tyson and William and Henry Walters. There are also no fewer than fifteen Civil War generals (nine Confederate, six Union), eight Maryland governors and seven Baltimore mayors within Green Mount's walls. The headstone reading "After life's fitful fever, she sleeps well" belongs to Betsy Bonaparte Patterson. It's a fitting epitaph for a Baltimore belle who, as a teenager in 1803, was wooed by and wed to visiting French naval officer Jérôme Bonaparte—only to have a certain Napoleon annul the union and draw his kid brother back home to Europe (and an arranged marriage of diplomatic value). The quirkiest headstone belongs to Elijah Bond, who patented the Ouija board in Baltimore. A collector of the boards installed a headstone shaped like one of Bond's "spirit boards" in 2006. The tall obelisk marked "Booth" is for the thespian family of that name, including father Junius and son Edwin. The name John Wilkes, another son, doesn't appear in the family plot, but his remains were moved here from Washington, D.C., in 1869. Cemetery visitors leave pennies—Lincoln side up—on a small, unmarked headstone here. Perched on high, the octagonal Gothic Revival 1850s chapel has flying buttresses supporting a 102-foot spire. Its design, by the prolific firm Niernsee and Neilson, was inspired by a monument to Sir Walter Scott in Edinburgh. Visitor information and maps are available at the Tudor-Gothic main entrance for a small fee.

Johns Hopkins Medical Complex

601 North Broadway (Billings Building) • East

This sprawling hilltop complex presents a seemingly impenetrable thicket of buildings of various ages and architectural styles. Residing here are Johns Hopkins Hospital and the Johns Hopkins University schools of medicine, public health and nursing, alongside sundry institutes, clinics and labs. This high-ground location has been used for healing since the eighteenth century, when yellow fever victims were housed here in temporary structures. Later, it was home to the Maryland Hospital for the Insane. That institution was already relocating when Johns Hopkins acquired the thirteen-acre site and leveled what remained. He died shortly thereafter, leaving trustees to build the new hospital. Of the three original buildings, the most prominent is the four-story brick Queen Anne–style Administration Building, topped with a now-iconic dome. Although ground was broken for it in 1877, it took twelve

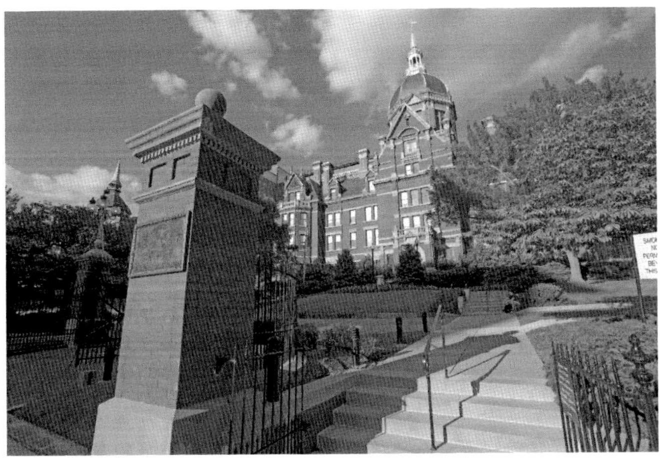

Original main building of the Johns Hopkins Hospital, completed in 1889. *Courtesy of Visit Baltimore.*

years to complete because of funding shortfalls. It is named the Billings Administration Building in honor of John Billings, a Civil War battlefield surgeon who designed the medical aspects of the initial hospital buildings and served as construction manager.

Any list of medical breakthroughs and firsts developed at this now world-class medical center would be exhaustive, from the mundane—first use of rubber gloves in surgery—to such daily lifesavers as the invention of CPR.

Chapter 8

BRICK, MORTAR, MARBLE AND STEEL

A LOOK AT THE CITY'S ARCHITECTURE AND URBAN DESIGN

Baltimore, as a built environment, is best appreciated up close, at street level. Compared to the skylines of Philadelphia, New York and Boston, Baltimore's profile is modest in acreage and not vertically ambitious. A first-time visitor, depending on how he or she came into town, could be forgiven for thinking that the city consists mainly of row houses. But if you look and linger, the town offers unique spaces, elegant design, sheer craft, curious details, stories and histories, local idiosyncrasies and—pardon the expression—charm. The mid-twentieth-century Baltimore that loyal son H.L. Mencken described as looking "like the ruins of a once-great medieval city" has lost some of its medieval qualities, but its 250 years of history have left their traces in the homes of the humble and the rich, the houses of worship and the places of business and industry. This wide-ranging section is about the forms and textures of Baltimore's hardscape: the raw materials of walls and streets, the passing and recurring architectural styles, the uses and reuses of buildings and the peculiar icons of our somewhat prickly skyline.

To paint with a very broad brush, Baltimore is mostly a reddish-brown town. The existing historic core of the city is chiefly built of brick; Fell's Point preserves just a few examples of the sort of wooden houses that circled the harbor circa 1800. Brick took over not only because it was more durable than wood, but also because it was locally available and cheap. Brickyards sprouted along the south edge of the Inner Harbor, where raw clay was dug right out of the ground. Bricks also arrived as ballast in British ships and were offered for sale at dockside. Red brick walls with white trim (of local marble

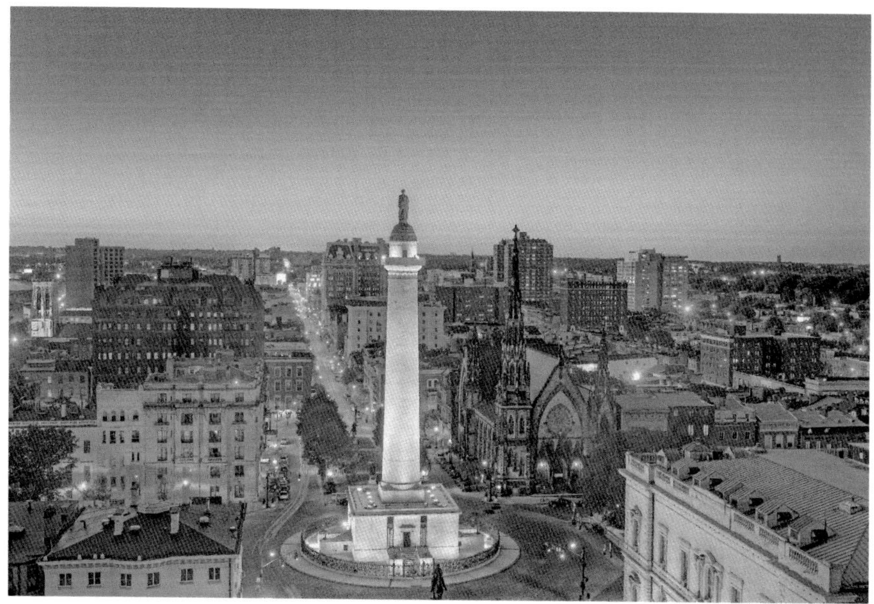

The Washington Monument is the centerpiece of Mount Vernon Place. *Courtesy of Sean Pavone.*

or painted wood) characterized the Georgian and Federal architectural styles that dominated the early city, including public buildings, churches, mansions and commonplace row homes. The brick-and-white-trim look has never entirely gone away; it enjoyed a local revival with the construction of the Johns Hopkins University's Homewood Campus in 1904, which inspired architects working in the nearby neighborhood of Guilford (opened 1913) and the southern end of Roland Park (circa 1910).

Early stone buildings also survive in Baltimore, especially in the industrialized Jones Falls valley and the old mill villages of Dickeyville and Franklintown. The massive, flood-resistant mill complexes of the early nineteenth century were typically made of tough, streaky, gray to brown or black gneiss, a half-billion-year-old stone quarried right out of the city's streambanks. Especially in the Jones Falls valley, buildings of stone and brick that started as water- and steam-powered factories survived into the twentieth century as hives of electrified light industry. Many now contain offices, art studios, gyms, restaurants and coffee shops, where hand-built stone walls and aged bricks lend a comforting sense of connection with the past.

Baltimore prospered in the decades prior to the Civil War, and wealthy citizens developed lofty, aspirational tastes. The city's architects, including

European-trained craftsmen and homegrown builders, drifted toward classical revival styles, favoring local Cockeysville marble for pillars, pediments and cornices in the Greco-Roman tradition and moving on to classically derived Renaissance models and other European styles. While the pale, dignified look was especially popular for downtown churches and public buildings—from City Hall to the Clarence Mitchell Courthouse—classical elements also made their way onto the façades of upscale row houses and were grafted onto otherwise unremarkable brick façades. The continuum of Georgian, Federal and classical revival styles can be easily seen by walking around Mount Vernon and the blocks to its south and west.

Blacksmiths and foundries made their own contributions to the look and form of nineteenth-century Baltimore. To this day, upscale antebellum row houses around Mount Vernon boast hand-wrought railings, boot-scrapers and window grates, some with cast-iron ornaments. Cast iron, in turn, was crafted into entire façades beginning in the 1850s. Cast in molds, molten iron was capable of elaborate forms that could be replicated, so that a façade could be fabricated from repeated castings of the same ornate window frame or cornice mold. By the end of the nineteenth century, scores of cast-iron façades lined the city's commercial blocks in downtown Baltimore, encrusted with pillars and moldings on every floor.

As the nineteenth century progressed, increasingly ornate and exotic styles overtook the orderly world of brick and marble. Gothic architecture, persistently popular for churches, spiked the skyline with elaborate spires and towers. Homebuilders and architects alike borrowed from foreign styles; fads came and went and collided with one another. Some prominent architects, seeming to frown on the distractions of ornament, revived the somber, early medieval dignity of Romanesque, especially for banks and churches. The general trend, however, was toward increasing ornamentation; chronologically, it would not be wrong to sum up the multiple styles as Victorian.

Baltimoreans of past centuries enjoyed wrapping practical structures in incongruously exotic garb: consider the Bromo-Seltzer Tower, part Italian Renaissance, part patent-medicine billboard; the Roland Park Shopping Center, said to be America's oldest strip mall, disguised as a Tudor manor; Engine House 6, another imitation-Renaissance tower with a fire hall at its feet; and the Hansa House, from 1912, a downtown commercial building lifted from sixteenth-century Germany.

By the 1890s, densely packed, smoky Baltimore was bursting at its boundaries. Upscale three-story row houses marched out the main roads as the city encroached on, and eventually absorbed, formerly rural villages, mill towns and "railroad suburbs" of patrician summer homes. Industry, commerce and banking created a growing middle class, hankering for fresh air and sunlight. On what were then the outskirts of town, developers carved up old estates. Some venerable mansions were torn down, while others were repurposed. Trolley lines rolled out the main thoroughfares, sprouting commercial centers and new housing tracts. The Roland Park Company planned and developed a new concept: the garden community, dedicated to the most privileged strata of Baltimore society. Roland Park and the other "Olmsted neighborhoods" that followed were playgrounds for domestic architects, where traditional brick mansions alternated with romantic, one-of-a-kind dream houses. Elsewhere on the suburban frontier, less grandiose developers bought up cow pastures and truck farms along the main roads, planted row houses along the thoroughfares and lined the rolling hills with row houses, duplexes and free-standing cottages for middle-class workers and professionals.

Just as suburbia was taking root, downtown suffered a disaster that, in retrospect, performed a service by clearing the way for a new, less crowded central Baltimore and spurring modernization of the city's water and sewer systems. The Great Baltimore Fire of 1904, blamed on a discarded cigar or cigarette, devastated 140 acres of the city's commercial core and working wharves, from Liberty Street on the west to the outlet of the Jones Falls on the east and from the harbor's edge north to Lexington Street. Driven by strong winds, flames consumed hundreds of nineteenth-century commercial buildings, including most of downtown's showy cast-iron fronts. Fire companies rushed in from Washington, D.C., and Philadelphia only to find their hose couplings didn't fit Baltimore's fire hydrants. A few rugged buildings, like the stout fortress of the Mercantile Bank (now the Chesapeake Shakespeare Company), were gutted by flames but remained structurally sound.

Remarkably, no one was killed in the thirty-hour conflagration, whose glow could be seen from Washington, D.C. Well, such was the official body count city boosters latched onto and promoted for decades. A twenty-first-century historian found an overlooked newspaper account from the era describing the charred remains of a body pulled from the harbor. Still, that there was only one death is miraculous given the scale of the calamity, which pitted steam-powered fire equipment against a sixteen-story building burning like a torch. The city quickly rebuilt, widening the streets and instituting structural codes to prevent future infernos. Somewhat belatedly and haltingly, Baltimore fully entered the age of skyscrapers.

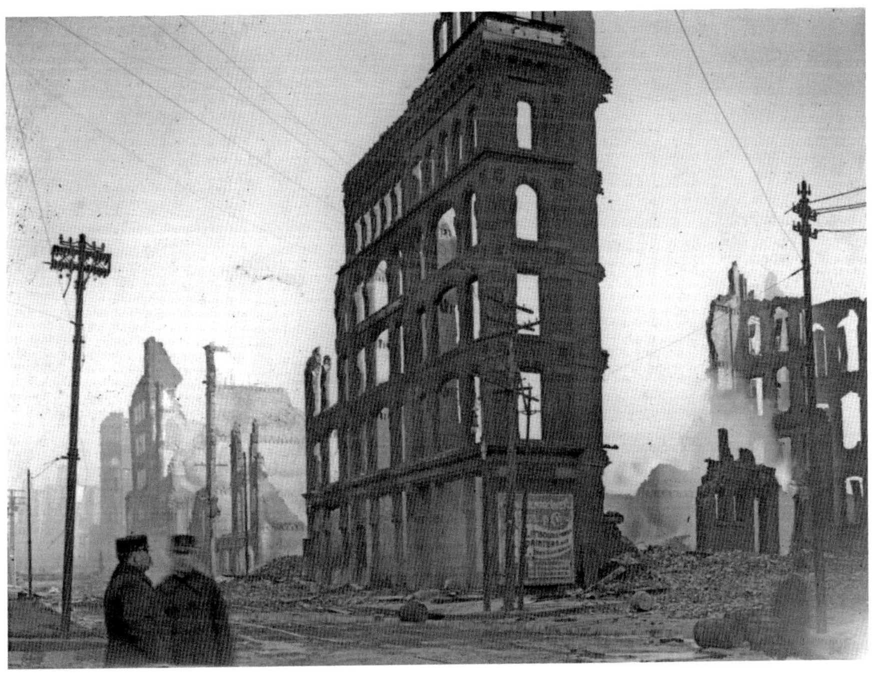

The Great Baltimore Fire of 1904 left much of downtown in smoking ruins. *Courtesy of Library of Congress.*

The higher the buildings climbed, the more engineering took precedence over craft. The soaring Art Deco masterpiece at 10 Light Street, from 1929, stands at the boundary between the richly patterned past and the mechanized severity of architectural modernism. Not surprisingly, the years of the Depression and World War II contributed little to Baltimore's skyline, although the city's population burgeoned and street-level construction boomed.

The full embrace of modernism didn't come until midcentury, when civic leaders and planners tackled a moribund downtown with Charles Center, an ambitious remaking of much of the commercial and financial district. Select older buildings were preserved, but many were demolished as irregular street patterns were ironed out to create building lots across twenty-two acres. Urban activity was focused on a pair of interior plazas in a plan that literally turned its back on the streets by channeling foot traffic to a series of elevated cement walkways. (In this prospective new world order, pedestrians need never set foot on a city sidewalk or encounter a street corner.) A number of notable new buildings bloomed in its wake, beginning with Mies van der Rohe's black-glass One Charles Center in 1962. A cultural intrusion into

Charles Center's capitalist bustle was noted modernist architect John M. Johansen's Brutalist Morris A. Mechanic Theater, erected in 1967 at 1 South Charles Street as a study in blocky cast-concrete forms. (Deemed undersized for contemporary Broadway shows, the theater shuttered in 2004; many found the soot-stained "brutal" walls hard to love, and it met the wrecking ball in 2014 over the protest of ardent admirers.)

Charles Center was largely successful in keeping the downtown office market current and competitive until forces beyond the drafting board emerged: an explosion of mergers and acquisitions that saw Baltimore become more and more of a branch-office town, exemplified when Maryland National Bank got gobbled up in 1993 by a North Carolina financial institution; the eventual successor, Bank of America, ultimately parted with its landmark Art Deco skyscraper on Light Street. Some of the midcentury urban planning just didn't age well, including the largely unpeopled plazas and the overhead walkways—derided as hamster "Habitrails" in some circles—that have since been torn down.

In the 1970s, the Inner Harbor's proverbial "rotting wharves" and wholesale markets were cleared away and replaced with sleek towers, like I.M. Pei's World Trade Center, and one-of-a-kind, tourist-tempting confections

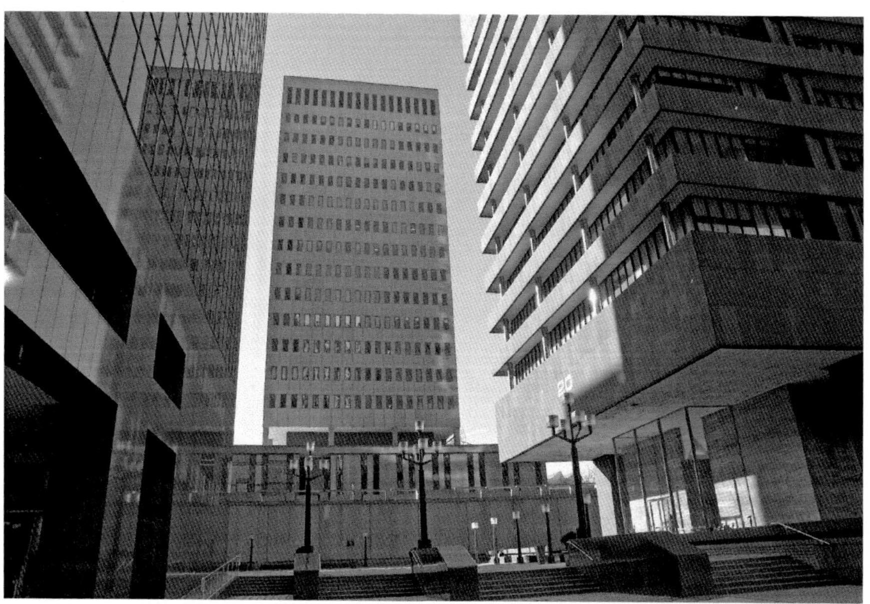

Breaking ground in the 1960s, the Charles Center Plan sought to modernize downtown. *Courtesy of Brennen Jensen.*

like the National Aquarium and repurposed Power Plant building. Baltimore planners also bolstered the era's back-to-the-city movement with a nationally lauded Urban Homesteading Program, better known simply as the "Dollar Houses." The city lightened its inventory of decaying properties—including blocks of row houses condemned for canceled highways—by selling them for one dollar to buyers who pledged to renovate them and live in them for a specified period of time. Handsome neighborhoods, such as Otterbein just west of the Inner Harbor, emerged from the program. House prices there have gone from $1 to north of $400,000.

By the 1980s, many architects had decided that pure modernism was just not that much fun, and so began the ongoing public experiment of postmodernism. While Baltimoreans have coined sarcastic nicknames for some of downtown's more attention-grabbing postmodern towers (for example, the "Bug Zapper Building" for Harbor View Towers), street-level Baltimore has discovered the joys of adaptive reuse: new buildings tucked behind or grafted onto old façades, stabilized ruins and all sorts of old structures—industrial, civic, commercial and religious—converted into rental units, condominiums, restaurants and classrooms. The cheerful eclecticism that results is in keeping with the city's self-reinvention as a creative incubator, a town that appreciates its past while not being stuck in it. (Baltimore's significant colonial and early 1800s architecture is discussed in Chapters 1 and 2. The city's landmark churches and temples are detailed in Chapter 4; a few notable buildings pop up in other chapters as well.)

YOUR GUIDE TO HISTORY

Baltimore Architecture Foundation

(410) 625-2585 • www.baltimorearchitecture.org

Founded in 1987, this offshoot of the Baltimore chapter of the American Institute of Architects (dating to 1871) helps citizens discover Baltimore's built environment through tours, lectures and educational programs. A highlight is its annual Doors Open Baltimore, a weekend-long event each fall where more than fifty significant Baltimore buildings can be explored for free. Plans are underway to open the Center for Architecture and Design on the retail level at One Charles Center with a gallery, classrooms, public event space and an architecture-focused retail store.

Row Houses

Ubiquitous

Travel through almost any Baltimore neighborhood and sooner or later you will see row houses of some kind. Although the first row houses in America sprouted in Philadelphia, modeled on styles from London, Baltimore was just a few years behind. This practical, inexpensive and, for builders, profitable approach to housing is still the best option for many Baltimoreans. Row houses have been defined—debatably—as buildings that are not only stuck together but also built together, with a uniform style, by a single builder. They can be tall and grand, as in Mount Vernon or Bolton Hill; they can be tiny, as in parts of Fell's Point and Federal Hill; and they can be simple or ornate, depending on when they were built and for what set of buyers. Generally, the style of row houses reflected the dominant architectural trends of their times, from the simple dignity of the early Federal period to the fussy eclecticism of the Late Victorians, the spartan, mass-produced blocks thrown up for twentieth-century industrial workers and the wider, brighter "daylight row houses" of outer city communities. If you live in Baltimore long enough, and pay attention to such things, you can develop a sharp eye for the age of neighborhoods based on their row house styles.

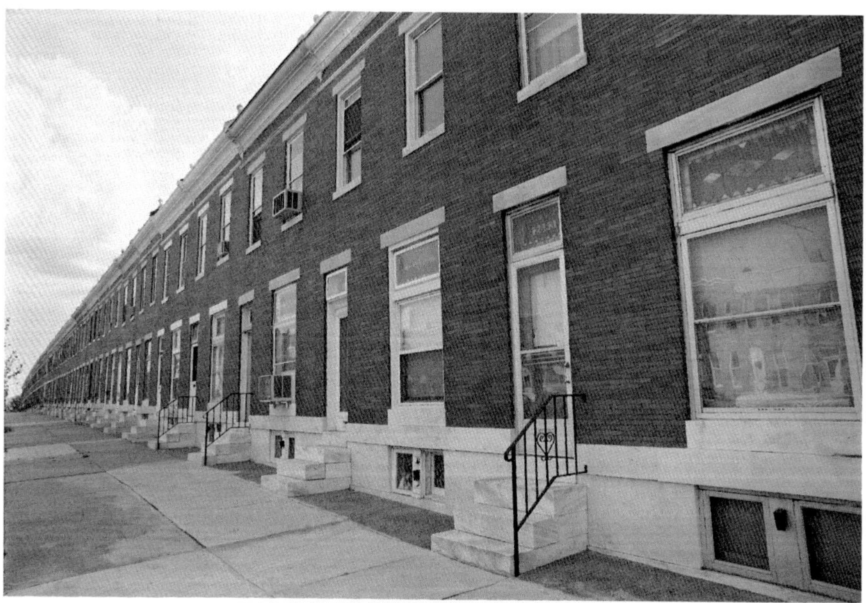

Baltimore's longest row of row houses. *Courtesy of Jim Burger.*

One crucial bit of Baltimore row house lore: The longest continuous row of identical row houses in Baltimore is found on the 2600 block of Wilkens Avenue, in the southeast corner of town. Built by Walter Westphal in 1903, the row consists of fifty-four dwellings with orange glazed brick, white trim and simple white cornices divided between houses by brackets. The dividers are topped by Westphal's trademark ball-on-pedestal motif, also seen on several less famous rows around town. The 2600 block of Wilkens is so well known that it has a nickname, the "Mill Hill Deck of Cards."

Marble Steps

Midtown, East, Southeast, South and West

The famed "marble steps of Baltimore" aren't as famous as they used to be, but the ubiquitous white steps maintain their status as a collective local icon. Many tons of marble brighten the older parts of the town, almost all of it coming from the quarries of Cockeysville, ten miles north of the city line. Not only steps but also countless window frames, doorways, columns, cornices, entire façades and two Washington monuments (in Baltimore and Washington, D.C.) have been carved out of the half-billion-year-old

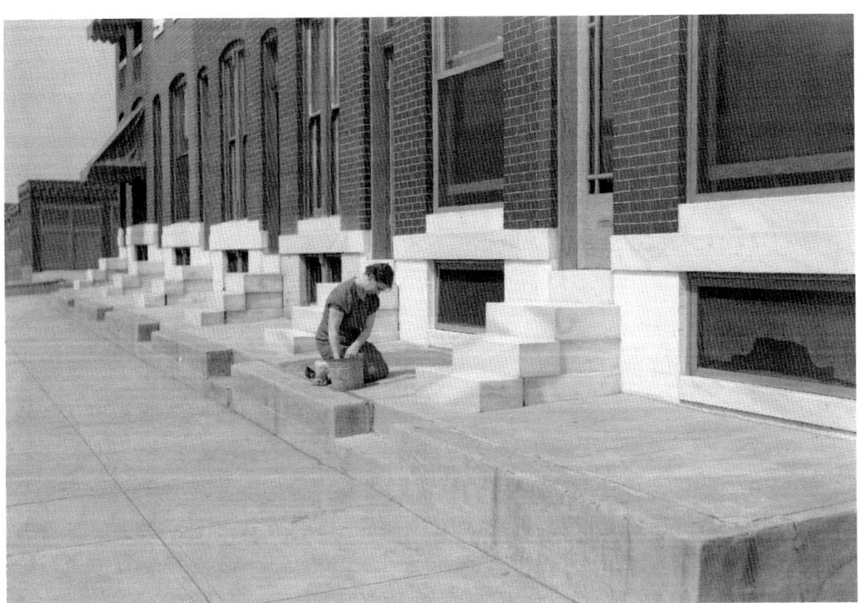

Keeping your white marble steps white required regular work. *Courtesy of Library of Congress.*

Cockeysville marble formation. What seems to have cemented the fame of the steps, in particular, was the once-common sight of Baltimore housewives on Saturday mornings, scouring their white front steps and socializing on the sidewalks. The steps needed regular scouring because industrial Baltimore was a sooty place; without a regular scrubbing, those glittery white steps would have quickly turned a blotchy gray. Especially in neighborhoods such as Highlandtown, where entire blocks consist of identical row houses, gleaming white steps became a matter of household pride and even competition. Scrubbing them was something of a civic and social ritual for housewives. After the federal Clean Air Act, and with the decline of Baltimore's smokestack economy, the urgency of step-scrubbing faded. It might also be pointed out that "housewife" has been a declining occupation for decades. Baltimore's women have jobs outside their homes and social lives beyond their blocks. So, in some respects, the decline of this quaint local custom was also a side effect of social and environmental progress.

Formstone

Found in many Baltimore neighborhoods, especially East, Southeast and South Baltimore

In 1937, the Lasting Products Company of Baltimore patented Formstone, a kind of imitation masonry that was applied by hand to thousands of row houses, businesses and even churches throughout the city's working-class neighborhoods. The product was intended to preserve and beautify houses that were built of cheap, erosion-prone brick. Lasting Products trained hundreds of home-improvement contractors in the craft of applying the cement-like material to walls and then coloring and sculpting it to resemble stone. A sprinkling of mica dust could be added for sparkle. Formstone and its inevitable competitors gained popularity in a number of American cities, but it seems to be more visible in Baltimore than anywhere else. At any rate, the product is strongly identified with this city. (John Waters, homegrown filmmaker and connoisseur of bad taste, calls it the "polyester of brick.") Formstone's popularity peaked in the 1950s and then dropped as cheaper "improvements" such as aluminum siding undercut the market. In recent decades, the gentrification of old Formstone-clad communities has led to disagreements between neighbors who like the familiar hometown look and the generally newer neighbors who prefer to have it removed, exposing the original (and often low quality) brick. Unfortunately, in spite of its preservative intention, Formstone (like aluminum siding) can crack and leak over time, allowing moisture to be trapped in spaces behind the facing and hastening the decay of underlying bricks. Homeowners who remove Formstone may incur the double expense of removing the facing and having to repair damaged bricks. While acres of Formstone have been removed since the 1980s, many more acres survive.

Iron-Front Buildings

Multiple locations

While Baltimore is thought of as a city of red brick, it was also among the pioneers and prolific adopters of iron-fronted buildings during their period of cachet in the latter half of the nineteenth century. Bolted-together cast-iron façades were popular for commercial structures, offering durability, convenience and fanciful designs. The Bartlett-Hayward & Company in the city's Pigtown neighborhood was among the nation's largest iron foundries and a national leader in cast- and wrought-iron architecture, shipping materials all over the country. By the early twentieth century, when steel construction replaced iron, Baltimore was home to more than one hundred iron fronts. Only a handful remain today. Gleaming beneath white paint, the five-story iron front at 300 West Pratt Street (Inner Harbor) began as a brush company in 1871 and received an award-winning renovation into office space in 1990. The deep-red, four-story iron front at 33 South Front Street (Inner Harbor) is folded like an accordion. The 1869 façade once belonged to Fava Fruit Company, whose downtown building was demolished in 1976. The salvaged iron front sat in storage until relocated here and reinstalled in its folded fashion in 1996. A striking example of interior iron work can be seen at the Peabody Library, discussed in Chapter 7.

World Trade Center Baltimore

401 East Pratt Street • Inner Harbor
(410) 837-8439 • www.viewbaltimore.org • Admission Fee

For the history lover, the main attraction of this world's tallest pentagonal office tower, built in 1977, is its twenty-seventh-floor "Top of the World" observation deck, from which visitors can peer down at a number of the venerable sites featured in this book. Much of historical interest is hidden behind tall modern downtown buildings, but to the west, in plain view, stands the 1,116-foot-long brick warehouse built by the B&O Railroad, now part of Oriole Park at Camden Yards; below and to the south lies the innermost Inner Harbor, with a nice aerial view of the USS *Constellation* and a clear look at Federal Hill across the water. The view east is the best, dominated by the great sheltered waterway that gave Baltimore its reason for being. From the innermost waters where the World Trade Center stands, Baltimore Harbor, also known as the Northwest Branch of the Patapsco River, zigzags eastward, joining the Middle Branch of the Patapsco beyond the wooded headland of Fort McHenry, which is marginally visible from the Top of the World. Six miles from downtown, Key Bridge crosses the Patapsco River. Beyond the bridge lies the Chesapeake Bay.

The tower, designed by I.M. Pei, is well suited for its sightseeing function, with sixty-five-foot-wide windows dominating its five sides, interrupted only by the stout piers at the corners. Also on the observation level is a standing exhibit called "Built to Last," featuring large-scale black-and-white photographs of landmark Baltimore buildings.

Just outside the building, at street level, stands Baltimore's memorial to the Marylanders who died in the terrorist attacks of September 11, 2001. This is a marble-clad platform engraved with individual names of victims and a quietly mournful chronology of the attacks. Resting on the platform is a cluster of scorched, twisted steel girders from New York's World Trade Center.

One Charles Center

100 North Charles Street • Downtown

This twenty-three-story, dark-glass office tower in the International style by famed modernist architect Mies van der Rohe was completed in 1962 as the first office building in the ambitious Charles Center downtown renewal project. Its retail level is currently slated to become home to the Baltimore Architecture Foundation's Center for Architecture and Design. Some forty blocks farther north on Charles Street stands the city's second Mies van der Rohe building, the fifteen-story Highfield House Condominium (4000 North Charles Street, North), completed in 1964.

10 Light Street

Downtown • Exterior Only

Easily the city's most handsome skyscraper, this thirty-four-story brick tower topped with a mansard roof of oxidized copper and gilt has aesthetics you could describe as "Art Deco meets Gothic." And some of its carved gargoyle-like features appear almost Mayan. It opened in 1929 as home of the Baltimore Trust Bank, but that institution didn't last long because...well, 1929. It was largely a soaring white elephant throughout the Depression that followed the stock market crash. After changing hands a few times—including a stint as the O'Sullivan Rubber Company Building—it returned to banking in 1961 and had a good run until mergers and acquisitions sent bank offices out of state in 2012. It has since been carved up into apartments. Though the city's tallest building for decades (and the tallest office tower south of New York when built), its small details dazzle as well. Ornate and symbolic limestone carvings and small bronze figures on window and door surrounds depict crabs, clipper ships and the Baltimore Fire of 1904, as well as more generic symbols, such as beehives and hourglasses.

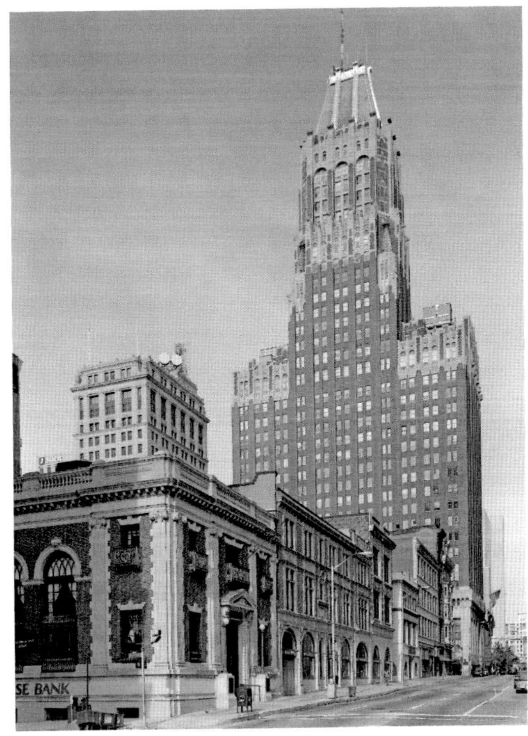

Baltimore Trust Bank built the city's most notable skyscraper in 1929. *Courtesy of Library of Congress.*

Baltimore City Hall
100 Holliday Street • Downtown
(410) 396-3100 • www.facebook.com/baltimorecityhall

Apart from the deeds of mayors and city councils, City Hall boasts its own remarkable history. This mansard-roofed palace, with its tall central dome, was the work of a precocious twenty-one-year-old named George Frederick, who won the city's design competition in 1864. The contest had at that point dragged on since 1860, mostly due to the Civil War breaking out in 1861, throwing the city into disarray. In May of that year, following the violent anti-Union riot on Pratt Street, President Lincoln had ordered Baltimore's mayor and city council imprisoned, while Union army troops occupied Federal Hill and aimed cannons at the city's heart. While Frederick's winning design sat on the shelf, the Peale Museum building continued to serve as a stopgap City Hall, as it had done since 1830. Construction of the new seat of government finally began in 1867, with George Frederick serving as the supervising architect. Eight years later, when the building was finally dedicated, the architect was thirty-four years old. Surprisingly, the long-awaited building came in under its projected budget. Frederick, known for his versatility, went on to create a number of highly visible, very dissimilar buildings in Baltimore, including the Cylburn Mansion and the glass-and-steel Palm House at the Rawlings Conservatory. His City Hall soldiered on into the twentieth century. At one point in the demolition-happy 1970s, officials contemplated tearing down this quaint Victorian structure. Instead, it was decided to modernize and expand its office space, while preserving the 1800s pomp of the city council chamber, cleaning and repairing the complicated façades and restoring the beautiful three-story rotunda. Call ahead to inquire about tours.

Bromo-Seltzer Arts Tower
21 South Eutaw Street at Lombard Street • Downtown
(443) 874-3596 • www.bromoseltzertower.com • Fee for tours

This 288-foot structure is a beloved icon, a quintessentially Baltimorean pastiche of classical beauty, commercial crassness and cultural eccentricity. Modeled loosely on the somewhat taller Palazzo Vecchio in Florence, the tower features a working clock with four dials, each twenty-four feet in

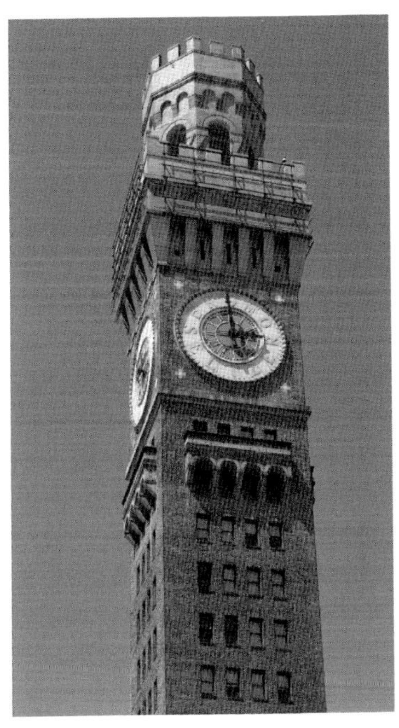

The quirky and beloved Bromo-Seltzer Arts Tower. *Courtesy of Andrew Horne.*

diameter, facing the points of the compass. In place of numerals, the clock face spells out "BROMOSELTZER." Erected in 1911 as part of the Emerson Drug Company's office complex, the tower was originally topped with a fifty-one-foot, seventeen-ton replica of the trademark blue "Bromo" bottle, bedecked with nearly six hundred lightbulbs and revolving twice per minute. The giant Bromo bottle came down in 1936 after cracks appeared in the structure. As for the product, Bromo-Seltzer is no longer manufactured. The once-popular over-the-counter headache remedy started out in 1888 as a hazardous quack medication but went through various, purportedly safer reformulations over many years until it was discontinued in 1975. The tower is now managed by the Baltimore Office of Promotion and the Arts. Former office spaces serve as studios for Baltimore artists, whose work is publicly displayed in the stairwells. Enthusiastic volunteers provide tours and entertaining lectures about the building's (and the product's) checkered history. The highlight of the tour is a visit to the gigantic clockworks, now powered by electricity.

Chesapeake Shakespeare Company

7 South Calvert Street • Downtown

(410) 244-8471 • www.chesapeakeshakespeare.com

The home of this important regional theater company is a dark, squat fortress, with massive load-bearing brick walls and solemn arches, a vivid example of the late nineteenth-century style known as Richardsonian Romanesque. Designed in 1886 by the prolific Baltimore firm Wyatt and Sperry, it was the headquarters of the powerful Mercantile Safe Deposit and Trust Company until 1970, when "Merc" moved its main office to a concrete tower on Hopkins Plaza, leaving behind a branch office that held on until 1993. The architects, in collaboration with their clients, conceived this building as an impenetrable treasure house with fireproof, burglar-proof vaults. In fact, the building was one of a scant dozen structures said to have survived the great fire of 1904, although it was actually set ablaze inside by debris falling through its skylights from the nearby Continental Trust Building (ironically, another so-called survivor of the fire). The bank's fireproof vaults performed as advertised. Ornately restored after the disaster, the bank's lofty, columned interior became an attractive space for modern reuse. In 2000, after a long vacancy and a costly renovation, it changed hands repeatedly, mostly serving a series of doomed nightclubs until a private foundation bought it for the Chesapeake Shakespeare Company in 2013. After another costly remodeling, the Company staged its first production there a year later. The Chesapeake Shakespeare Company alternates performances of the Bard's works with classic plays by other giants of theater.

Clarence Mitchell Jr. Courthouse

100 North Calvert Street • Downtown
(410) 333-3732

Built in 1900, this stately structure claims an architectural world record: each of the thirty-one-foot Ionic columns on its eastern façade is carved from a single block of stone, making them—there are eight columns—the largest monolithic columns on the planet. (The ancient Greeks and Romans built their columns in sections, or "drums," as have most of their successors over the last 2,500 years.) The western entrance, facing St. Paul Street, is guarded by a statue of Cecil Calvert, the English lord who, without leaving England, received a royal charter to establish the colony of Maryland in 1633. According to the late Gil Sandler, collector of Baltimore stories, the model for the statue was Francis X. Bushman, a handsome native of Baltimore's Hamilton neighborhood who was soon to gain fame as a star in silent movies. In the 1980s, the courthouse was named after the great Baltimore-born lawyer who, as a lobbyist, represented the civil rights movement in the halls of Congress, winning key legislation in the struggle for racial equality.

Although you must pass through a metal detector on your way in, the Mitchell Courthouse has some real charms hidden down its glum gray corridors. The former Orphan's Court, now the Museum of Legal History, is restored to Late Victorian glory. The true gem, however, is the multistory eastern lobby, one of the most visually stimulating interior spaces in the city, featuring marble steps, a forest of columns supporting a vaulted ceiling, art-glass windows and murals depicting romanticized scenes from Maryland and U.S. history.

Hansa Haus
11 South Charles Street • Downtown • Exterior Only

This half-timbered building of German Renaissance design interjects old-world whimsy into downtown. It was built in 1912 as the offices of the North German Lloyd steamship line, whose ships began plying the waters between Bremerhaven, Germany, and Baltimore in 1866. During World War I, German Americans and recent German immigrants were subject to a great deal of prejudice and suspicion. Most of it was unfair. However, it's been subsequently revealed that pro-German conspirators met in the Hansa Haus attic during the war to plan sabotage explosions that rocked New Jersey and New York.

Lord Baltimore Hotel
20 West Baltimore Street • Downtown
(410) 539-8400 • www.lordbaltimorehotel.com

The last old-school hostelry operating downtown, the twenty-three-story, French Renaissance Revival Lord Baltimore Hotel opened in 1928 as the city's last classically designed high-rise and the state's largest hotel. It was fully renovated in 2014. Keeping amenities up to date has helped the business keep the lights on, such as the recent addition of the swanky rooftop Sky Bar, which draws a chic set up to the nineteenth floor for al fresco schmoozing on clement evenings. Ask to see what is said to be a former speakeasy off the Versailles Room, uncovered during restorations. Now, if you spy a little girl in white playing with a red ball, it might be Molly—one of the resident ghosts contributing to the Lord Baltimore being ranked among the most haunted hotels in America.

The Belvedere

1 East Chase Street • Midtown

(410) 659-5287 • www.thebelvederebaltimore.com

Baltimore's grand dame hotel raised its busy, Beaux Arts–style mansard roof above midtown in 1903 and quickly became a magnet for society happenings and smoky barroom deal making. It's named after the Howard family's eighteenth-century estate that once rambled in the vicinity. For all its glamor, the Belvedere struggled as a hotel over the years, perhaps because it's orphaned away from downtown. Ownership revolved as much as its entrance doors. (In the 1920s, a circus clown-cum-hotelier was in charge—one with a penchant for walking the halls naked.) By the 1970s, it had been reduced to a student flophouse but finally found success as a condominium and catered-event space in the 1990s. The handsome Owl Bar remains a popular watering hole with its baronial interior of ornate brickwork, stained glass, carved wood and mounted animal heads. With the site being a speakeasy during Prohibition, it is said that the lightbulb eyes within the namesake pair of owl statues above the bar blinked when it was safe to order booze. The birds remain in place, although their mission is moot amid all the bracing cocktails and house-brand craft beers. The muraled walls of the sumptuous John Eager Howard room off the lobby depict Baltimore's bucolic early days. It is said that a small service elevator in this room was routinely commandeered for private use by Wallis Warfield Simpson whenever she was in residence with the Duke of Windsor, the man who abdicated the British throne in 1936 to marry the Baltimore divorcée.

Washington Monument

Mount Vernon Place • Midtown

(410) 962-5070 • www.mvpconservancy.org • Admission Fee (to climb)

Completed in 1829, more than fifty years before that *other* Washington Monument down in the nation's capital, this marble Doric column soars 162 feet and is then topped with a 16-foot-tall statue of George Washington resigning his commission as commander of the Continental Army, which occurred at Annapolis, Maryland, in 1783. Designed by Robert Mills (who also designed Washington, D.C.'s monument), originally it was intended to stand near where the Battle Monument does today. City leaders, unconvinced of the era's engineering ability, instead erected it on what was then undeveloped land donated by John Eager Howard, thinking that if it ever toppled over, it wouldn't damage any residences. The city soon swallowed it up, and Mount Vernon Place (the park surrounding it) and Mount Vernon (the neighborhood it is in) both take their name from Washington's Virginia estate. For a fee, you can climb the 227 steps winding up the column to a four-windowed viewing chamber. Entry to the gallery at the base is free and includes video exhibits and touchscreens detailing the monument's history and its extensive 2015 renovations.

Mount Washington

Neighborhood bounded by Northern Parkway, Falls Road and Smith Avenue • North

In the nineteenth century, summer in Baltimore City was smelly, smoky and sweltering. It's no wonder that the wealthiest city merchants spent summers at rural estates in the cooler highlands outside town. By midcentury, the growing upper middle class hankered for summer getaways of their own. So began "railroad suburbs," clusters of airy summer homes along rail lines. Mount Washington, on the northern boundary of modern Baltimore, started this way in 1854 as the "Mount Washington Rural Retreat," a planned community on the steep hills along the west bank of the Jones Falls, eight miles from the city center. Immediately upstream from the new development stood the large Washington Mill, a water-powered cotton-weaving complex built circa 1810, and a settlement called Washingtonville, where mill employees lived. A small commercial town grew up in the narrow stretch where the river, railroad, mill town and bedroom community came together. This entire area was annexed by Baltimore City in 1918. Historically, its attractions are the old mill complex, now occupied by an assortment of upscale commercial enterprises, and the lively pre–Civil War wood-frame architecture of the Dixon's Hill neighborhood, named for the prolific architect Thomas Dixon. A master of inventive angles, shapes and proportions, Dixon designed many imaginative wooden houses in the neighborhood, as well as the Mount Washington Octagon, built in 1855, a large, ornate eight-sided building that overlooks the present-day light rail station.

The "Olmsted Neighborhoods"
Roland Park • Guilford • Homeland • Original Northwood • North
www.olmstedmaryland.org

In the 1880s, Baltimore's Gilded Age economy stimulated demand for homes with luxury, privacy, park-like settings and trolley service to downtown. Seeing an opportunity in the city's expansion, a Chicago investment firm bought a five-hundred-acre tract just north of what was then the Baltimore city line. In 1891, it founded the Roland Park Company and hired a Kansas City developer, Edward Bouton, to create one of America's first planned suburban communities. On the first plat, north of Cold Spring Lane, planner George Kessler laid out a street grid that rapidly filled in with "catalogue houses," customized from basic designs, alongside increasingly large and elaborate one-of-a-kind homes for the more well-to-do buyers. Every house was required to have indoor plumbing.

In 1897, Kessler was replaced by the firm of the Olmsted brothers, whose father, Frederick Law Olmsted, had co-designed New York's Central Park and more or less invented the profession of landscape architecture. The Olmsteds took their cues from the natural lay of the land, creating an irregular pattern of streets interspersed with a network of artfully named footpaths. Bouton's company, meanwhile, encouraged the region's most talented architects to create showpiece mansions in the new suburb. At the same time, the Roland Park Company invented America's first racially and ethnically restrictive covenants: Roland Park properties were, in the first half of the twentieth century, for sale or rent only to White people; Black citizens were allowed to reside in the development only if they were live-in servants. Jews were excluded as a matter of unspoken policy. Such practices were just one way in which Baltimore instituted discriminatory patterns that persist today.

While Roland Park expanded along the corridors of Roland Avenue and University Parkway, Bouton and the Olmsteds started a second planned community in 1913. Guilford, between North Charles Street and York Road, was intended from the start to serve the wealthiest Baltimoreans. Where Roland Park offered such middle-class options as catalogue houses, duplexes and apartment buildings, Guilford was more consistently upscale by design, dominated by extra-large houses with handcrafted details and natural materials, in a variety of styles: Federal (inspired by the Hopkins campus), Arts and Crafts houses with Gothic and rustic details, stucco-sided Mission-style mansions and Tudor-style houses that evoked the half-timbered cottages of old England. In the same vein, but with a greater admixture of truly middle-class homes, the Bouton-Olmsted team built a third suburb, Homeland, which opened in 1924, north of Guilford. Here, the average house is relatively modest by Guilford standards, but many are adorned with quaint hand-wrought details and your choice of slate roof and three or four kinds of siding: stone and/or brick and/or stucco and/or clapboard and/or shingles. Some of the smaller homes are so encrusted with hand-wrought features that the term "jewel-box" comes to mind. A fourth and last Olmsted neighborhood, now called Original Northwood, opened in 1930, about a mile west of Guilford along Argonne Drive. It's the most solidly middle class of the Olmsted projects, with beautifully crafted row houses and small, gem-like cottages mixed in with conventional "colonials." Taken together, the "Olmsted Neighborhoods" occupy a large chunk of northern Baltimore. While the residential streets offer windshield tourism, a few notable features of the Olmsted communities are open to the public.

Roland Park Shopping Center

4700 block of Roland Avenue • North

This Tudor-style complex, built by the Roland Park Company, opened in 1907. It incorporates six street-level shops, a number of second-floor offices and the neighborhood's fire hall, all of which are still in use. Although small by today's standards, it is generally regarded as the first purpose-built shopping center in America. Early in its history, the north end of the shopping center abutted the terminus of the Roland Park trolley line.

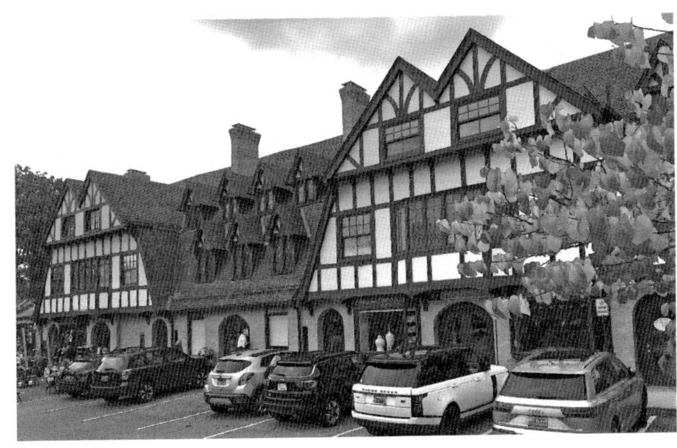

The 1907 Roland Park Shopping Center might be the oldest purpose-built shopping center in the country; it's certainly among the most handsome. *Courtesy of Tom Chalkley.*

The Roland Water Tower
4400 block of Roland Avenue • North • Exterior Only

Rising handsomely over the treetops, this 148-foot octagonal structure is so strongly associated with the Roland Park neighborhood that it's usually called the Roland Park Water Tower. Built in 1905, it was designed for beauty as well as function, with a green tile roof, ornate arches and glazed brick walls. For twenty-five years, it served as part of the city's water system. Since 1930, when the city converted to a reservoir-based system, the tower has been essentially an ornamental landmark and community icon. As such, it fell into neglect for many years. In August 2020, the Roland Park Civic League came to the rescue, having raised funds to renovate the structure and evict its long-standing population of pigeons.

Engine House 6
414 Gay Street • East
(410) 727-2414 • www.facebook.com/box414association

Distinguished by its unusual tower, this building is the oldest surviving fire hall in the city. The wedge-shaped structure at the base of the tower dates to 1853, but earlier firefighting facilities had occupied the same Oldtown location since 1819. When the existing station was built, fire companies were essentially men's clubs that competed, sometimes violently, for the glory and rewards of putting out a fire. That changed in 1858, when the city merged the fractious independent companies into the municipal fire department. The tower, erected in 1879, originally served as a lookout post for urban fire spotters; it is equipped with a bell to ring alarms. The clock at the top of the tower was a later, pre-1900 addition. The building continued to serve as a fire hall until the mid-'70s. Since 1979, it has been home to the Baltimore City Fire Museum, which displays firefighting equipment, antique pump wagons, documents, books, photographs and twenty-five helmets that belonged to firefighters who died doing their jobs. The museum is operated by Box 414, an association of self-described fire buffs and retired firefighters who, as a public service, provide volunteer canteen service to firefighters on the job. The organization takes its name from the sidewalk alarm box that first warned of the great 1904 fire.

McKim Community Center
1120 East Baltimore Street • East
(410) 276-5519 • www.mckimcenter.org

For nearly two hundred years, this small but distinguished building has served the needs of struggling families and their children, following the wishes of John McKim, a Quaker mill owner who provided the funds "for the education of indigent youth." The building, completed in 1833, was designed in the Neoclassical style then popular in Baltimore, with a stern façade modeled closely on ancient Greek temples. In the 1890s, Baltimore's public education system reduced the need for such independent schools, so the McKim building was converted to a kindergarten and later to its present function as a community center.

Phoenix Shot Tower
801 East Fayette Street • East
(410) 605-2964 • www.carrollmuseums.org • Admission Fee

Erected in 1828 using more than 1 million bricks, this 215-foot-tall "vertical factory" for making lead shot was the tallest building in the country until 1846, when it was bested by Manhattan's Trinity Church. It could almost be mistaken for a smokestack were it not for the occasional double-hung windows along its soaring flanks. Molten lead was fed through a colander-like device at various levels to create drops that formed spheres as they plunged downward to land in vat of water. The shot was used for small game hunting. (The business papers of the company that built it have been lost and, with them, the origin of the name Phoenix; perhaps it was a byproduct of the era's vogue for Greek terms.) Shot towers of this sort were obsolete by 1898, and this was the last of the city's four such towers still standing in

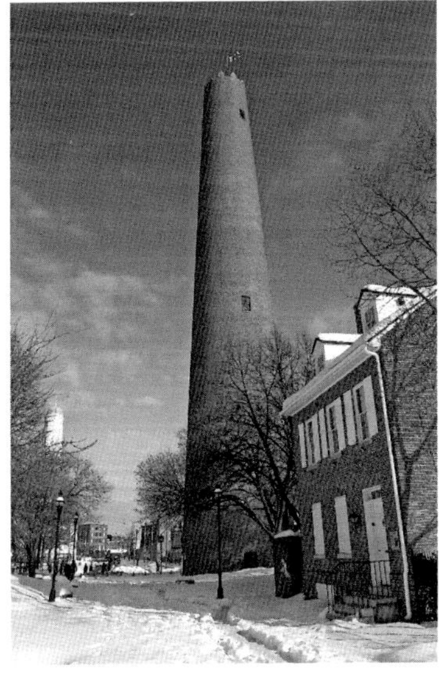

Once the tallest building in the country, the Phoenix Shot Tower began making lead shot in 1828. *Courtesy of Mark Peters.*

1924 when it was slated to be pushed over to make way for a gas station. Baltimoreans rallied in an early historic preservation win, raising $17,000 to buy the tower and donate it to the city. After recent renovations, visitors are now allowed to climb the three hundred or so winding stairs to the top. The upward trek is pulse-pounding for multiple reasons, but the al fresco views from on high are stunning and worth the effort. Without trooping up, you can enter and admire the three-and-a-half-foot-thick walls and the old elevator system for raising lead. The tower is managed by the nearby Carroll Mansion Museum, about two blocks south at 800 East Lombard Street.

Chapter 9

ARTS AND LETTERS

A CITY'S CONTRIBUTIONS TO BEAUTY AND BOOKSHELVES

Over the course of 250 years, Baltimore's artistic landscape has undergone a long and slow but dramatic shift, roughly parallel to its rise and decline as a leading American city. In the first half of the nineteenth century, the fast-growing (and, in 1814, heroic) town decorated itself with two grand Neoclassical sculptural works, the Battle Monument and the Washington Monument, earning the honorific name of the "Monumental City." Seemingly content, the city didn't bother with any more statues or monuments until after the Civil War. The city's foremost painter in those prewar days—and for the rest of the nineteenth century—was the talented, entrepreneurial Rembrandt Peale, founder of, and exhibitor at, the Peale Museum on Holliday Street (discussed in Chapter 1). Peale's specialty was idealized but convincingly realistic portraiture, in the style and tradition of his father, the Philadelphia painter and polymath Charles Willson Peale. Rembrandt Peale's portraits, some of which are still on display at the museum, flatteringly capture their sitters' features and personalities, while expressing an air of patriotic self-confidence. Two other Baltimore painters deserve mention. A local contemporary of Peale's, Joshua Johnson, is notable as the first African American artist known to have made a career out of painting pictures. Born into slavery, he taught himself to be a "limner," or free-lance portraitist, and opened a studio on South Charles Street. His careful likenesses of Baltimoreans offer a glimpse of the style and manners of his times. Some of his portraits are displayed at the Maryland Center for History and Culture, the BMA and the Peale

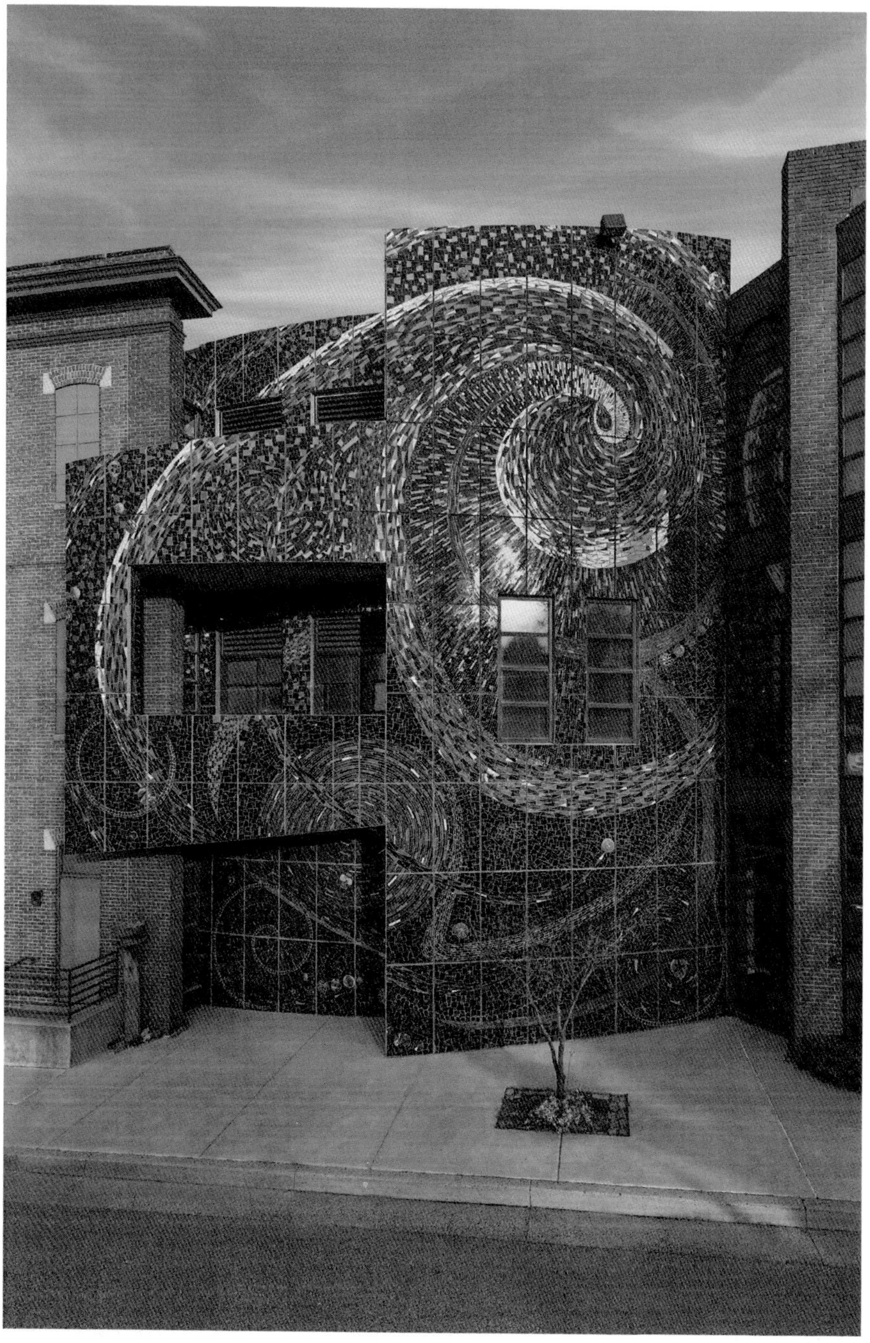

The American Visionary Art Museum celebrates creativity both self-taught and self-styled. *Courtesy of AVAM.*

Museum. Richard Caton Woodville, a scion of Baltimore's wealthy Caton family, grew up here but moved to Germany in 1845 to study art. He died there at thirty-six, leaving behind only a handful of finished works. Two of his paintings, both obliquely referring to contemporary events, hang at the Walters Art Museum. In the graphic arts, Baltimore's most notorious nineteenth-century exponent was the cartoonist Adalbert Volck, a Bavarian-born dentist and Confederate sympathizer whose best-known works are harsh lampoons of Abraham Lincoln and General Benjamin Butler, who led the Union army's occupation of Baltimore. (Volck also sculpted the portrait of Edgar Allan Poe that stares from the poet's monument in the Westminster Hall burial ground.) As for the rest of the 1800s, the city had its share of skilled local painters and portraitists whose work is chiefly of documentary interest today.

Following the Civil War, the city's industrial and commercial sectors boomed, and public art in Baltimore (as in much of the country) settled into a ceremoniously realistic style that lasted for nearly a century. The postwar period saw a huge spate of statuary, much of it commemorating military heroes, a trend that would continue as America fought war after war overseas. While major public sculpture generally represented White men in suits or soldierly garb, lesser works typically featured symbolic and decorative figures of men, women and children, usually nude or half-draped, in the durable tradition of Ancient Greece and Rome by way of Europe. (A stroll around Mount Vernon Park provides specimens of all these motifs.) Major cultural institutions, including the Maryland Institute College of Art (MICA, founded in 1826), the Walters Art Gallery (opened 1909; became a public institution in 1934) and the Baltimore Museum of Art (founded 1914; opened 1929) promoted art and exhibited great works of the past. They enjoyed mainstream patronage and support while conforming to standard tastes that had prevailed for decades.

While Baltimore was not exactly a cultural backwater, its public art was strikingly conservative. Art critic John Dorsey, surveying the city's sculptural landscape between 1914 and 1954, wrote that "one would never know… that such movements as expressionism, cubism and abstract art had ever appeared in the world." Prior to 1950, the only notable local artist who strayed from naturalistic classicism was the singular local sculptor Grace Turnbull, who dabbled in medieval abstraction after pushing naturalism as far as she was able. Artists who yearned for greater innovation and self-expression either left town or confined themselves to the humble, more perishable fields of illustration, as did the talented social chronicler

Aaron Sopher and the charming cartoonist Richard "Moco" Yardley, whose works are mainly preserved in private collections. Still, among the conservatives, there were some outstanding masters, notably the prolific Hans Schuler, responsible for six major public monumental works in the city and a number of private memorials scattered around city cemeteries.

Soon after the BMA opened, the Great Depression settled over America. In the ferment of hard times, long-repressed voices began to rise against conventional notions of beauty and value. Local collectors, critics, teachers and artists decried the museum's narrow appeal. Modernity finally arrived in 1949, when the BMA received the bequest of the wealthy sisters Claribel and Etta Cone, a huge collection that turned the BMA into a belated shrine for lovers of early modern art, particularly fans of Henri Matisse. As they and other wealthy collectors passed on their treasures, the museum added gallery space to accommodate them. At MICA, the increasingly modernist faculty asserted itself following the 1951 death of its fiercely traditionalist president, the sculptor Hans Schuler. While MICA continued to teach traditional media, skills and techniques, the school developed a more adventurous and broad-minded approach to art education. The more progressive philosophy flowered after the Yale-trained painter Eugene Leake became the school's president in 1961.

The confident, heroic realism of the past lost its footing as the city declined from its peak population in 1960 and its economic base eroded. In 1964, in a bid to keep public art alive, Baltimore enacted a "one percent for art" policy pertaining to all buildings constructed with public money. This led to an explosion of minor but highly visible sculptures and mural works throughout the city, mostly abstract in nature, employing the fullest possible range of materials instead of traditional stone and bronze.

Since the 1970s, artists, both homegrown and MICA-trained, have increasingly embraced nontraditional media, popular culture and the gritty aesthetic of their urban environment. Looming large among Baltimore's noted working artists is MICA alumna Joyce J. Scott—veteran printmaker, weaver, sculptor and performance artist perhaps best known for her delicate beadwork pieces confronting the prickliest social issues. Also in residence is rising-star painter Amy Sherald, who earned an MFA from MICA and was tapped to paint Michelle Obama's official portrait. The artist (and former part-time server) recently sold one of her African American portraits for seven figures.

Thanks in part to its relatively cheap housing stock, the city is a haven for experimental, eccentric and independent-minded artists. City-sponsored murals and graffiti (legal and illegal) have created an unavoidable "gallery of the streets," and our foremost contemporary art institution, the American Visionary Art Museum, devotes itself to what used to be called "outsider art." Contemporary art by Marylanders is reliably on view at the galleries of MICA and at smaller private venues such as Maryland Art Place and the Creative Alliance at the Patterson, in Highlandtown, as well as small independent galleries sprinkled around hip neighborhoods.

In terms of literature, Baltimore's story arc is very different. The city has never been a center of publishing or literary culture, but it has always been a way station for literary cranks, iconoclasts and outsiders, as well as for writers, such as Edgar Allan Poe and Upton Sinclair, who have focused on the shadows and the rot behind the glittering façades of their times. Sinclair lived here as the ward of a wealthy aunt and uncle, who unwittingly schooled him in the class system that he decried in *The Jungle* and other novels. Gertrude Stein, later famous for her Parisian salon and a handful of cryptic one-liners, lived in Baltimore only long enough to attend medical school and write her first two novels.

The journalist and editor H.L. Mencken, a proud and prickly Baltimorean, built his career mocking American culture, but he deserves some credit for launching one of the most enduring genres in American popular literature: "hard-boiled" detective fiction. To support his highbrow but unprofitable publication the *American Mercury* (published in New York), the cynical Mencken started several sensational mass-audience magazines, including *Black Mask*, a proving ground for crime writers. To fill its pages, Mencken fostered two remarkable local talents: Dashiell Hammett, who grew up on the city's old East Side, and Mencken's fellow *Sunpapers* journalist James M. Cain, author of *The Postman Always Rings Twice* and *Double Indemnity*. Hammett and Cain are still listed among the most literary of crime novelists. Their stories gave rise to hundreds of imitations and dozens of American film noir classics, which are a genre unto themselves.

Except for Mencken, none of these writers ever really settled in Baltimore, and even Mencken commuted to New York City for years (a necessary evil for one who called that city a "third-rate Babylon"). Mencken's pal, the Jazz Age novelist F. Scott Fitzgerald, sojourned in Baltimore for nearly five years in the 1930s while his wife, Zelda, was hospitalized at Johns Hopkins Phipps Psychiatric Institute and other facilities—one of the longest stops of his nomadic career. "I belong here, where everything is civilized and gay and rotted and polite," he said of the city. (His full name, Francis Scott Key Fitzgerald, is a nod to his anthem-penning distant cousin and underscores the deep Maryland roots on his father's side.) The author and his wife are buried in a family plot in Rockville, Maryland. While sequestered in addresses that included a Bolton Hill row house and a suburban cottage in nearby Towson, he published what he hoped would be his great comeback novel, *Tender Is the Night.* (It had been more than a decade since his smash *The Great Gatsby*, and finances were strained). The novel deals with mental breakdown and the dissipation of a man of early promise and clearly rings autobiographical. Zelda's struggle was with schizophrenia; his was with the bottle. Mencken, the first to publish Fitzgerald when he bought his short story "Babes in the Woods" back in 1919, called Fitzgerald an "excellent companion when sober" but said "liquor sets him wild." Though widely acclaimed today, sales of *Tender Is the Night* proved lackluster. It was his final novel. (Curiously, despite all Zelda was dealing with, she wrote her one and only novel, *Save Me the Waltz*, while in town.)

The city continues to enjoy the company of contemporary authors who come and go from teaching positions at the Johns Hopkins Writing Seminars, a program founded in 1947, and similar programs at other local colleges. Edward Albee, John Barth, Alice McDermott and Robert Stone are among the luminaries who have taught at the Hopkins program; many notable writers have graduated from it. But the only current A-list novelist who really calls Baltimore her home is the prolific Anne Tyler, many of whose earlier books are set in unnamed but recognizable neighborhoods—particularly the somewhat reclusive author's own leafy Roland Park. After two of her Baltimore-based novels were Pulitzer Prize finalists, her 1988 effort *Breathing Lessons* finally took the top literary prize. Meanwhile, a film version of her 1985 novel *The Accidental Tourist* garnered four Oscar nominations. A keen observer of ordinary lives, she seems to revel in Baltimore's ordinariness.

One of the most potent, largely nonfiction voices of the last few years belongs to Baltimore native Ta-Nehisi Coates, now living in New York City. A keen observer of America's structures of racial privilege, his *Between the World and Me* won the National Book Award in 2015. Like his earlier memoir *The Beautiful Struggle*, much of it draws on his experiences growing up in Baltimore. Other local writers, such as former journalist David Simon (discussed in Chapter 9), have made their most lasting marks in television and film; Simon's wife, Laura Lippman, is a prolific mystery writer who sets many of her yarns in her gritty hometown.

YOUR GUIDE TO HISTORY

Bolton Hill
Neighborhood bounded on the north by North Avenue, on the south by Dolphin Street, on the east by Mount Royal Avenue and on the west by Eutaw Place • Midtown
https://boltonhillmd.org

This genteel neighborhood, sometimes likened to Boston's Beacon Hill or Washington, D.C.'s Georgetown, is a fine place to stroll along shady, often brick-paved sidewalks. Groomed squares and boulevard parks break up the stately rows of largely post–Civil War row houses of brick and stone, while tucked into the mix is the neighborhood's oldest building: a detached Italianate house (232 West Lanvale Street) dating to 1848. Bolton Hill could easily fit in the chapter on architecture but is included here because among its who's who of famous former residents—from Alger Hiss to Woodrow Wilson—are a goodly number of writers, including James M. Cain and William Manchester. Borrowing a scheme used in London, houses with famous former residents bear informative blue plaques. The staid row house at 1307 Bolton wears one as the last address F. Scott Fitzgerald shared with his wife, Zelda, and daughter "Scottie" amid dark-cloud days for a couple who'd defined the Jazz Age good life. Journalist Russell Baker spent much of his early years in Baltimore, as described in his autobiography *Growing Up*, awarded one of his two Pulitzer Prizes. Baker was a Johns Hopkins University grad and one-time *Baltimore Sun* police reporter, and his Bolton Hill stop was at 1501 Park Avenue.

On the art side, the eleven-story Marlborough (1601 Eutaw Place—see separate listing) was where sisters Etta and Claribel Cone quietly amassed and lived amid their amazing modern art collection. Art also enlivens some of Bolton's button-down stodginess thanks to the nearby Maryland Institute College of Art, whose students often rent apartments here. If you see a clutch of young people toting canvases or cameras, they're likely MICA students. Sadly, Bolton Hill is bereft of many places to eat and drink. Just a stone's toss outside its border, however, is the singular Mount Royal Tavern (1204 Mount Royal Avenue). With a Sistine Chapel knockoff ceiling, an eclectic juke box and an overall atmosphere of artful shabbiness, it's no wonder *Esquire* magazine called it "a great dive bar" and put it on its list of America's best drinkeries.

Mount Vernon Park

Mount Vernon Place and Washington Place • Midtown
http://mvpconservancy.org

This four-part park, converging on Baltimore's Washington Monument, is the centerpiece of Baltimore's most historic community, where it serves as both a public gathering space and a showcase of pre-1950 public sculpture. When the monument was built, this area was part of the estate of the Revolutionary hero John Eager Howard, whose heirs laid out the park and its bounding streets. In the 1840s, the former Howard property filled in with private mansions and public buildings; in the 1890s, the park began to accumulate statuary. Aside from George Washington atop his pillar, the park boasts thirteen works of sculpture, including military equestrian statues of the aforementioned John Eager Howard and the Marquis de Lafayette, plus two statues of civilians, philanthropist George Peabody (near the Peabody Conservatory) and, downhill from Peabody, the pro-Confederate Maryland politician Severn Teackle Wallis. A third figure was removed in 2017: Chief Justice Roger Taney, author of the Dred Scott decision, which declared that African Americans did not have civil rights. On the west end of the park is a helmeted figure symbolizing Military Courage. The rest of the human-figure statues in Mount Vernon are nude or semi-nude, in the classical mode: three charming fountain figures and four small, stodgy, allegorical figures by the great French animal sculptor Antoine Louis Barye. Barye is also represented by one of his excellent animals, *Seated Lion*.

Maryland Institute College of Art

1200–1500 blocks West Mount Royal Avenue • Midtown
(410) 669-9200 • www.mica.edu

MICA, as it is known, ranks as one of the top art schools in the United States. Its presence in mid-Baltimore has contributed hugely to the city's rising reputation as an art center, as every year a fraction of the school's students decide they want to stick around and be part of the city's free-spirited, creative, socially engaged community. The campus includes ten galleries that display contemporary work by students, graduates and other notable artists from around the world. Student work also shows up on the medians of Mount Royal Avenue and North Avenue.

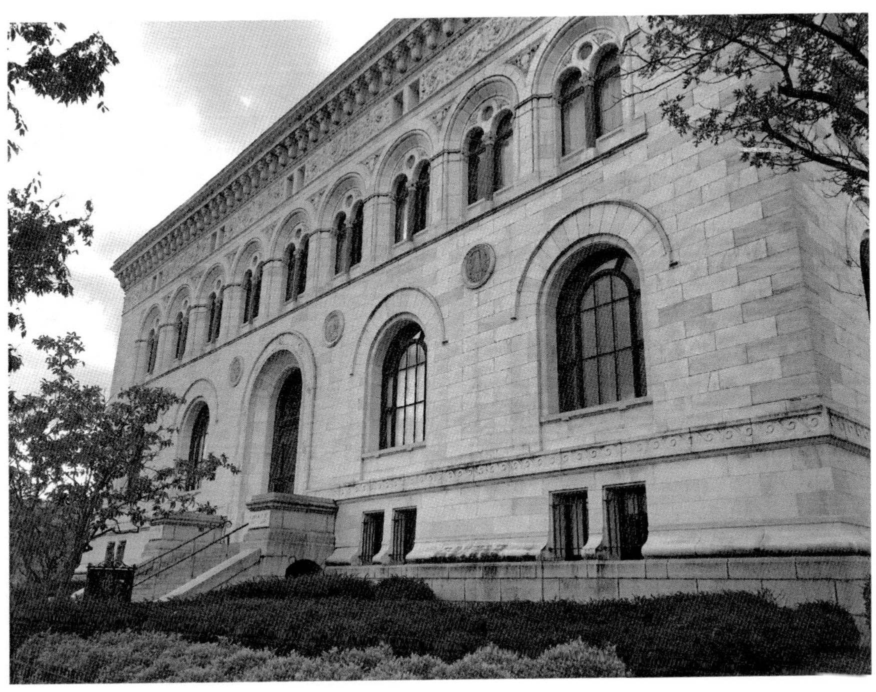

The Maryland Institute College of Art dates to 1826, its marbled main building to 1908. *Courtesy of Tom Chalkley.*

Forward-thinking as it is, MICA has its roots in a classic, conservative approach to art education. Founded in 1826 as the Maryland Institute for the Promotion of the Mechanic Arts, the school originally offered classes in not only art but also a broad range of applied arts and sciences, including engineering and architecture. MICA's present-day Main Building, clad in white marble, was built in 1908. Stylistically, it evokes the Italian Renaissance; the lofty central court features one of the grandest stairways in Baltimore, making it a popular venue for weddings and receptions.

The rest of the academic campus is distributed along Mount Royal Avenue and on West North Avenue, across the Howard Street Bridge. Several MICA buildings are striking examples of adaptive reuse of older structures: the 1896 Mount Royal railroad station, at Dolphin Street; the Fox building, a former shoe factory; and the Lazarus Building, on North Avenue, a former sewing factory. The Brown Building, on Mount Royal across from the Main Building, is an intriguing and thoroughly modern work of glass-clad geometry.

Baltimore Museum of Art
10 Art Museum Drive • North
(443) 573-1700 • www.artbma.org • Free

Divided into three architecturally distinct sections, plus two sculpture gardens, the BMA is an important museum that strives for modern relevance while preserving a fine collection of European "Old Masters," as well as the prized Cone Collection, a world-class trove of early modern art from Europe. The BMA's sculpture gardens feature works by major twentieth-century artists including Henry Moore, Alexander Calder and Isamu Noguchi. Other BMA galleries highlight traditional arts from Africa, Asia and the Pacific, Native American and Euro-American arts spanning three centuries and modern works of the last few decades. In 2020, the BMA resolved to purchase new works only by female artists in an effort to redress the traditional art-world dominance of males.

The original museum building, completed by 1929, was designed by John Russell Pope, architect of the National Gallery of Art in Washington, D.C. Like the much larger National Gallery, Pope's Baltimore museum is presented as a classical temple to the arts, with a broad sweep of stairs leading visitors up to an austere Grecian portico. Appropriately, the oldest section houses the museum's original core collections of European and American art; later galleries were added to display private art collections that have been donated over subsequent decades. The east wing, built in 1982, added a new lobby and other amenities and connected the museum to its two sculpture gardens. The west wing, added in 1994, has an assertively modern metal façade and a collection of contemporary works.

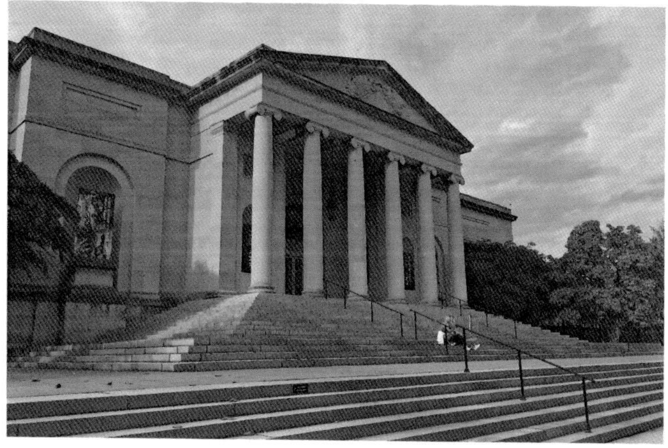

The Baltimore Museum of Art. *Courtesy of Tom Chalkley.*

Marlborough Apartments

1701 Eutaw Place • Midtown • Exterior Only

When it was built in 1905, the handsome, luxurious eleven-story Marlborough Apartment House was the city's largest rental property, featuring units with as many as ten rooms, affordable only by the wealthiest of renters. Today, the Marlborough is renowned as the former home of two such wealthy tenants: the Cone sisters, Claribel and Etta, pioneering collectors of post-impressionist and cubist art. The sisters' wealth was based on the family's wholesale grocery business in Baltimore and their brothers' successful textile plants in Greensboro, North Carolina. Dr. Claribel Cone, elder of the pair, was a groundbreaking medical researcher and professor and a forceful personality; Etta, a talented pianist, was more reserved. In 1903, the sisters traveled to Europe together and met up with their expatriate Baltimore friends Gertrude and Leo Stein. At the Steins' apartments in Paris, the sisters were introduced to Pablo Picasso, then hungry and unknown, and later to Henri Matisse. So began the sisters' collection of thousands of pieces of mostly French art encompassing Courbet, Degas, Cézanne, Van Gogh, Pissarro, Gauguin and, most prominently, Matisse. In 1920, together with their brother Fred (who dabbled at collecting), the Cones took three adjoining apartments on the Marlborough's eighth floor. Claribel's apartment eventually became so cluttered with art that she abandoned it as is and took an apartment on the sixth floor for sleeping. The sisters continued to collect long after their friendship with the Steins went awry. Claribel died in 1929; Etta, who died twenty years later, bequeathed most of the sisters' collection to the Baltimore Museum of Art—pursuant to Claribel's condition that "the spirit of appreciation of modern art in Baltimore became improved." The Cone Collection, which includes the world's largest public holding of Matisse works, is still considered the crown jewel of the BMA. Matisse himself visited Etta in her apartment in 1930.

Schuler School of Fine Arts

7 West Lafayette Street • Midtown
(410) 685-3568 • www.schulerschool.com

Smack in the middle of the city's official Station/North Arts District, the Schuler School stands, draped with ivy, in quiet defiance of the surrounding blocks of graffiti murals, experimental theater and arthouse cinema. The school serves as a refuge for the traditional techniques and values of the Old Masters of Europe, carrying on the legacy of sculptor Hans K. Schuler, who started his studio at this address in 1906 and served as president of the Maryland Institute College of Art from 1925 until his death in 1951. Schuler's heirs and former students started the present-day school in 1959 as an alternative to the modernism that had overtaken the Maryland Institute. The school continues to attract students pursuing classic approaches to drawing, painting, printmaking and sculpture. The elder Schuler's sky-lit sculpture studio is preserved next door to the school, at 5 East Lafayette. Schuler's finished works, notably the Pulaski Monument in Patterson Park and the Johns Hopkins Fountain at North Charles and 33rd Streets, are indispensable city landmarks.

American Visionary Art Museum
800 Key Highway • Inner Harbor
(410) 244-1900 • avam.org • Admission Fee

AVAM, as it's known, sprang from the mind of Rebecca Alban Hoffberger, a native Baltimorean whose creative vision was shaped by her professional work with psychiatric patients. Hoffberger has applied the name "Visionary Art" to a broad cross-section of non-mainstream creative work, but at the heart of the AVAM collection are the inventive, untutored works of so-called outsider artists. Some, like the late mechanic Vollis Simpson, are compulsive gadgeteers with big imaginations, working in isolation. (One of Simpson's towering whirligigs is permanently installed outside the museum.) Others, coming from many walks of life, create art from a fierce inner need to communicate a personal religious or cosmic vision. Hoffberger has said that the museum was not created in opposition to academic art, but rather to make space for "the best of self-taught, intuitive contributions of all kinds." The main museum building, which opened to the public in 1995, is itself an inventive and unexpected dual structure situated immediately east of Federal Hill. The eastern half of the structure is the repurposed former headquarters of the Baltimore Copper Paint Company, built in 1913; the façade of the old building, facing Key Highway, curves broadly to match the arc of the road. The newer part of the building, from 1995, continues the same curve. Mirror-glass mosaics, executed by teams of apprenticed Baltimore youths, cover the big convex wall facing Key Highway and part of the rear, facing Federal Hill.

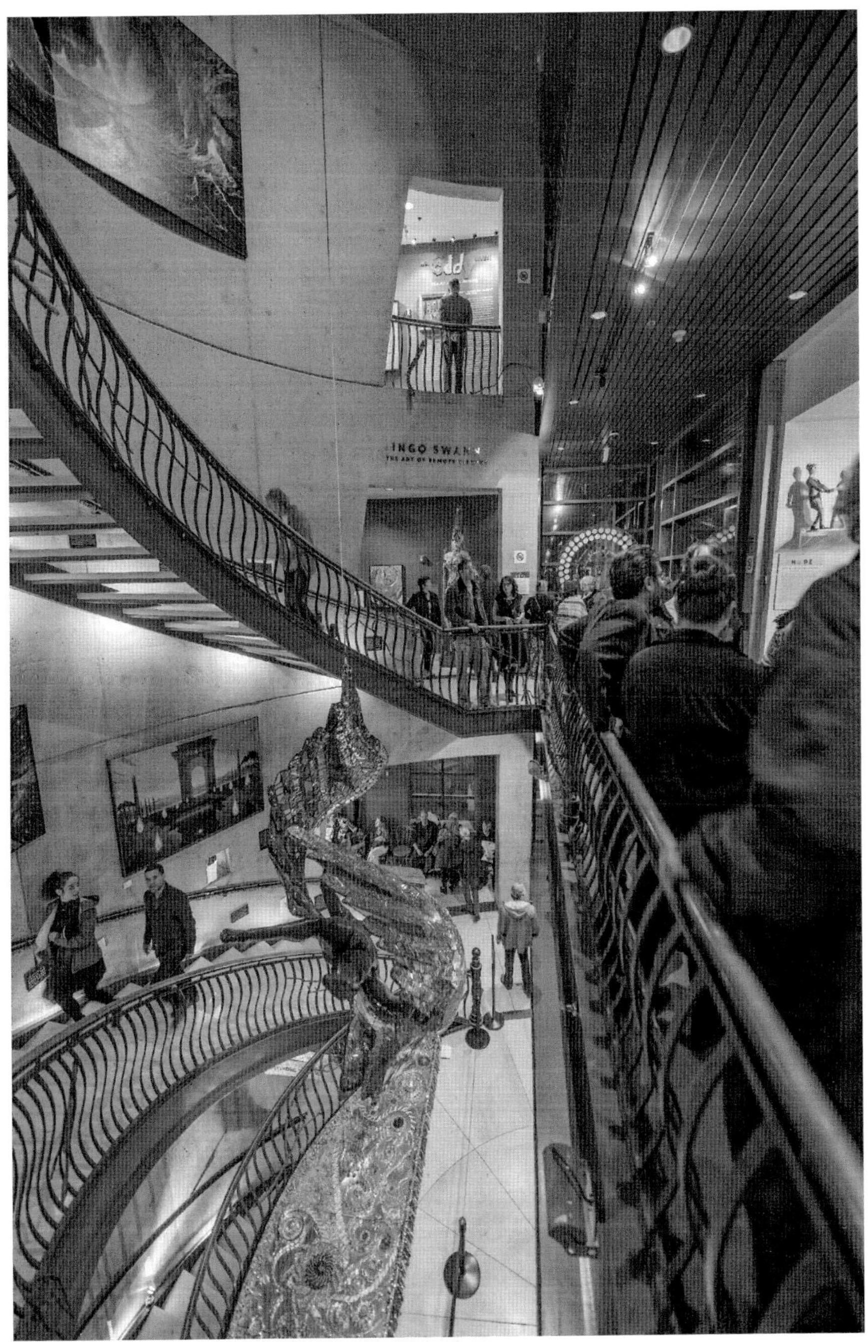

The American Visionary Art Museum. *Courtesy of AVAM.*

One Calvert Plaza

Southeast corner of Calvert and Baltimore Streets • Downtown • Exterior Only

Dashiell Hammett, the author of *The Maltese Falcon* and numerous other literary crime novels, was born in southern Maryland and grew up on Stricker Street in Southwest Baltimore. The family's house no longer exists, so the prime Hammett shrine in town is this handsome sixteen-story office tower erected in 1901 as the Continental Trust Building—the city's only structure designed by Chicago's skyscraper pioneer D.H. Burnham. This was the headquarters of the legendary Pinkerton Detective Agency, where young Hammett, a somewhat aimless jack-of-all-trades, took a job in 1915. As a junior detective, he assisted a seasoned professional who became the model for Hammett's recurring character, the "Continental Op," an unglamorous but dogged investigator with his own code of honor. In 1922, Hammett quit the Pinkerton agency because of its involvement in union-busting. For the rest of his life, Hammett was a political progressive who, during the red-baiting mania of the 1950s, went to jail for refusing to "name names" of suspected subversives in the literary and movie world. Without real evidence, local legend credits the old office building's sculpted birds of prey, perched on a cornice above the grand entrance, as the inspiration for the author's famous falcon. Years prior to Hammett's service with Pinkerton, the building was gutted but not destroyed by the 1904 fire.

Gertrude Stein Sites

2408 Linden Avenue • West

215 East Biddle Street • 214 East Eager Street • Midtown • All Exterior Only

The experimental novelist and art-world matriarch Gertrude Stein spent a number of formative years in Baltimore before relocating to Paris in 1903. She and her siblings came here first in 1892, after the death of their parents, to live with their aunt and uncle, the Bachrachs, on Linden Avenue in Reservoir Hill. There, as a teenager and between semesters at Radcliffe College, she mingled with the Bachrachs' artistic social circle and gained a reputation as an irreverent, independent young woman. Today, recently rescued from long decay, the Bachrach house is sometimes referenced as the "Gertrude Stein House." In 1897, when Stein began studies at the Johns Hopkins School of Medicine, she and her brother Leo moved to a place of their own at 215 East Biddle Street in Mount Vernon. Three years later, Leo took off for Paris, and Gertrude resettled nearby at "a funny little house" at 214 East Eager Street. This phase of her life informs her earliest novels. In *Three Lives*, published in 1909, she rhapsodizes about urban street life and describes the row houses on East Eager as looking like "a row of dominoes" as they stagger down the steep hill between Calvert Street and Guilford Avenue. They still look that way. Stein's next chapter was set in Paris, where she assumed a central role in the artistic avant-garde.

Lizette Woodworth Reese Monument

1000 block of East 33rd Street • East

The gifted, eccentric Grace Turnbull created this singular monument for Reese (1856–1935), a published poet who lived in the nearby Waverly neighborhood. A schoolteacher who wrote traditional, formal lyrics about nature, emotions and small-town life, Reese was admired by H.L. Mencken but is little remembered today. Turnbull, for her part, was a woman born into wealth, a scholar of classical philosophy and a free-spirited artist who experimented with various materials and styles. The Reese memorial, depicting the proverbial good shepherd surrounded by stylized sheep, has a studied simplicity that seems to acknowledge cubism as well as medieval European sculpture. In yet another twist of style, Turnbull carved the sleekly modern but unassuming *King Penguin* in the Inner Harbor. Her best-known work, however, is the naturalistic, strikingly sensuous *Naiad* in East Mount Vernon Park.

Edgar Allan Poe Sites

Westminster Hall Cemetery, East Fayette Street at North Greene Street • Downtown
"The Poe House" • 203 Amity Street • West Baltimore
Latrobe House • 11 West Mulberry Street • Downtown • Exterior Only
Poe Statue • Mount Royal Avenue at Maryland Avenue • Midtown
www.poeinbaltimore.org

Best known for his grotesque imagination, his invention of the detective story and his parody-prone poetry, Edgar Poe might seem to be an incongruous icon for a down-to-earth, pragmatic town like Baltimore. Nevertheless, he is a bona fide hometown hero: died here, buried here, had his first work published here and, in his twenties, lived with his aunt and cousins in a small brick house on the east side of town. Baltimore's NFL team is called the Ravens, and there are bars and restaurants and local beers whose names trade (and pun) on his famous titles. Other cities—Richmond, New York, Boston and Philadelphia—claim their own Poe sites because the chronically unemployable writer bounced around in search of editorial jobs. But no other town embraces this haunted poet with such beyond-literary ardor.

Fittingly, the chief shrine to the morbid author is his burial site on the grounds of Westminster Hall, formerly the Westminster Presbyterian Church. After his mysterious, scandalous death in 1849—he was found, disheveled and disoriented, on the streets of Fell's Point and died four days later—Poe was interred in what was then a Presbyterian burial ground. In 1852, the Presbyterian church was erected over much of the cemetery, preserving many graves in the dirt floor basement space known today as "the catacombs." Most of the sub-floor graves are still in their original beds, but fame, which Poe pursued all his life, caught up with him after death. Beginning in 1865, local educators led a fundraising drive to create a fitting monument for the famous Baltimorean, and in 1875, Poe's remains were exhumed and reburied outside the church walls. The monument was designed by the prominent local architect George Frederick, architect of City Hall, featuring a bronze relief portrait of Poe by Adalbert Volck, a Baltimore artist famed for anti-Lincoln cartoons he published during the Civil War. To this day, Poe's literary loyalists gather at the grave site on the anniversaries of his birth and death, as well as on Halloween. Visitors leave things, like personal notes to Poe and morbid souvenirs. For as many as seventy-five years, a mysterious figure was said to appear at Poe's grave annually on the poet's birthday, leaving behind three roses and an unfinished bottle of cognac.

Less visited, but still significant, is the simple house at Amity Street, occupied by Poe's aunt, Maria Clemm—along with Clemm's mother, children and nephew Edgar—between 1833 and 1835. Today, the site houses a Poe museum, which can be toured virtually when not physically open; in-person tours can be arranged through its website. Although Poe wrote many stories and poems during his sojourn, this is not the house where he wrote "The Raven," as has been sometimes claimed. "The Raven" was published in New York in 1845, a decade after the poet left Baltimore.

But the young Poe of Amity Street was already an aspiring writer, having self-published two collections of poetry. In 1833, he submitted a short story called "MS Found in a Bottle"—the tale of a nightmarish voyage—to a

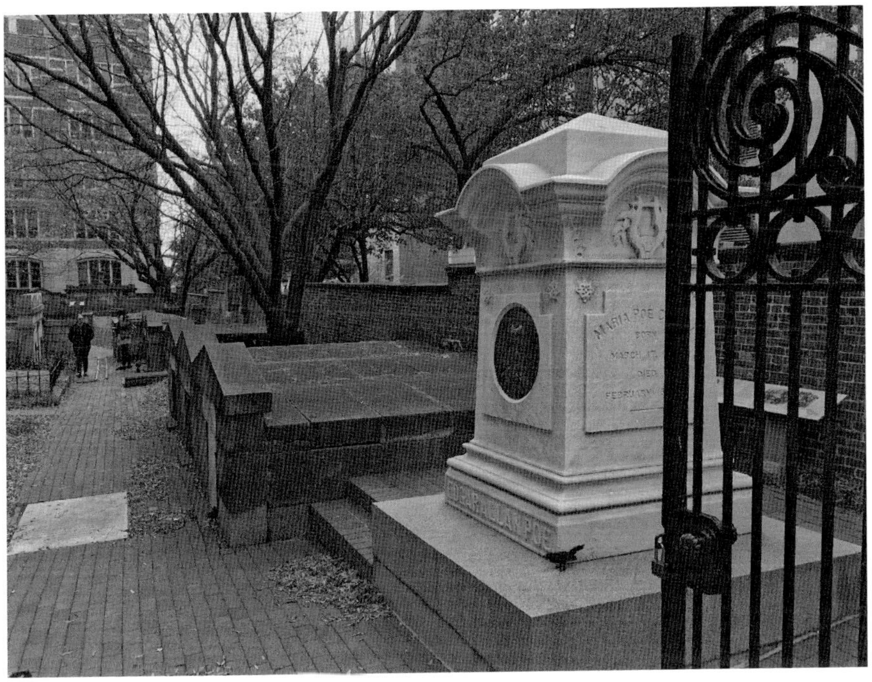

Master of the macabre, writer Edgar Allan Poe's grave is in the atmospheric Westminster Burial Ground dating to 1786. *Courtesy of Tom Chalkley.*

contest sponsored by a local literary publication, the *Saturday Morning Visiter.* That October, the contest judges met at the Mulberry Street home of John H.B. Latrobe, one of the sons of the famous U.S. Capitol architect Benjamin Latrobe. The judges, Latrobe among them, were unanimous in awarding the first prize to Poe's story. It was the *Saturday Morning Visiter* that launched Poe's career. A plaque at the Latrobe House features Poe's portrait. The house itself is a nice example of the elegant Federal-style designs favored by prosperous Baltimoreans at the time.

A fine statue of Poe sits facing Mount Royal Avenue from a courtyard on the University of Baltimore campus. The last and best-known work of sculptor Moses Ezekiel, it shows Poe seated, appearing somewhat off balance, with a bowed head and a hand half raised in a mysterious gesture. The sculpture itself seemed to have been cursed: the artist's working models were successively destroyed, one by fire and the second by an earthquake. The third version, finally cast in bronze in Berlin in 1916, was delayed five years by the First World War. By the time Poe's monument reached Baltimore in 1921, the artist was four years dead. The statue was not popular and languished for many years, obscured by weeds on a traffic island. It was rescued, restored and relocated in 1980s. Among the city's many public portrait-sculptures, this is one of the most vividly expressive of an actual personality.

H.L. Mencken House and Museum

1524 Hollins Street • West
(855) 853-1524 • www.menckenhouse.org

The house museum dedicated to journalist, essayist and razor-penned social and literary critic Henry Louis Mencken recently reopened after being shuttered for more than twenty years. It's a fully restored example of a classic, middle-class Baltimore row house from the 1880s. (So, even if you've little interest in its former owner, a visit will let you peek inside a residential style that defines the city.) Mencken lived his entire life within these walls, save for the five years he was married to writer Sarah Haardt before her death from meningitis in 1935. Though one of the most prominent writers and editors of the first half of the twentieth century, he rebuffed all offers to move to New York City to stay in his beloved Baltimore and a house he once

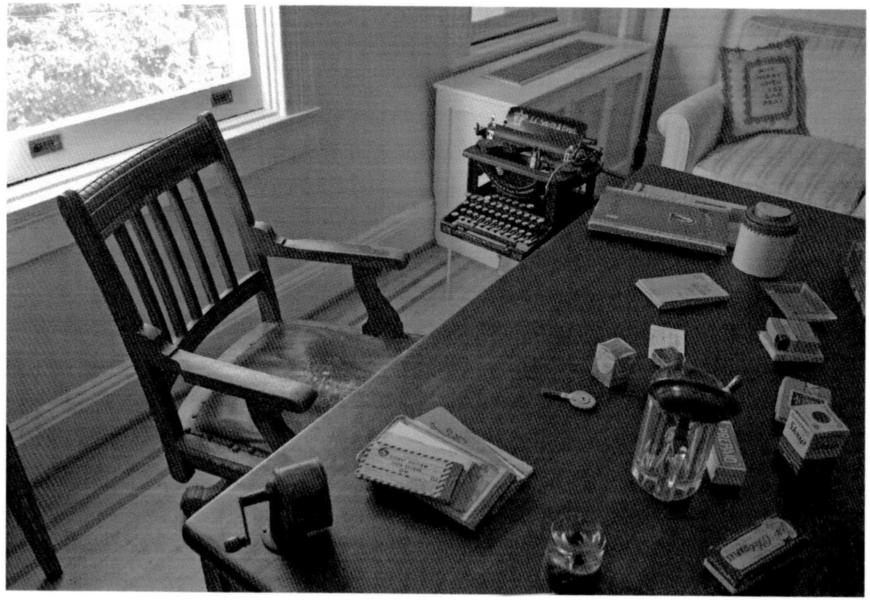

Writer H.L. Mencken's desk and typewriter within his house museum. *Courtesy of Brennen Jensen.*

called "as much a part of me as my two hands." Wistful depictions of his late nineteenth-century boyhood at the address can be found in his book *Happy Days*, the first in his three-volume autobiography. Mencken artifacts and household objects stored offsite have returned, and there are plenty: from the carpets on the floor to the piano in the corner to the pencil sharpener on the desk. Even the umbrella stand and umbrella by the door belonged to the cigar-chomping "Sage of Baltimore." A besotted F. Scott Fitzgerald is said to have crashed on the parlor sofa.

Mencken's second-floor office sports his rumpsprung chair parked beside the black typewriter he used to bang out blistering broadsides on politics, religion and the American "booboisie." (His quote "On some great and glorious day the plain folks of the land will reach their heart's desire at last and the White House will be adorned by a downright moron" has seen heavy use in social media.) Alas, among Mencken's millions of published words lurk some undeniably racist and anti-Semitic ones. Curiously, if one examines his life and output in toto—publishing Black writers when most White editors wouldn't, frequently writing about the folly of segregation and the idiocy of the Klan and counting Jews among his best friends—he's clearly more of a civil rights advocate than a racist. Still, you have to take the bad with the good when considering this enigmatic and prolific figure.

Chapter 10

OF STAGE AND SCREEN

TRIUMPH AND TRAGEDY ARE PART OF BALTIMORE'S ENTERTAINING HISTORY

When it comes to troubled theatrical dynasties—families where gifted acting can be paired with a penchant for madness and self-destruction—before Hollywood's Barrymore clan, there were the Baltimore Booths.

British-born actor Junius Brutus Booth (1796–1852) had a celebrated thirty-year stage career in the United States after immigrating in 1821 along with a London flower girl named Mary Anne Holmes as a common-law wife. While the theatrical life was rather nomadic, the Baltimore area was their principal home. In 1824, Booth acquired a log cabin in Bel Air, Maryland, some twenty-five miles northeast of the city, where they spent the warm-weather months—wintering at various city addresses or on the road—and where Holmes bore most of their ten children. (By 1847, the cabin had been replaced with the Gothic Revival Tudor Hall, which stands to this day.) Booth managed a Baltimore theater for a time, and the 1850 census places the family in the city (in a since-demolished house near Little Italy).

Booth's ability to bring Shakespeare's tragedies to life—with *Richard III* a specialty—was legendary. The critical praise was gushing. Alas, a personal tragedy was Booth's growing penchant for alcohol-fueled erratic behavior—wandering off mid-performance or having stage fights become all too real. He picked up a nickname: the "Mad Tragedian." And then there was the matter of his building a family in Maryland with Miss Holmes while secretly sending money home to a Mrs. Booth (and a son) in England. (It came to a dramatic head when Booth's English son came to Baltimore looking for him.)

Three of Booth's American sons followed him to the footlights, with Edwin Booth having the most success—outshining his father's talents on Baltimore boards and beyond, many said. But then the Booth name might dwell only in dusty theatrical histories if not for the stage work of Edwin's younger brother: a certain John Wilkes Booth. This budding thespian, of course, assassinated President Lincoln in Ford's Theatre in Washington, D.C. (and historians continue to ruminate on the roots of John's rapid radicalization).

The Booth clan rests quietly today beneath an obelisk in the city's Green Mount Cemetery. Ford's Theatre stands as a historic site, museum and working theater. It is named after Baltimore theater magnate John Ford, who owned and ran it. He managed a number of Baltimore theaters, and a few years after the Lincoln tragedy, Ford built a new theater in Baltimore he called Ford's Grand Opera House. Alas, it's gone now. It was pushed over in 1964. Demolition, either by wrecking ball or the odd fire, is a fate that has befallen many Baltimore theaters and music halls since the city's first such venue was erected back in 1782. Consider the drama at the 500 block of North Howard Street. Here, in 1875, arose the 1,200-seat Academy of Music, rivaling any venue in the nation for opulence and appointments, contemporary accounts suggest. In 1927, barely fifty years later, it was torn down and replaced with the Stanley Theater. This was a movie theater—or, more rightly, a movie *palace*. This was the golden age of sumptuous cinemas, and its resplendent Medieval Romanesque auditorium sat 4,000 as the largest theater ever built in town. The curtain fell on this terrazzo floor and chandelier grandeur in 1964, when it was unceremoniously replaced with a parking lot. And the wrecking ball keeps swinging: the Mechanic Theater, erected downtown in 1967 by noted modernist architect John M. Johansen, was demolished in 2014.

If Baltimore stages all too often disappear, the city had a hand in giving the world some performers who are, quite simply, immortal, including a trio of Black jazz/swing giants: Cab Calloway, Billie Holiday and Chick Webb. A few of the city's musical progeny defy pigeon-holing, such as experimental rocker Frank Zappa, head Talking Head David Byrne and pioneering composer Philip Glass, who helped birth the minimalist movement before moving into film soundtracks. (His father ran a record store in town and would bring his musical son all the classical discs that didn't sell—these were invariably the most avant-garde works of the day, giving young Philip a modernist bent from the start.) And before dreaming of California, "Mama" Cass Elliot, born Naomi Cohen, began her vocal career in Baltimore musical theater.

Overall, Baltimore doesn't have a "sound" like Philadelphia, Detroit and other cities (though dance music fans might be familiar with internationally recognized Baltimore Club, a sort of rap-meets-rave house music subgenre whose electric beats and looped vocals have been packing dance floors since the late 1980s). Nor is the city the birthplace or center of a musical genre the way New York, Nashville and New Orleans are. (Although the Orioles, a Baltimore R&B vocal group founded in 1946, helped create doo-wop music, and the modern banjo, of all things, was invented in town after an immigrant German drum maker named William Boucher brought western technology to an organic African instrument in the 1840s.)

Recent biographical scholarship says that Eleanora Fagan, the future Billie Holiday, was born in Philadelphia in 1915. (Her unwed teenaged parents briefly fled there from their native Baltimore.) Holiday spent a troubled childhood among the alley houses of upper Fell's Point. She endured a stint in a reform school and, while still a girl, was running errands—and possibly worse—for a brothel. But amid her hardscrabble life came a sonic epiphany: she heard Louis Armstrong and Bessie Smith sing on shellac records and began testing her own voice. "Lady Day" would learn to tap into personal privations for a unique, plaintive and blues-drenched vocal style. Holiday-themed murals and art can be found along the 200 block of South Durham Street, where she lived at multiple addresses before taking off for Harlem.

Calloway had an altogether different Baltimore childhood. Born in Rochester, New York, he spent his formative years in Baltimore, where his family was ensconced in the city's small Black middle class. Calloway drove his own car to Frederick Douglass High School, where he was voted class "heartbreaker" and wowed audiences in musical shows. He divided his free time between Pimlico Race Course and the musically jumping Black nightclubs along Pennsylvania Avenue. He was soon playing drums and singing in a four-piece band. Older sister Blanche Calloway saw showbiz success before he did and helped blaze a trail. (She would go on to lead her own band.) An athlete as well as entertainer, Calloway played pro basketball in town for a bit before seeking national musical fame, first in Chicago and, inevitably, Harlem. He came to be called the Hi-De-Ho Man from the scat singing in his 1931 mega-hit "Minnie the Moocher," which spawned a film showing him in one of his trademark capacious zoot suits. With his dexterous and playful wordplay and flashy style, some see Calloway as an early father of hip-hop.

Chick Webb might be the lesser-known figure, but his story of perseverance and triumph is the greatest of all. William Henry Webb was born into

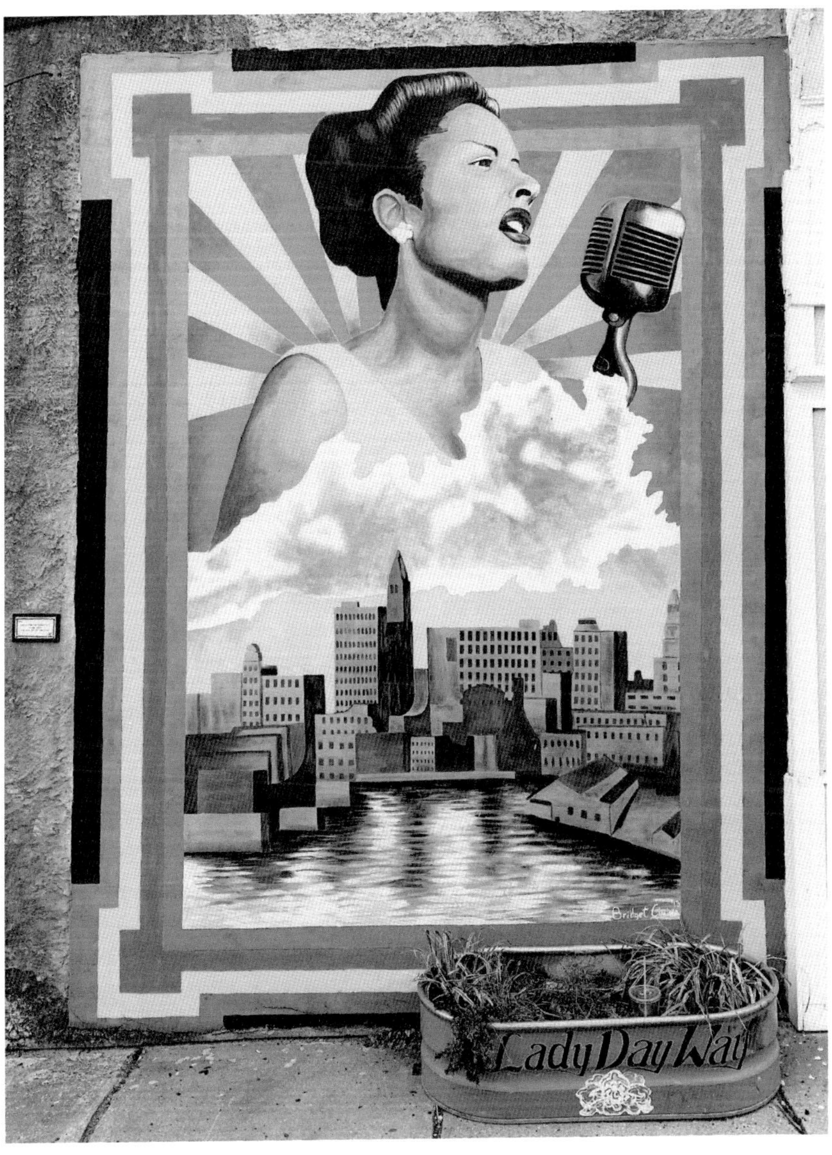

Artist Bridget Cimino's homage to Billie Holiday in the Fell's Point backstreet where "Lady Day" grew up. *Courtesy of Kathryn Skare.*

impoverished East Baltimore in 1909. An early childhood fall damaged his backbone and ultimately left him with tuberculosis of the spine and a severe deformity. ("Hunchbacked" is what he was called in the day; he never stood more than four feet tall, his scrunched stature engendering the nickname he adopted professionally.) It's said that young Webb took up drumming as physical therapy. He played on pots and pans at home and trash cans outside before selling enough papers out of a wagon he pulled through the streets to buy a drum set. He had a rhythmic gift. Barely out of boyhood, he played in a band for day-trippers on Chesapeake Bay excursion boats and was still a teen when he left for Harlem.

After some austere years, Webb had his own band, which took up residence at the storied and integrated Savoy Ballroom in the early 1930s. Here, in applause-driven "Battle of the Bands" competitions, he bested the greatest swing outfits of the day, including Benny Goodman's. In 1935, he added a shy, unknown teenage orphan vocalist to his band: future First Lady of Song, Ella Fitzgerald. Webb maintained familial ties to Baltimore, coming down to perform for Black audiences at the Royal Theater and at the Hippodrome Theater, where, because of segregated seating policies, his mother had to watch him from the corner of the stage. While the hit records racked up, his spinal condition worsened, but he played through pain. In the spring of 1939, Webb left his band's national tour seeking treatment at Johns Hopkins Hospital. He died there on June 16 at age thirty. His Baltimore funeral was one of the largest the city had ever seen, as giants of the entertainment world, Black and White, descended on East Baltimore. Webb is buried at Baltimore County's Arbutus Memorial Park beneath a headstone bearing a crown and a drum.

Moving from sound to cinema, a pair of decidedly different homegrown auteurs put Baltimore on the big screen: Barry Levinson and John Waters. While the former is known for such award-winning blockbusters as *Good Morning Vietnam* and *Rain Man*, he also made a labor-of-love quartet of Baltimore-based films, at times personal and autobiographical, beginning with his directorial debut *Diner* in 1982. The 1987 comedy *Tin Men* stars Danny DeVito as a dodgy aluminum siding salesman (although it was really about Formstone, the localized fake-stone "home improvement" hustle). The 1990 film *Avalon* presents a multigenerational tale of Jewish assimilation—what is gained and what is lost as immigrants and their progeny move

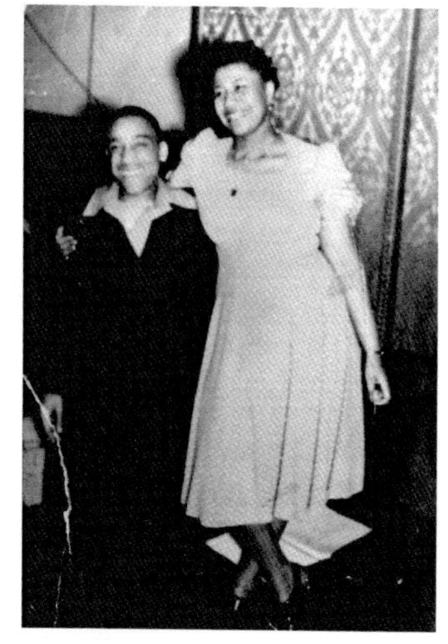

Rare image of drummer and bandleader Chick Webb with his protégé, Ella Fitzgerald. *Courtesy of the Webb family and Michelle Gienow.*

up Baltimore's economic ladder. Judaic and racial themes intertwine in his 1999 comedy-drama *Liberty Heights* (named after a city neighborhood), wherein a group of Jewish teenagers lance the tightly delineated racial, religious and social lines of 1950s Baltimore.

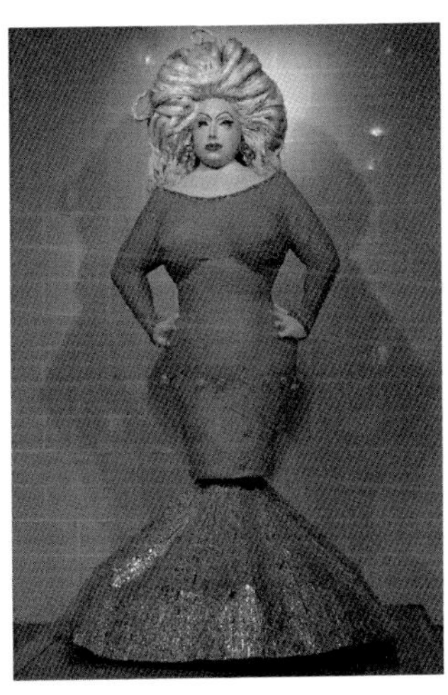

John Waters's star Divine, as depicted by artist Andrew Logan at the American Visionary Art Museum. *Courtesy of AVAM.*

As for Waters, describing his plots is a fool's errand, especially his pocket change–budgeted early works made with the Dreamlanders, a like-minded band of shock-celebrating cinematic eccentrics. (It's perhaps enough to say that the protagonists in his 1972 film *Pink Flamingos* compete for the title of "filthiest person alive.") For the bulk of his oeuvre, his leading lady was the late Harris Glenn Milstead, better known as the corpulent drag queen Divine, whose made-up and bewigged visage is now an international icon. Their ribald tales of depravity played before howling college-aged audiences at midnight screenings, while raising the ire (and blood pressure) of state censor Mary Avara. (Maryland was the last state with its own board of censors reviewing and rating films; Avara branded the Dreamlanders "sickies" before her board was dissolved in 1981.) The self-styled "Pope of Trash" began to get bigger budgets and bona fide Hollywood stars and celebs, such as Kathleen Turner and Sonny Bono, but his scripts maintained some warped sensibilities.

Perhaps the wildest tale of all is how an outsider like Waters, whose *Pink Flamingos* features a singing anus (literally) and Divine eating dog feces (really), became a revered favorite son. His reappraisal sped along after the tuneful stage adaptation of his 1988 film *Hairspray* became a Broadway smash in 2002 (its story inspired by a segregated Baltimore televised teenage dance show Waters grew up watching). The writer/director keeps a house in Baltimore, and his pencil-thin mustache is frequently seen around town, including a favorite haunt, Hampden's Atomic Books.

Baltimore's small-screen story is dominated by David Simon, a TV writer and transplant from the Washington, D.C., suburbs. He immersed himself in the politics of the street corner and City Hall as a longtime reporter for the *Baltimore Sun*. Simon spent a year shadowing city homicide detectives for a book that spawned NBC's popular 1990s police drama *Homicide: Life on the*

Street. (Barry Levinson was an executive producer of the show, which was filmed entirely in town.) A second book he coauthored about a year of an inner-city Baltimore drug corner spawned the Emmy Award–winning HBO mini-series *The Corner* in 2000. But it is HBO's *The Wire*, the celebrated five-season series premiering in 2002, that made Simon's name. Created and principally written by him, this gritty and violent saga of police versus drug gangs is set against a backdrop of institutional failure: unions, schools, the media and more. For all its savagery, Simon's deft writing and hard-won journalistic insight into the morass humanizes the "soldiers" on both sides of the so-called war on drugs. For city boosters lamenting Simon's bleak depiction of Baltimore, it's cold comfort that *The Wire*, while snubbed by the major awards, is a critical darling. (*Rolling Stone* places it second only to *The Sopranos* as the best television show of all time.) While versions of his dark, illicit-drug opera play out in cities and towns across the country, Baltimore got the primetime black eye (but also years of work for local actors and production crews).

To bring this back around to the world of acting, the late Howard Rollins was born in Baltimore and dropped out of what's now Towson University just north of the city in 1970 for a role in the Maryland Public Broadcasting serial *Our Street.* About ten years later came his Academy Award–nominated performance in *Ragtime.* Film and TV actor Josh Charles did standup comedy at Baltimore clubs while still a child, and his big acting break came in John Waters's *Hairspray.* A pre-Smith Jada Pinkett graduated from the Baltimore School for the Arts in 1989 (one year after Charles did). And long before having a certain hit show in California, the first bay this actor likely watched was the Chesapeake. Yes, David "*Baywatch*" Hasselhoff is from Baltimore.

YOUR GUIDE TO HISTORY

MECU Pavilion

731 Eastern Avenue • Inner Harbor

(410) 547-7200 • www.livenation.com

This waterside open-air concert venue opened in 1981 and was known as Pier Six Pavilion until the Municipal Employees Credit Union bought naming rights in 2018. It seats 2,800 under its striking white tent structure, with another 1,800 or so out on the lawn.

Arena Players

801 McCulloh Street • Downtown
(410) 728-6500 • www.arenaplayersinc.com

Billed as the oldest continuously operating African American community theater in the United States, Arena Players was founded in 1953 as an outgrowth of the Negro Little Theater Movement begun during the Harlem Renaissance to create venues for dramatic works written and performed by Black artists. Itinerant for its first decade, it has long had its own three-hundred-seat theater and classroom space for youth drama programs. Famous actors who strode its boards include the late Howard Rollins and Tony Award winners Trazana Beverley and André De Shields.

"The Block"

400 East Baltimore Street • Downtown

The nickname for the city's historic tenderloin is literally true today: it has shrunk to a single sketchy block of strip clubs. But for much of the twentieth century, the gaudy neon lights stretched for nearly eight blocks and Baltimore enjoyed a lively reputation as a bustling burlesque town.

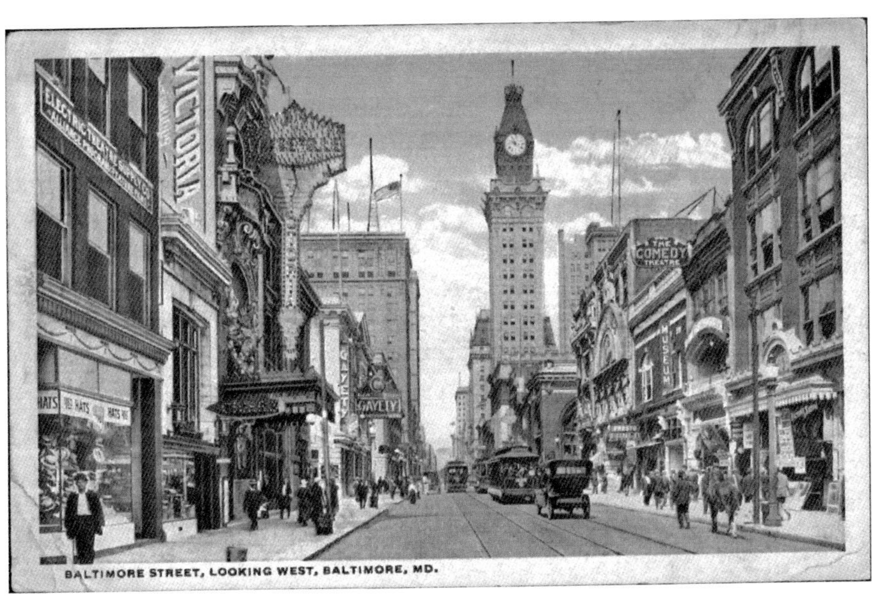

Vintage postcard of the once-bustling burlesque district along East Baltimore Street. *Author's collection.*

During the Block's midcentury heyday—before all-nude pole dancing became the norm—pasties-and-G-string striptease shows might include a jazz combo and salty-tongued comics. The Gayety Theater (405 East Baltimore Street) opened in 1906 with seating for a whopping 1,600. Fires and interior renovations have long obliterated the auditorium, although its ornate façade, with its sweeping arches and decorative human faces, largely survives. Its marquee once used the Brit-spelling "Burlesk," and its stage saw Red Skelton, Jackie Gleason and Phil Silvers take up the mic and Gypsy Rose Lee take off her clothes. Perhaps the most famous denizen of the Block was Blaze Starr, the curvy West Virginian who earned her moniker as "the Hottest Blaze in Burlesque" performing at the 2 O'Clock Club (414 East Baltimore Street) in striptease shows incorporating everything from a burning sofa to a live panther. A 1954 *Esquire* magazine profile brought her national fame, as did a tabloid-fodder affair with married Louisiana governor Earl Long a few years later (subject of the 1989 Paul Newman film *Blaze*). She later owned the 2 O'Clock Club and was dubbed "Mayor of the Block." It's all rather seedy today, although the adventurous might want to visit Midway Bar (421 East Baltimore Street). No nude shows here, just some vintage photos of the burlesque queens who shimmied and teased during the Block's good-old, not-so-bad days.

Chesapeake Shakespeare Company

This theatrical group and its historic downtown stage at 7 South Calvert Street are described in Chapter 8.

Everyman Theatre

315 West Fayette Street • Downtown
(410) 752-2208 • www.everymantheatre.org

This professional theater company debuted in 1990, and the award-winning ensemble moved into a 253-seat home in the former Town Theater in 2013. The Town began as a vaudeville and burlesque venue called the Empire in 1911. Unable to find its footing in the competitive live performance market, the Empire's curtain fell in 1937, and the building was converted into a multi-level parking garage. A decade later, it was reconverted back to theatrical use—movies this time—as the Town Theater. Decaying and vacant by the 1990s, the Town might have again taken up parking duty if not for Everyman's dramatic intervention.

Hippodrome Theatre at the France-Merrick Performing Arts Center
12 North Eutaw Street • Downtown
(800) 343-3103 • www.france-merrickpac.com

In a city that hasn't been kind to its historic theaters, the Hippodrome became a glittering outlier in 2004 when the vacant 1914 vaudeville house was reborn as a $63 million, state-of-the-art venue for even the largest and most elaborate Broadway shows and musical performances. Built with three thousand seats, it was billed as the largest theater south of Philadelphia upon its debut. Movies were soon added to live shows that included everything from performing elephants to jugglers to cross-talk comedians. A skinny twentysomething named Frank Sinatra, fresh from performing as a singing waiter in his native New Jersey, made a pivotal first appearance with the Harry James Orchestra here in 1939. The Hippodrome eventually became a full-time movie house and achieved rundown white elephant status in the age of suburban multiplexes. The redevelopment incorporates a pair of adjacent nineteenth-century bank buildings to expand lobby space.

Baltimore School for the Arts
712 Cathedral Street • Midtown
(443) 642-5165 • www.bsfa.org

Founded in 1979, this four-year public high school prepares students for careers in music, visual arts, theater (acting, design and production), dance and film. It resides in a seven-story, Italian Renaissance–style building built in 1926 as the Hotel Alcazar. The late rapper Tupac Shakur was a theater student here for two years in the 1980s, studying alongside his friend, actor Jada Pinkett (who graduated in 1989). Actor Josh Charles, fashion designer Christian Siriano and ballet dancer Jacqueline Green are also alums. Performances and exhibitions are often open to the public.

Baltimore Theatre Project
45 West Preston Street • Midtown
(410) 539-3091 • www.theatreproject.org

Founded in 1971 by producer and contemporary theater aficionado Philip Arnoult and Antioch College, Baltimore Theatre Project is the city's home for original and experimental theater, music and dance via various in-house companies and visiting national and international artists and ensembles. Its 150-seat theater is carved out of an 1897 building initially erected for a fraternal organization that later served as early home for the city's Center Stage theater.

Baltimore Center Stage
700 North Calvert Street • Midtown
(410) 332-0033 • www.centerstage.org

This is a happy story in which an accomplished but homeless acting company is rescued by kindly priests. Center Stage, the organization, started out in 1963 on North Avenue, but its building, the unintended target of an arsonist, burned to the ground in 1974. Meanwhile, the Jesuit priests in charge of St. Ignatius Church, at Calvert and Read Streets, were sitting on about three times as much space as they needed. The Jesuits owned the entire west side of the 700 block of Calvert Street, but their church, built in 1856, took up only the northern one-third of the space. The rest of the Jesuit complex, built in 1899, lay vacant; it had been the home of Loyola College until 1922, when Loyola moved to Cold Spring Lane. In 1975, the Jesuits donated the entire school complex to Center Stage. The architectural firm of James R. Grieves radically redesigned the interior. In the hollow of the old auditorium, it built a theater, while the rest of the school building became the lobby, business offices and two restaurant/café spaces. In 1991, a second architectural team, Ziger/Snead, tucked a second performance space, the smaller Head Theater, into the vacant space above the main theater. Center Stage is by most measures the leading dramatic organization in Baltimore. A $28 million renovation completed in 2017 tweaked theatrical spaccs anew and saw it formally add "Baltimore" to its name.

Eubie Blake Cultural Center
847 North Howard Street • Midtown
(410) 225-3130 • www.eubieblake.org

Pianist and composer James Hubert "Eubie" Blake was born in the city's Dunbar-Broadway neighborhood in 1887 to parents who had formerly been enslaved. (Blake maintained that he was born in 1883, but available records indicate the later date.) Life was hard: he was the only of the couple's ten children to survive past infancy. Blake's musical genius showed early, and his parents scrimped for a pump organ and lessons in church music. However, he soon followed his ear to saucier, secular sounds, writing his first piano rag at sixteen and playing at a bordello and a nightclub owned by Black pro boxer Joe Gans. After relocating to New York City, he and lyricist Noble Sissle wrote the music for Broadway's first all-Black musical revue, *Shuffle Along*, in 1921, which played to packed houses for more than five hundred performances. Additional Broadway shows and songs followed, as did a period of retirement. But Blake's dexterous, sinewy fingers were working the ivories—from symphony halls to TV's *Saturday Night Live*—right up to his death in 1983 at age ninety-six. The primary goal of his namesake Cultural Center is to help Baltimore youth develop their creative abilities through classes in music and dance. The Center also includes an art gallery and a performance venue called Eubie Live!

Joseph Meyerhoff Symphony Hall
1212 Cathedral Street • Midtown
(410) 783-8000 • www.bsomusic.org

The Baltimore Symphony debuted in 1916 as the nation's first publicly funded orchestra, becoming a private entity in 1942. Its current 2,443-seat home opened in 1982 as a study in the curvilinear: from the vast oval exterior to the sweeping lines of the hall's boxes, balconies and circular sound baffles fine-tuning the acoustics. A *Washington Post* architecture critic praised its "no-nonsense elegance" and the "sleek romance" it added to the streetscape. It is named for the Ukrainian-born founder of a successful Baltimore construction company and a longtime BSO president who ponied up nearly half of the $22 million cost of the hall. The symphony made history in 2007 when Marin Alsop shattered the proverbial concert hall glass ceiling to become the BSO's music director—the first woman to achieve this title at a major American orchestra.

Modell Performing Arts Center at the Lyric
140 West Mount Royal Avenue • Midtown
(410) 900-1150 • www.modell-lyric.com

Opened simply as the Music Hall in 1894 and known for most of its life as the Lyric Opera House, the city's grand dame performance venue assumed its present moniker in 2010 to acknowledge a $3.5 million gift toward renovations from the Modell family, former owners of the NFL's Cleveland Browns/Baltimore Ravens. The exterior of the 2,564-seat hall has been covered with numerous additions over the years, so you can no longer tell that it is essentially a big brick rectangle. And that's by design—partly. Maryland-born architect T. Henry Randall followed the "shoebox" manner of concert hall layout notably employed at Leipzig, Germany's once-celebrated nineteenth-century Neues Gewandhaus (destroyed in World War II). Alas, a grand semicircular protruding front of baroque design, housing expanded lobby space, got axed for budgetary reasons in the early going. It wasn't until 1981 that proper front of house space was added (albeit a drab, tan brick thing of questionable architectural merit). Still, the acoustics are pretty good in the big box, and a who's who of musical greats have performed within, from Caruso to George Gershwin to Patti LaBelle. Baltimore's own champion boxer Joe Gans fought to a rare non-victory here in 1906 (it was a draw). It has also been the setting for innumerable graduation ceremonies and the blueblood set's annual Bachelor Cotillion (the archaic and ritualized "coming out" of "society" debutantes). Recent renovations updated the antiquated back of house, where hemp ropes were still used to move scenery.

SNF Parkway Theatre
5 West North Avenue • Midtown
(443) 438-6144 • mdfilmfest.com

In a striking feat of adaptive reuse, this classic movie theater has been massively remodeled and reborn as...a movie theater. The Parkway originally opened in 1915; its first feature was *Zaza*, a silent flick accompanied by live organ music. Through the age of "talkies" to the dawn of Technicolor, the Parkway operated as a mainstream movie house until 1952, when a new owner bought it and, soon after, closed it. The space reopened in 1956 under the name 5 West Art Theatre, showing foreign

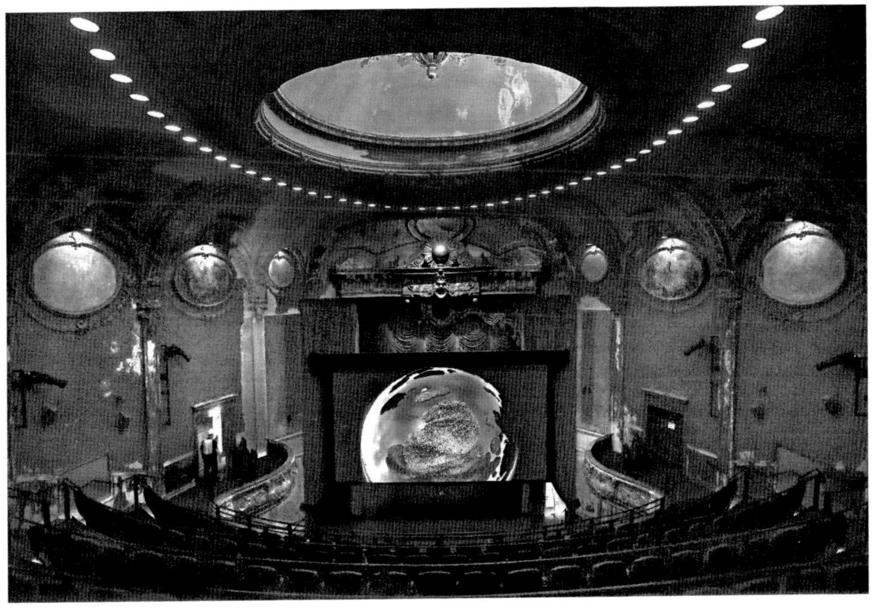

SNF Parkway Theater. *Courtesy and copyright of Amy Davis.*

and classic films until it closed in 1978. In 2012, local film buffs made their way into the almost century-old theatrical space and were amazed at its dusty, decaying splendor. To rescue the building, a partnership including the Maryland Film Festival, the Maryland Institute College of Art and Johns Hopkins University garnered a grant of $5 million from the Stavros Niarchos Foundation. Rather than painstakingly restoring the interior to its original opulence, the Baltimore architectural firm Ziger/Snead stabilized the decay into what's been described as a state of "suspended deterioration." The renamed SNF Parkway reopened in 2017.

The Senator Theatre

5904 York Road • North
(410) 323-4424 • www.thesenatortheatre.com

Through much of the twentieth century, almost every Baltimore neighborhood had a movie theater. In the heyday of "movie palaces," dozens of glittering marquees loomed over city sidewalks promoting feature films, cartoons, newsreels and short subjects. In sweltering summers, the best of the theaters were air-cooled. Television and home air conditioning

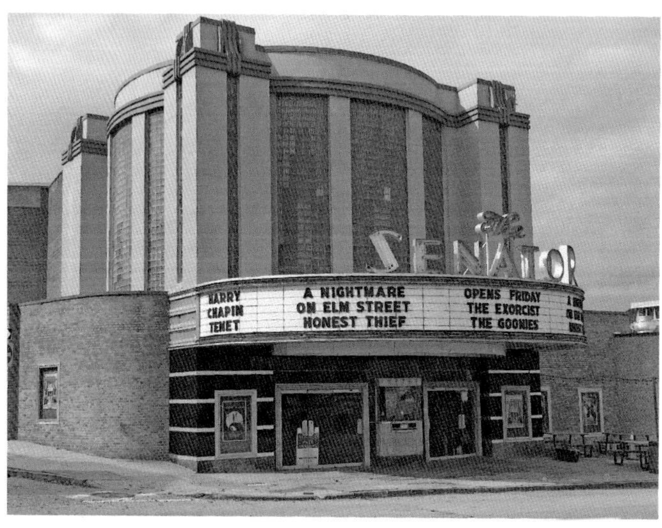

The Senator Theater is a gem from 1939. *Courtesy of Tom Chalkley.*

undercut the theatrical market, and the onslaught of cable TV and streaming videos has brought it close to extinction.

Today, the city has only six movie theaters, including the Senator, the Charles (which occupies a former streetcar barn), two chain franchises of recent construction and one, the Parkway, a classic that has been saved from ruin and restored to functionality. Among this half dozen, the theater that best preserves the old moviegoing experience is the Senator, which opened in 1939, the year of *The Wizard of Oz*, Disney's *Snow White and the Seven Dwarfs* and *Gone with the Wind.*

Designed in the Streamline Moderne style by architect John Zink and much restored in recent years, the Senator sports a semicircular marquee and a convex façade illuminated by neon tubes behind tall panels of glass brick. Inside, the circular lobby features restored Art Deco–flavored murals symbolizing the history of visual entertainment. The main theater, with one thousand seats, focuses on a forty-foot-wide screen. The irony is that the Senator, now much loved as a relic of the age of movie palaces, was a fairly ordinary neighborhood theater showing second-run movies. Renovated by new owners circa 1990, the Senator made the most of its status as cinematic survivor, hosting gala opening events especially for films by hometown heroes Barry Levinson and John Waters, complete with commemorative Hollywood-style imprints in wet cement on the sidewalk.

Creative Alliance at the Patterson

3124 Eastern Avenue • Southeast

(410) 276-1651 • www.creativealliance.org

When it closed in 1995, the Patterson Theater in Highlandtown was one of the last and oldest neighborhood movie houses operating in Baltimore. There had been a Patterson Theater on the corner of Eastern Avenue and East Street since 1910. The current building, in its somewhat stolid original form, opened in 1930; it survived the Depression and a devastating fire in 1958. By the 1990s, however, the Patterson's fortunes had sunk along with the economic conditions of the neighborhood: it was a discount movie house showing second-run features, with cheap tickets and stickier-than-average floors. The place went dark in 1995 and languished for the next five years. Then along came a somewhat scruffy arts organization that had started the same year the movie theater closed. The Fell's Point Creative Alliance had begun as an innovative fusion of café, art gallery and performance space run by an artists' organization. Spearheaded by Margaret Footner and Megan Hamilton, the Alliance had a vision of creating a multifunctional art center that would engage with its immediate neighborhood while offering its programs to the world. With a federal grant and foundation support, the old theater was gutted and redesigned inside the brick shell. Its unique but time-ravaged "blade"-style sign, from 1930, was painstakingly recreated. The reborn, renamed Creative Alliance at the Patterson opened in 2003. True to its vision, the Creative Alliance provides classes to local children, studio space for a few lucky artists, bold and intriguing art shows, a bar and a packed schedule of live performances, from bluegrass to hip-hop and from hand-made "crankie" performances to bawdy burlesque shows.

Frank Zappa Bust

3601 Eastern Avenue • Southeast

Musician and composer Frank Zappa—who first emerged in the 1960s as a member of the experimental rock group the Mothers of Invention before going on to enjoy a genre-warping sonic career in avant-garde rock, jazz and classical music—was born in Baltimore in 1940. He spent a good chunk of his childhood in the city and nearby Edgewood, Maryland. The eclectic figure, an erudite champion of artistic freedom and foe of censorship, died of cancer in 1993 at age fifty-two. This bust of the mustachioed Mr. Zappa sits atop a twelve-foot pole and was erected in 2010, a gift to the city from a Zappa fan club in Lithuania.

Billie Holiday Statue

Northwest corner of Pennsylvania Avenue and West Lafayette Avenue • West

Mouth thrown open in song and wearing a trademark gardenia in her hair, this larger-than-life bronze statue depicts legendary jazz vocalist Billie Holiday. She grew up in Baltimore as Eleanora Fagan before heading off to Harlem to become "Lady Day," with a bluesy song style all her own. The statue's black granite base includes imagery relating to a pair of her most famous recordings: "God Bless the Child" (which she co-wrote) and the chilling, anti-lynching song "Strange Fruit." Catty-cornered across the intersection from her stands a replica of the Royal Theater marquee. Holiday performed at this former venue many times. Opened initially as the Douglass in 1922, the Royal became a major venue for Black entertainers, and many lament the decision to demolish it in 1971. In 2019, much of this historic stretch became the Pennsylvania Avenue Black Arts and Entertainment District, with tax breaks and other incentives to encourage arts-focused development. Group tours of the area can be arranged through the Baltimore Heritage Area Association (www.explorebaltimore.org).

Chapter 11

SPORTING LIFE

FROM BALLFIELD TO BLEACHERS, BOWLING ALLEYS TO BOXING RINGS, A CITY COMPETES

They were champions. Again. "After a long season of hard, earnest work and uninterrupted triumphs, the Orioles were like a lot of happy boys just out of school," the *Baltimore Sun* proclaimed. "Joy reigns supreme among the three-time champions of the world where every man on the team did heroic work."

The paper was describing a great October day when the Baltimore Orioles baseball team returned home after winning the pennant—their third straight!

Okay, if you follow major-league ball, you might be a bit confused by this stellar, black-and-orange triumph—as of this writing, the current American League Orioles are rebuilding and haven't enjoyed the ultimate October victory in more than thirty-seven years. And never three in a row. But this *Sun* article is from 1896 and describes an old National League Orioles franchise. This was when "Foxy" Ned Hanlon assembled and managed a scrappy band of seeming misfits into a team that dominated the diamond like few before or since. It might be easy to dismiss hardball from so long ago, but the 1890s Orioles helped birth modern baseball—full stop. They not only pioneered the Baltimore chop at long-demolished Union Park, but their aggressive, heads-up play also engendered the hit-and-run, squeeze play and sacrifice bunt.

The weirdest twists of all? Despite their winning ways, the moneyed machinations of pro sports (some things never change) saw the team cut from the National League in 1900. The birds were reborn in the new American

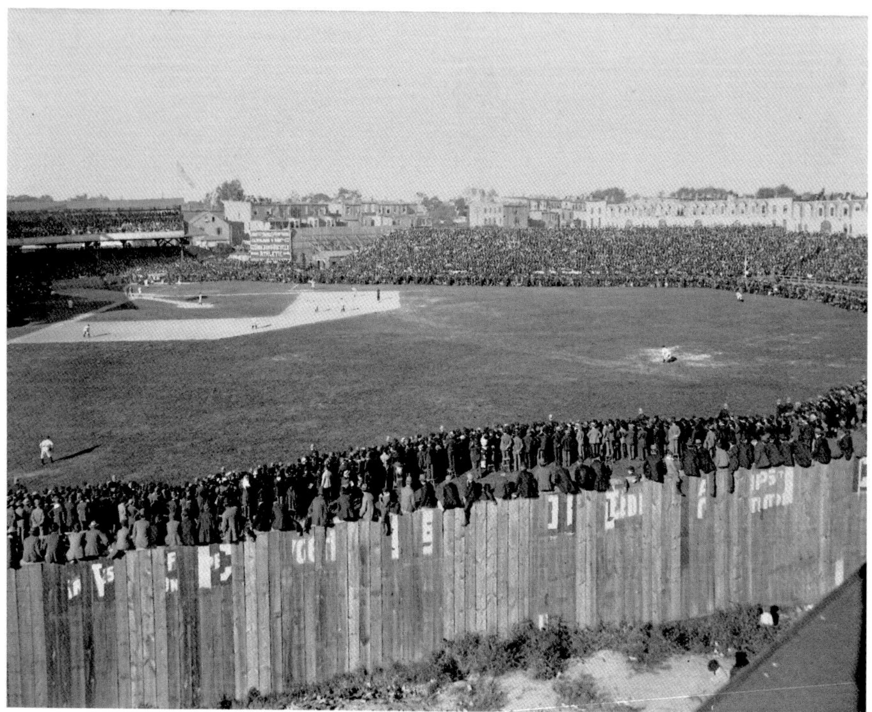

Baltimore Orioles playing at long-demolished Union Park in 1897. *Courtesy of Library of Congress.*

League the following year with veteran player/manager John McGraw at the helm, but then that team up and relocated to New York City in 1903. Initially renamed the Highlanders, in 1913 the former Orioles became the Yankees—yes, *those* Yankees, the perennial nemesis of today's Eastern Division Orioles. Oh, and Babe Ruth, the most storied ballplayer to wear Yankee pinstripes—or perhaps any baseball uniform, for that matter—was born in Baltimore and played his first ball for a minor-league Orioles team.

Meanwhile, on the gridiron, the old Baltimore Colts helped make the modern NFL. The nail-biting, nationally televised 1958 National Football Championship game where legendary Colts quarterback Johnny Unitas led the team to a sudden-death overtime win against the New York Giants is widely hailed as the "Greatest Game Ever Played." It helped position football as our most popular televised sport. And while many cities have longer pro-football histories, the NFL's 100 Greatest Players list includes nine who played for either the Baltimore Colts or the Ravens—a number few cities can match.

The city's pro hoops history is less dramatic. A Baltimore Bullets basketball team first appeared in 1944, playing initially in the American Basketball Association and then the Basketball Association of America before joining the National Basketball Association in 1949. The team folded during the 1954 season. A reformed NBA Baltimore Bullets played here from 1963 to 1973 before relocating to suburban Washington, D.C., and eventually becoming the Washington Wizards. Legendary center Wes Unseld earned Rookie of the Year accolades in a Baltimore Bullets jersey in 1969.

And as to the other football game, the Baltimore Blast is an indoor soccer team in the Major Arena Soccer League presently playing games at Towson University's SECU Arena.

Sports, like most American institutions, was originally segregated. Professional Black baseball teams were playing in Baltimore as early as the 1870s. During the golden age of Negro League ball (1920–51), the city had various teams and won three championships. The Baltimore Black Sox took the pennant in 1929, and the Baltimore Elite Giants (pronounced "*ee*-light") were league champions in 1939 and 1949. Future MLB Hall of Famers Roy Campanella, Leon Day and "Biz" Mackey played for the Elites, and Jud Wilson and legendary pitcher Leroy Robert "Satchel" Paige wore Black Sox jerseys.

The old Negro League ballfields have long since disappeared. But some of the league's amazing stats continue to impress, and thanks to a recent decision by Major League Baseball, they are now included in the MLB record book. Take those of infielder John Beckwith—the Black Bomber—who spent a few years in an Elites uniform, including the 1930 season when he finished with a .464 batting average. Babe Ruth himself said that Beckwith hit harder than any man in the world.

Speaking of hitting hard, Baltimore's Joe Gans was the country's first Black boxing champion, reigning as the top lightweight between 1902 and 1908. Born Joe Gant in 1874 (Gans was a newspaper typo that stuck), it's said that he gained forearm strength shucking oysters on the Baltimore waterfront. A pro pugilist since age seventeen, his most famous bout was a successful 1906 title defense against Danish-born Oscar Nelson—a grueling forty-two-rounder that is still the longest fight in pro boxing history.

With his considerable winnings, Gans opened the handsome Goldfield Hotel on Baltimore's east side in 1907, naming it after the Nevada town where he'd bested Nelson. The three-story hostelry included a lively, integrated nightspot—likely the first such Black-owned establishment in the city—where composer and pianist Eubie Blake, then a teenager, honed his ragtime chops as a hired pianist.

Though nicknamed "the Old Master" for his skillful ways, Gans didn't make it to old age. Tuberculosis felled him in 1910 at age thirty-five. The Goldfield, later made into apartments, was pushed over in 1960 to make way for Baltimore's main post office. A historical marker stands near the Goldfield site at the corner of Colvin Street and East Lexington Street, and Gans is buried at Mount Auburn Cemetery (discussed in Chapter 6).

Moving on to four-legged athletes, Pimlico Race Track is one of the nation's oldest horse racing ovals. It opened in 1870 and is famous for its annual Preakness Stakes, center jewel of racing's Triple Crown. The track's fortunes have waxed and waned over the years (currently in a protracted wane), but highlights of its twentieth-century glory days include 1938's "Match of the Century," the stallion versus stallion race between Seabiscuit and War Admiral. Tens of thousands of spectators packed the stands and lined the rail on race day, while an estimated 40 million listened on the radio. War Admiral, the Triple Crown winner the year before, was well favored but lost to a charging Seabiscuit by four lengths.

By the mid-1950s, Baltimore was a big-league town. The St. Louis Browns relocated here in 1954 to become the American League Orioles, joining an NFL Colts team founded the year before. Both teams played at Memorial Stadium, erected in 1950 (and enlarged in 1954) on the northeast Baltimore site where there'd been a municipal stadium since the 1920s. The Orioles enjoyed a golden era between 1966 and 1983, when they had the best record in all of baseball, appearing in six World Series and winning half of them.

Memorial was showing its age by the 1980s, when dual-sport stadiums were falling out of favor. The owner of the Colts sought better facilities and locked horns with city leaders. It came to an ignoble end on March 27, 1984, when, without warning, an armada of Mayflower trucks moved the team to Indianapolis under cover of darkness and a sloppy snowstorm. The city would endure a dozen-year NFL drought until the Cleveland Browns moved here in 1996 to become the Ravens, the name a nod to Edgar Allan Poe's famous poem. (Cleveland had a new Browns team within three years.) During the no-NFL period, the Baltimore Stallions in the Canadian Football League sprang up here in 1994—as it happened, winning that league's ultimate prize, the Gray Cup, their first year. The team moved on after the following season. The Orioles moved to their new downtown stadium Oriole Park at Camden Yards in 1991, and the Ravens, after one season

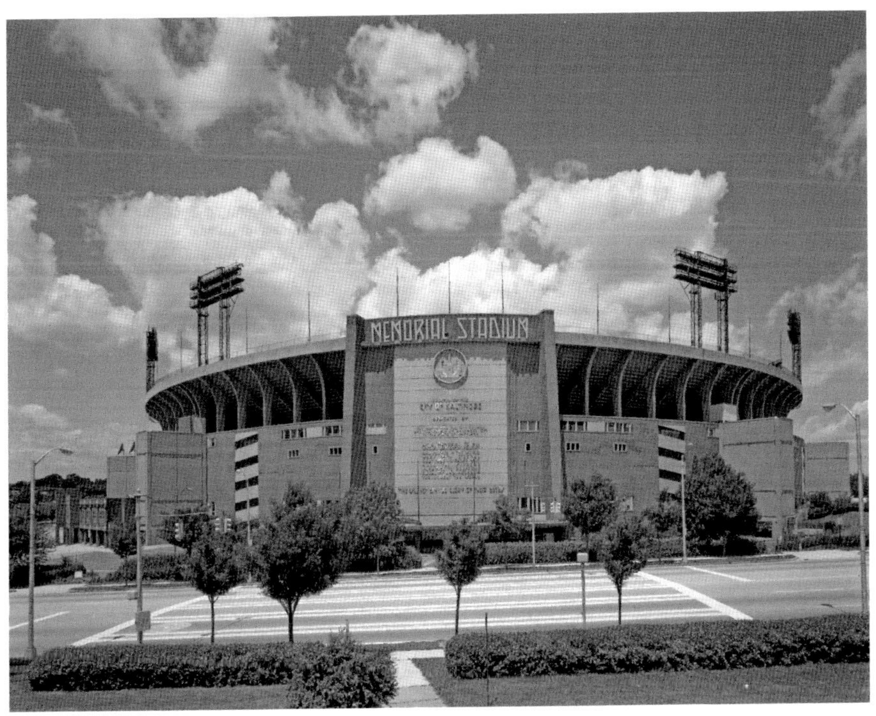

Both the Baltimore Colts and the Orioles enjoyed victories in now-demolished Memorial Stadium. *Courtesy of Library of Congress.*

at Memorial, relocated to their new nest for the 1998 season. Memorial Stadium was demolished in 2002.

It's said that when Baltimoreans ask someone where they went to school, they mean high school, not college. A spirited rivalry exists between students and alumni of the city's two premier public high schools: Baltimore City College (founded in 1839) and Baltimore Polytechnic Institute (founded in 1883). The annual November clash of their football teams is one of the oldest such rivalries in the country, dating to at least 1889. At this writing, City leads the series, but just barely, 63-62, with 6 ties.

Among the individual homegrown sports heroes celebrated here are tennis dynamo Pam Shriver, who won 133 titles in the 1980s and '90s (and is now a busy net-side broadcaster and pundit), and swimmer Michael Phelps, who trained his massive fingertip-to-fingertip wingspan in a number of area pools. The "Baltimore Bullet" became the most-medaled Olympian in history—a twenty-eight-medal splash in four straight Olympic Games, beginning in 2004.

Baltimoreans love to kick back and watch games, but they enjoy playing them as well. For some years now, lacrosse has been the nation's fastest-growing youth sport, but its popularity is old news in Baltimore. Though bearing the French name for "stick," lacrosse has its origins in games Native Americans played, especially in Canada's St. Lawrence River Valley. The sport came to Baltimore in 1878 after members of the city's Athletic Club saw it played in Rhode Island, where they'd gone for a track meet. The game, now Maryland's official team sport, put down serious roots here, at least in the tonier zip codes. Johns Hopkins University was only six years old when it fielded a team in 1882, and it's now the nation's winningest collegiate men's program, with forty-four national championships—nine since National Collegiate Athletic Association (NCAA) tournament play began in 1971. (After many years on the Johns Hopkins University's Homewood Campus, the National Lacrosse Hall of Fame and Museum relocated to suburban Sparks, Maryland.) Baltimore's Bryn Mawr School, a private prep school in Roland Park, fielded this country's first women's lacrosse team in 1926.

Another local sport just happens to also involve a few of those storied 1890s Orioles players—well, maybe. The latest research on the origins of duckpin bowling—a small-ball version of tenpin—shows the game being first mentioned in a Lowell, Massachusetts newspaper back in 1894. But the story most Baltimoreans grew up with has the game invented here at (long demolished) Diamond Alleys in 1900 by Orioles player/owners Wilbert Robinson and John McGraw, who were looking for a less strenuous form of bowling for the warm-weather months. Avid hunters, they likened the scattering pins to startled ducks taking flight. Whether these baseballers were the first to fashion the downsized game or were just early adopters, the city soon became a duckpin epicenter. The sport's governing body, the National Duckpin Bowling Congress, was founded in Baltimore in 1927 (and now resides in the suburbs). The television show *Duckpin & Dollars*, seen from 1962 to 1974, was but one of the duckpin shows that aired locally (contestants vied to roll strikes for cash). Televised duckpin bowling contributed to the success and regional fame of another of Baltimore's hometown heroes: Elizabeth "Toots" Barger, who "won every honor duckpin bowling had to offer," to quote a 1998 obituary. Between 1947 and 1968, the sport's golden age, Barger was the sport's top-ranked woman bowler thirteen times. In its 1960s heyday, there were more than one thousand duckpin lanes in the metro area. Its demise here and in the few other states where it cropped up can be chalked up to the rise of television, the loss of company leagues and general changes in how Americans spend their free time.

YOUR GUIDE TO HISTORY

Royal Farms Arena
201 West Baltimore Street • Downtown
(410) 347-2020 • www.royalfarmsarena.com

Opened in 1962 as the Baltimore Civic Center, the city's principal indoor arena seats anywhere from eleven thousand to fourteen thousand depending on the configuration (small by today's big-city arena standards, where most NBA-caliber facilities seat more than twenty thousand). The NBA's Baltimore Bullets played here between 1963 and 1973, but sports-wise it's mostly hosted minor-league outfits, including four hockey teams over the years—Baltimore Clippers, Blades, Skipjacks and Bandits—and "sports" such as pro wrestling and monster truck rallies. Musically, the "Bawlmerena" has echoed with innumerable A-listers, such as Sinatra, Jimi Hendrix, Led Zeppelin and Prince. The Beatles played back-to-back shows here in September 1964 during their first U.S. tour, and a jumpsuit-clad Elvis Presley took its stage during his final tour. With the structure undersized and outdated, there is frequent talk of replacing the arena.

Pimlico Race Track
5201 Park Heights Avenue • North
(410) 542-9400 • www.pimlico.com

Opened in 1870, Pimlico's dirt oval is among the oldest thoroughbred racetracks in the nation and site of the annual Preakness Stakes. (Of major tracks, only Saratoga Race Course is older.) It was built and is still administered by the Maryland Jockey Club, founded in colonial Annapolis in 1743 and considered the nation's oldest sporting association. (George Washington attended Jockey Club meetings and races.) A 1966 fire destroyed Pimlico's ornate Victorian clubhouse, leaving little infrastructure from its historic glory days. When its oval is quiet, other races are simulcast for handicappers here. Also known as Old Hilltop after a raised section of the infield where trainers once assembled, the track has declined along with horse racing's popularity (outside of marquee events). As of this writing, the first steps of a $375 million redevelopment project are underway.

Preakness Stakes

Baltimore becomes a city of horse racing fans each spring as the celebrated Preakness Stakes at Pimlico Race Track, held the third Saturday in May, fuels a weeklong civic celebration. On race day, billionaire Thoroughbred owners line the clubhouse rails, while the infield draws tens of thousands of youthful partiers. (Depending on the fickle spring weather, their revelry is either sunbaked or muddy.) First run in 1873 and named after a winning colt in Pimlico's 1870 premiere season, the Preakness is known as the middle jewel in the horse racing's Triple Crown between the Kentucky Derby (run the first Saturday in May) and the Belmont Stakes (run the first or second Saturday in June). The race is also called "The Run for the Black-Eyed Susans" after the Maryland state flower. Alas, the black-and-yellow flowers don't bloom in May. For many years, the winning horse was presented with a blanket of white daisies hand-painted to resemble Susans. Of late, a type of yellow chrysanthemum has served as a state flower stand-in.

Memorial Field at the Y

900 block of East 33rd Street • East

This youth baseball diamond is roughly positioned where the ballfield was within Memorial Stadium, demolished in 2002. Here fans cheered MLB's Baltimore Orioles (1954–91) and the NFL's Baltimore Colts (1953–83) and Ravens (1996–97). The barebones oval was dowdy but long-beloved—dubbed the "World's Largest Outdoor Insane Asylum" for all the chaotic fan energy within. The Orioles played in six World Series at Memorial (clinching two of the three they won there). A senior housing complex and YMCA occupy part of the site today. The former stadium's stylized metal letters honoring war dead and reading "Time Will Not Dim the Glory of Their Deeds" were reinstalled at a memorial site outside Oriole Park at Camden Yards.

Patterson Bowling Center

2105 Eastern Avenue • Southeast
(410) 675-1011 www.pattersonbolwingcenter.com

Billed as the nation's oldest duckpin bowling alley, this bi-level facility opened in 1927 with six lanes on each floor. It has added things like karaoke nights

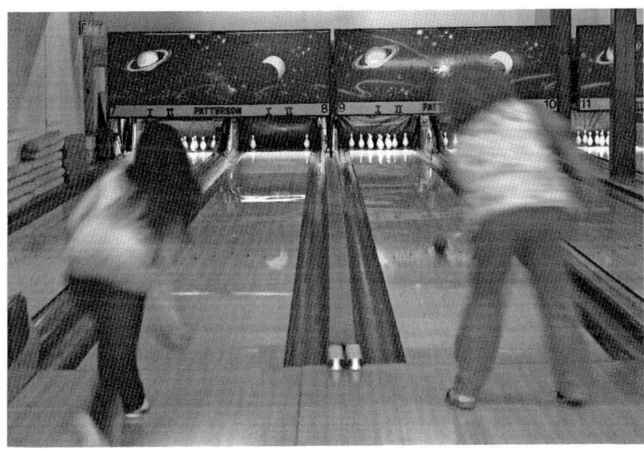

Duckpin bowling at Patterson Lanes. *Courtesy of Chris Myers.*

to broaden the appeal, but the throwback alley is still rolling along with both bowling leagues and open bowling. Curiously, duckpin bowling is both easier and harder than traditional bowling. On the one hand, the grapefruit-sized balls are much easier to wield, especially for children, than the weighty and finger-holed balls of tenpin. But the squat pins are much harder to knock down. No one has ever bowled a perfect game in duckpins—twelve strikes in a row, scoring 300—although such a feat is not uncommon among pro tenpin bowlers.

Babe Ruth Birthplace and Museum

216 Emory Street • South
(410) 727-1539 • www.baberuthmuseum.org • Admission Fee

The story goes that Kate Ruth didn't want to give birth to her first child at her tiny apartment above her husband's saloon, so George Herman "Babe" Ruth Jr. entered the world in 1895 at her parent's house at 216 Emory Street. This slender three-story row house and three adjacent to it have been run as a Babe-focused museum since 1974. The man who would be the Sultan of Swat began as a rough-and-tumble Baltimore street kid—one his bar-busy father and sometimes sickly mother couldn't handle. At age seven, they packed George Jr. off to St. Mary's Industrial School for Boys, a Catholic orphanage and reform school north of downtown. He learned to behave here, and he learned something else. When Ruth left for good twelve years later, he had a baseball contract in his pocket. A few rooms of period furnishing at the museum provide a glimpse of domestic life for working-class Baltimoreans more than one hundred years ago. And there are all manner of artifacts

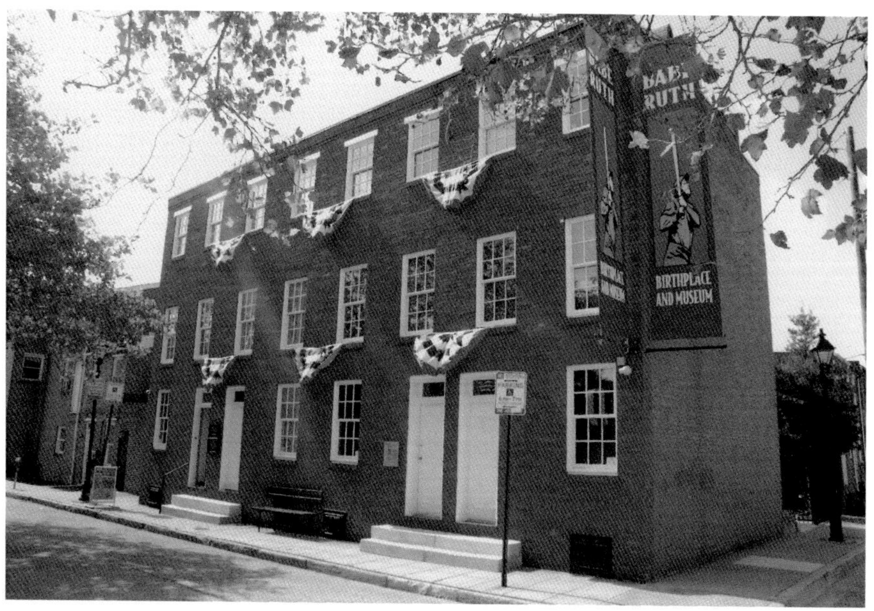

Babe Ruth's 1895 birthplace is now a museum. *Courtesy of Babe Ruth Birthplace and Museum.*

relating to Ruth's stellar career with the Red Sox and (mostly) the Yankees. Rarest of all are items from the few months he was a teenage pitcher for a minor-league Baltimore Orioles outfit managed by Jack Dunn. It is said that the wide-eyed and wet-behind-the-ears Ruth was called "Dunn's Baby," and a modified version of this moniker stuck. The Babe—hardly tyke-sized at six-foot-two and more than two hundred pounds—bashed 714 home runs during a twenty-two-year career.

M&T Bank Stadium

1101 Russell Street • South

Tickets and Tours: (410) 261-7283 • www.baltimoreravens.com • Fee

Home of the NFL's Baltimore Ravens, the two-time Super Bowl–winning team (as of this writing) was established in 1996 following the relocation of the Cleveland Browns. The $220 million stadium opened in 1998 and seats just over seventy-one thousand. Once called PSINet Stadium (until that name-buying internet provider went bankrupt), outside of NFL action, college and high school football, lacrosse and soccer have been played within.

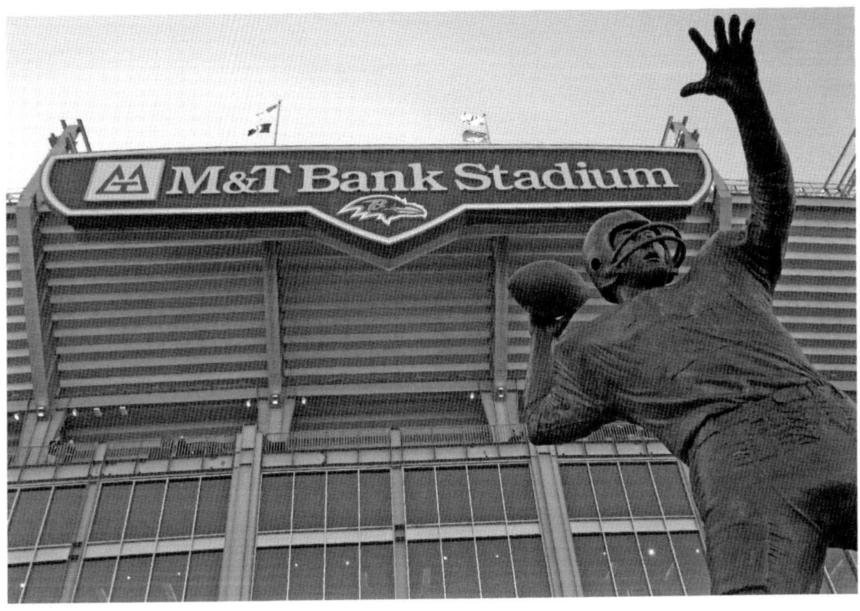

A bronze Johnny Unitas drops back to pass in front of M&T Bank Stadium. *Courtesy of Austin Kirk.*

A statue of thirteen-time Pro Bowler and Super Bowl MVP Ray Lewis guards the Hamburg Street entrance. The formidable middle linebacker played his entire seventeen-year career in Ravens purple. Nearby stands a statue of an arm-cocked Johnny Unitas—the Golden Arm—the Hall of Famer who never wore purple but is beloved as a storied quarterback for the old Baltimore Colts. Stadium tours are available.

Oriole Park at Camden Yards
333 West Camden Street • South
Tours: (410) 547-6234 • www.mlb.com/orioles/ballpark/tours • Fee
Orioles tickets: 888-848-2473 • www.mlb.com/orioles • Fee

With its graceful brick arches, exposed steel beams and asymmetrical playing field, the home of the Baltimore Orioles birthed the retro-ballpark movement after its first pitch in 1992. Camden Yards (as it's generally called—that, or just "The Yard") is named after a railroad facility that once stood on site and replaced the dual-purpose (and since demolished) Memorial Stadium out in North Baltimore's Waverly neighborhood. The

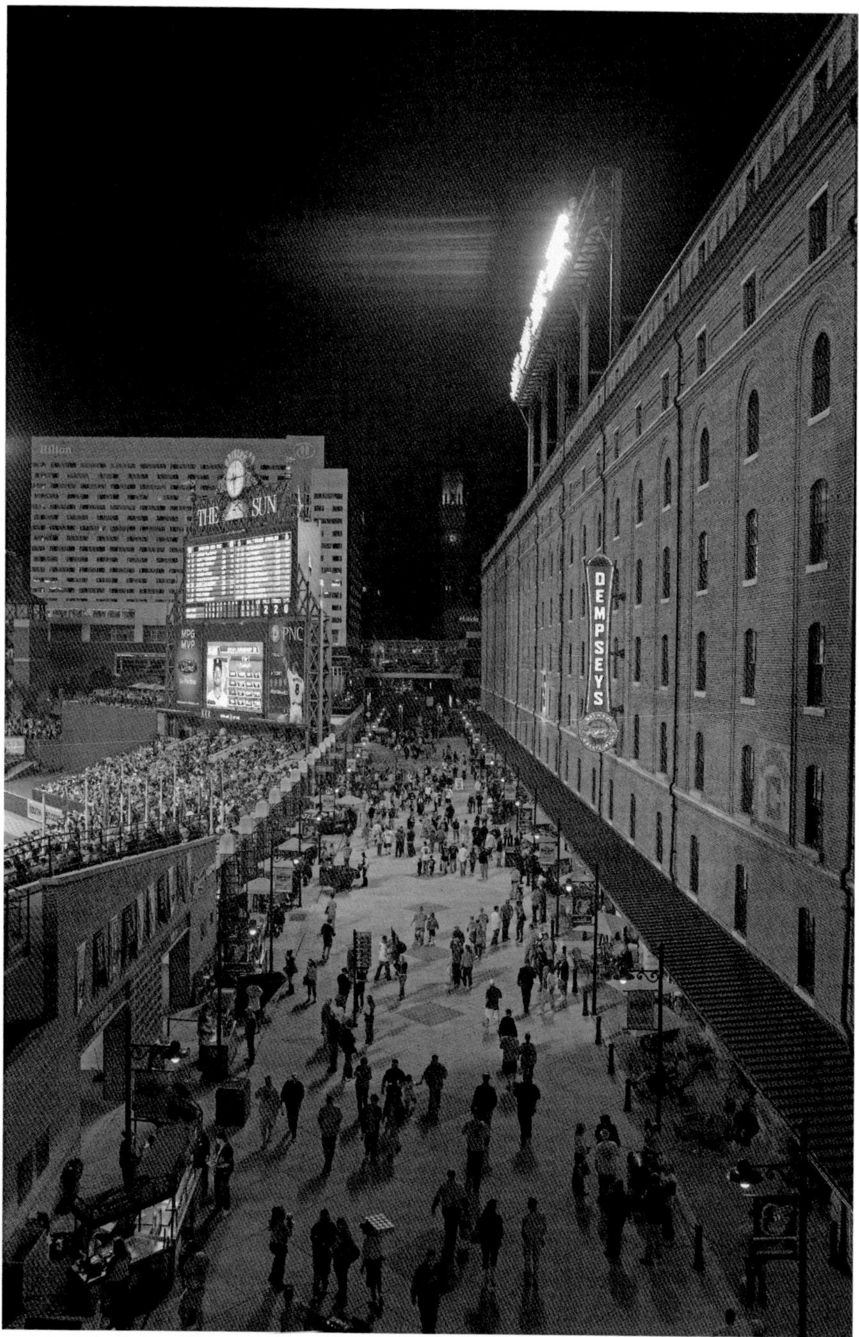

The massive and historic B&O warehouse is an integral part of Oriole Park at Camden Yards. *Courtesy of Visit Baltimore.*

ballpark has a historical leg up on its numerous copycats thanks to the incorporation of the eight-story, more than one-thousand-foot-long brick warehouse into its design beyond right field. (Initial stadium plans called for demolishing the hulking edifice, built by the B&O Railroad between 1889 and 1905, until a plucky college student's architectural thesis showed the advantages of the brick behemoth being preserved and celebrated.) Babe Ruth's birthplace stands but two blocks away, and the legendary hitter's father ran a saloon that stood near today's center field. The ballpark seats 45,971 (down from the original 48,876), and perhaps its most significant non-baseball event was when Pope John Paul II celebrated mass there in 1995. In 2012, Oriole Legends Park debuted in the picnic area behind the bullpen, home to six larger-than-life bronze statues of black-and-orange greats: Frank Robinson, Brooks Robinson, Earl Weaver, Jim Palmer, Eddie Murray and Cal Ripken Jr. Ballpark tours are available.

New Cathedral Cemetery
4300 Old Frederick Road • West
(410) 566-7770 • www.newcathedralcemetery.org

Covering 125 rolling acres and offering nice, distant views of downtown, New Cathedral was established by the Archdiocese of Baltimore in 1869 partly as a place to move hundreds of bodies and headstones from older graveyards being swallowed up by urban growth. While eternal home to a number of notables, including multiple Maryland governors and the city's first Black mayor, Clarence "Du" Burns, for baseball scholars the draw is the four members of the Baseball Hall of Fame—perhaps more than any other boneyard. Manager Ned Hanlon, left fielder Joe Kelley, third baseman/manager John McGraw and catcher Wilbert Robinson were all members of the glorious 1890s Orioles. While they went on to achieve hardball success in other cities and uniforms, they are reunited here beneath Baltimore soil.

Chapter 12

THE GREEN ESCAPE

PARKS AND GARDENS WHERE BALTIMOREANS GET BACK TO NATURE

Ever since the wealthy merchant William Patterson donated six acres of his property to be a "public walk," Baltimoreans have been creating parks to relieve the pressures of urban living. The latter half of the nineteenth century was the great age of park creation, here as in other East Coast cities, under the influence of Andrew Jackson Downing and Frederick Law Olmsted. Both of those pioneering landscape architects prescribed an approach inspired by the naturalistic country gardens of England, with swooping carriage lanes, fanciful buildings and shady spaces alternating with open fields.

Starting with Patterson's gift, the city expanded Patterson Park prior to the Civil War. Olmsted-inspired developments were put in place after the war was over. The grounds for Druid Hill Park, in private hands since 1688, were sold to the city in 1860. Clifton Park, the great "paradise on earth" estate of philanthropist Johns Hopkins, was sold to the city in 1894. A few years later, the city hired the Olmsted brothers' firm to create a plan for "the development of public grounds." The Olmsted plan, published in 1904, profoundly shaped Baltimore. It recommended adding two great, undeveloped stream valleys, Gwynns Falls Park and Herring Run Park, to the park system. Two smaller streams, Stony Run and Suwalt's Run, were joined together as Wyman Park, which today survives in fragments. To link these broad green spaces and turn them into a citywide system, the Olmsteds proposed building wide, shady connecting boulevards. Hence Clifton Park is linked to Herring Run Park by Norman Avenue, in the Mayfield neighborhood; Herring Run Park

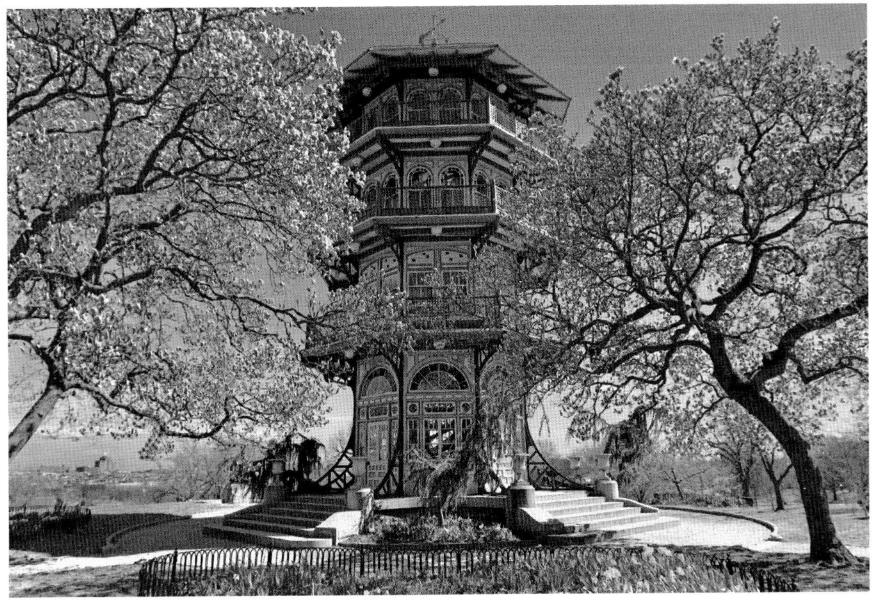

The Patterson Park Pagoda dates to 1890. *Courtesy of Aisha Springer.*

and Lake Montebello are (almost) connected to Wyman Park by 33rd Street; and Druid Hill Park is tied to Gwynns Falls/Park by Gwynns Falls Parkway. Meanwhile, in 1898, in the southwest end of town, the city had acquired Mount Clare, the colonial mansion of Charles Carroll, Barrister, along with its grounds, creating Carroll Park. Leakin Park, straddling the valley of Dead Run, was acquired in the 1940s. In 1946, the city acquired Cylburn, the north Baltimore mansion and estate of the chromium magnate Jesse Tyson. It became the Cylburn Wildflower Preserve in 1954, renamed the Cylburn Arboretum in 1982, the last major green space to be preserved within the city.

In the mid-twentieth century, as Baltimore's fortunes stalled and fell, many city parks suffered great neglect. That trend has been reversed to a large degree due to public demand and a growing understanding of the benefits of green space. The city's Department of Recreation and Parks, chronically underfunded, does its best to maintain good conditions, while many actual improvements have been led by private organizations, funders and volunteers. Each of the main city parks now has its own local volunteer support group, and a number of citywide organizations, such as the Parks and People Foundation and Blue Water Baltimore, advocate for both recreational use and environmental preservation.

Baltimore's embrace of bikes, bike lanes and trails is slowly gathering steam. A high point is the Jones Fall Trail, which follows the waterway (mostly) through town, often on handsome designated paths. The Baltimore Greenway Trails Coalition works to expand the trail network to better connect parks, neighborhoods and attractions. The group Flowering Tree Trails of Baltimore plants flowering trees alongside trails for springtime beauty.

YOUR GUIDE TO HISTORY

Jones Falls Trail

Baltimore Visitor's Center (Inner Harbor) to Mount Washington (North)

The Jones Falls, a roughly eighteen-mile-long stream gurgling through the city from headwaters in central Baltimore County, has been subject to centuries of ill-treatment. Pollution, of course, and sewage outflows are still a problem, but also willful indifference. Its lower reaches have long been channeled underground and out of sight, while upstream it often flows ignobly beneath an elevated six-lane highway. But in terms of engendering

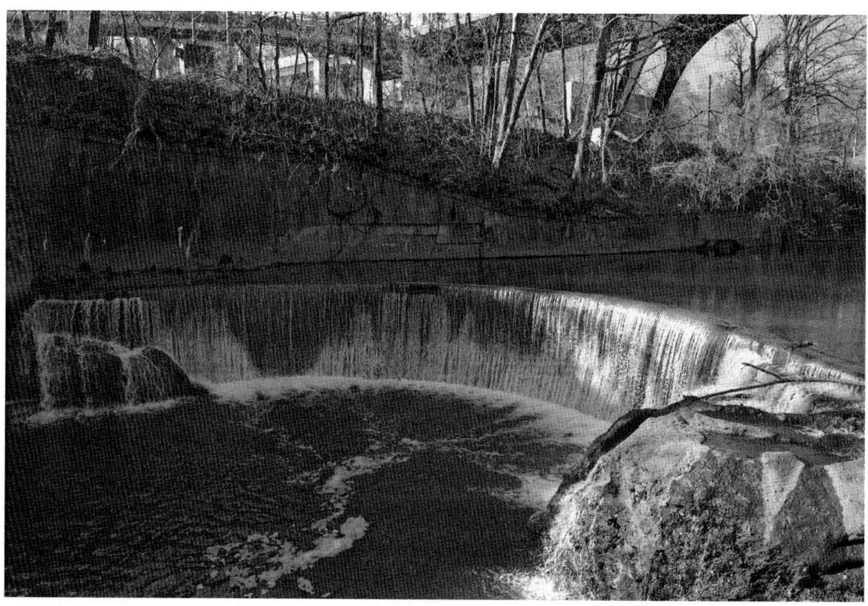

View from the trail. The Jones Falls' Round Falls is a vestige of an 1800s mill. *Courtesy of Brennen Jensen.*

industry and facilitating transportation, it's done as much to make Baltimore grow and prosper as the harbor itself.

Debuting in 1999 and still growing, the eleven-mile Jones Falls Trail throws some love to the waterway, roughly following it from the Inner Harbor to Mount Washington. The bike and hike path features some reclusive leafy stretches where you might see blue herons and kingfishers. Civic-minded historians, meanwhile, have installed interpretive signage along some of its length detailing the valley's rich industrial heritage, most of which involves textile mills that once employed thousands. It is named after David Jones, who settled near its mouth in 1661 as the first European resident in the Baltimore area. The origins of "falls," also used by a few other Baltimore-area streams, is murkier. (While water splashes over rocks in the Jones Falls, there aren't any sizable natural waterfalls of note.) One theory suggests the name goes back to Captain John Smith, who explored the bay in 1608 and described, in an Old English manner, how these streams often tumbled over "felles." Geologists might say that these waterways descend from piedmont to coastal plain across what's called a fall line, hence the name.

Cylburn Arboretum

4915 Greenspring Avenue • North
(410) 396-0180 • www.cylburn.org

This two-hundred-acre, city-owned arboretum, garden and nature preserve sprawls leafily around its namesake: a stone, Second Empire mansion built and expanded between 1863 and 1889 by Jesse Tyson, heir to a chromium empire. After giving up his long bachelorhood and moving his nineteen-year-old bride into a finalized Cylburn, a sixty-something Tyson modestly proclaimed, "I have the fairest wife, the fastest horses and the finest house in Maryland." The city acquired the property in 1942, and some of the period-detailed ground floor rooms are rented out for events. Along with all manner of trees, various themed gardens surround the property—plants arranged by flower color, scent and so forth. Formal gardens in the rear are watched over by a pair of somewhat weathered carved stone statues of seated women (the statues also incorporate an anvil, a gear, parts of a steam engine and a shield resting on a terrapin). Known as Baltimorea, they symbolize the city and once adorned a midtown bridge. Production greenhouses here supply other city parks and properties with greenery, and while off limits, they do host periodic public plant sales. The surrounding woods sport nature trails.

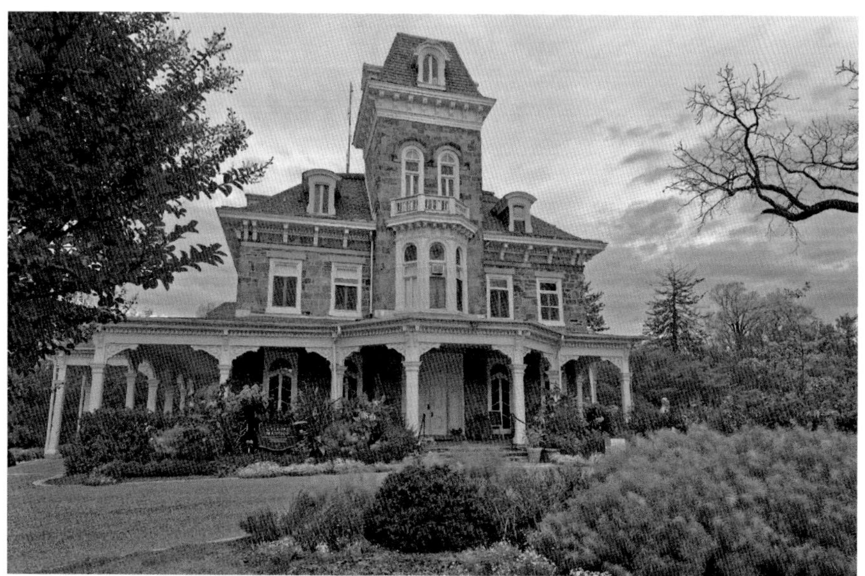

Cylburn Arboretum's diverse plants and trees surround its namesake mansion. *Courtesy of Brennen Jensen.*

Incidentally, Jesse's chromium-rich brother James built an Italianate stone mansion he called Ruscombe barely a half mile away in 1866. His surviving edifice, at 4901 Springarden Drive, houses medical offices today.

The Lakes of Homeland

Springlake Way and St. Dunstans Lane • North

This linear park in Homeland includes a series of six interconnected ponds and their landscaped surroundings, originally developed in 1843 around a natural stream on what was then the estate of the Perine family. The spring that originally fed the ponds dried up in the mid-twentieth century; ever since, the Homeland community has paid to pump city water through the system. Most of the park lies between the northbound and southbound sides of Springlake Way. This is an ideal place to take small children for a taste of managed adventure, watching the goldfish and wild ducks, jumping over the narrow channels that run from pond to pond and puzzling over the park's most peculiar feature, the bronze statue of *The Homeland Wolf*. It's the replacement for an original statue by the prominent local sculptor Edward Berge that disappeared in the 1930s.

Sherwood Gardens

Greenway at Stratford Road • North
www.sherwoodgardens.org

The Guilford Association maintains this park-like six-acre tract, famous for the eighty thousand tulips that electrify its flowerbeds in late April and early May. The gardens, sprawling across an Olmsted-designed park formerly known as Stratford Green, were created by John W. Sherwood, a wealthy tulip enthusiast whose former home overlooks the site. One day each year, gardeners from all over Baltimore are invited to dig up the past year's bulbs and take them home; volunteers plant fresh bulbs annually. Other blossoms and flowering trees, such as dogwoods and redbuds, come into bloom as the seasons progress.

Patterson Park

Bounded by East Baltimore Street, Eastern Avenue, South Patterson Park Avenue and South Linwood Avenue • Southeast
(410) 276-3676 • www.pattersonpark.com

In 1827, the wealthy Baltimore merchant William Patterson set aside 6 acres of his East Baltimore property as a "public walk" for neighbors to enjoy. After Patterson's death in 1835, the city set about acquiring adjacent parcels from Patterson's heirs and dedicated the collected property as a public park in 1853. This became the core of today's Patterson Park, which now sprawls across 137 rolling acres. Plans to develop the park were interrupted by the Civil War, during which Patterson Park became a Union army camp and hospital site; afterward, the city got busy laying out curving paths, a marble fountain, a boat lake and other amenities, creating one of most ambitious public parks in America at the time. After decades of neglect and decline in the twentieth century, the Friends of Patterson Park came together in 1998 to restore the space for community use.

On the west end of the park is Hampstead Hill, which was the fortified headquarters of the city's defenders during the 1814 Battle of Baltimore. Today, it is best known for its charming metal-framed observatory, popularly known as "the Pagoda," erected in 1891. The tower's designer, Charles H. Latrobe, represented the third generation of Baltimore's great architectural dynasty. From the Pagoda, the land slopes down dramatically, providing a sledding hill on snowy days and a natural amphitheater for summer concerts.

At the bottom of the slope, a former boat lake now serves as a scenic wetland and nature sanctuary, popular with birds and bird lovers. Also on the east end, along South Linwood Avenue, are public tennis courts, an ice skating rink and a public swimming pool.

Druid Hill Park

Bounded by Druid Park Lake Drive, Swann Drive, Druid Park Drive and I-83 • West
https://bcrp.baltimorecity.gov/parks/druid-hill

This sprawling, rambling city park contains a variety of recreational and scenic sites, linked by a maze of curving lanes. Founded in 1860 on land purchased from the Rogers family, Druid Hill Park was eventually expanded to more than seven hundred acres. It now incorporates the Maryland Zoo, the Howard Rawlings Conservatory, a public swimming pool, a network of bike trails, five baseball diamonds, a disc-golf course, tennis courts, multiple public-use pavilions, at least three historic monuments, the Rogers family cemetery, many acres of undeveloped woodland and the peculiar Model Safety City, which is used to educate young children about city traffic.

At its heart, Druid Hill Park is a creation of the Victorian era, with looping drives designed for horse-drawn carriages. Coming on the heels of New York's Central Park, Druid Hill's designers made use of natural landforms to provide scenic vistas and shady, romantic settings. Its exotic pavilions, now used for picnics and parties, were built in the 1860s to serve as stations along a miniature railway that no longer exists. Some of these pavilions were among the earliest works of George Frederick, architect of City Hall and other Baltimore landmarks. Lesser-known artists created the park's three commemorative statues, representing George Washington, Christopher Columbus and, incongruously, the legendary Scottish chieftain William Wallace (best known today as the hero of Mel Gibson's movie *Braveheart*). The Columbus statue, erected in 1882, has the non-distinction of being one of three Columbus monuments erected in Baltimore; all three have been attacked and damaged in recent years as symbols of colonialism and racism. Druid Hill Park's largest physical feature is Druid Lake, a reservoir belonging to the city's water system. At this writing, the western half of the lake is undergoing a massive engineering project to comply with federal water safety laws. The eastern end, with a commanding view of midtown Baltimore, is a great place for a stroll or a bike ride.

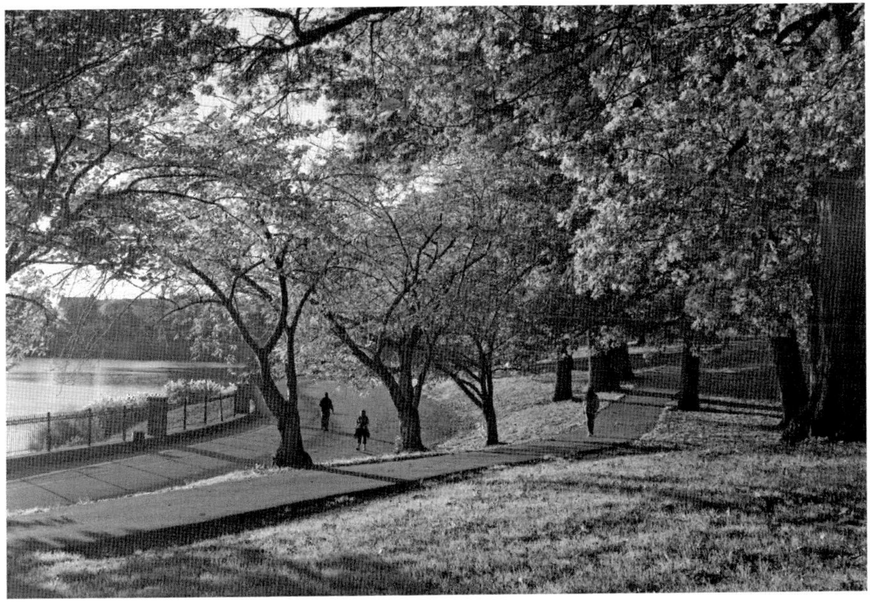

Leafy Druid Hill Park personifies the green escape. *Courtesy of Visit Baltimore.*

Howard P. Rawlings Conservatory and Botanic Gardens
3100 Swann Drive, Druid Hill Park • West
(410) 396-0008 • www.rawlingsconservatory.org

This complex of greenhouses includes displays of exotic flowers, fascinating collections of succulent desert plants and rainforest greenery and one of the most pleasant spaces in Baltimore: the original nineteenth-century conservatory building, now known as the Palm House, which accommodates thirty-foot trees with room to spare. Constructed in 1888, the Palm House is either the oldest or second-oldest public greenhouse in the United States. Its design, comprising a single glazed room that rises fifty feet to a central cupola, is credited to the prolific Baltimore architect George Frederick. An ambitious expansion of the conservatory, from 2002 to 2004, added two flanking pavilions and upgraded the three conjoined greenhouses; these now represent three climate zones: the Mediterranean, humid tropics and deserts. Outside the greenhouse lie formal gardens that feature a unique polygonal sundial: it tells the time in twelve locations around the planet, in addition to Baltimore. Admission to the conservatory is free but donations are welcome, and there is a small gift shop.

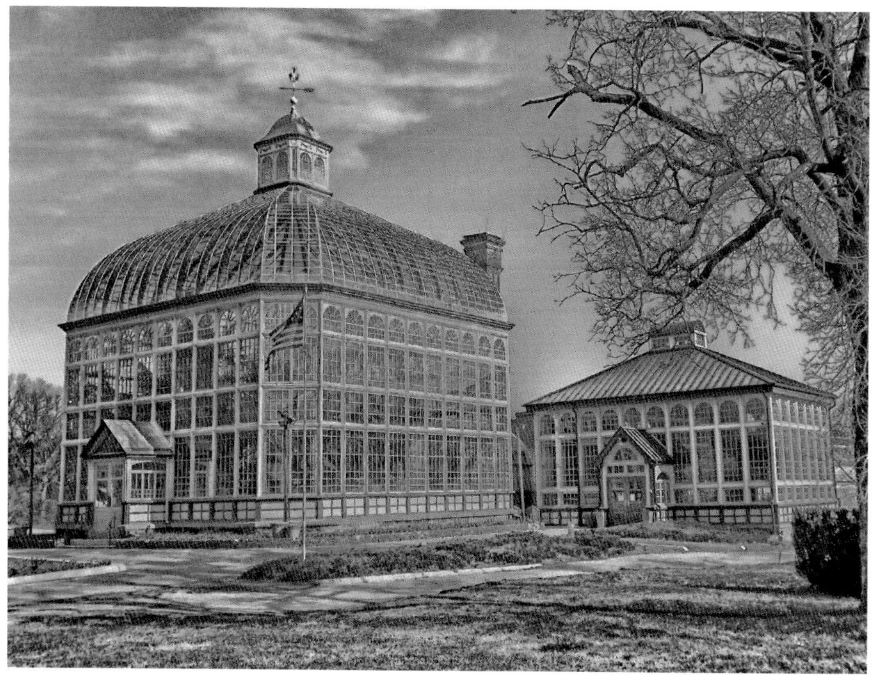

The Howard P. Rawlings Conservatory and Botanic Gardens and its 1895 Palm House. *Courtesy of Pixabay.*

Gwynns Falls/Leakin Park

Gwynns Falls valley between Dickeyville and Mount Clare • West
https://bcrp.baltimorecity.gov/parks • www.gwynnsfallstrail.org

Baltimore's biggest natural area, and the second-largest urban forest in the United States, is this 1,200-acre swath of green, incorporating the steep wooded valleys of Gwynns Falls and its tributary, Dead Run, which flow through West Baltimore. Although most of its acreage consists of wild second-growth forest, the sprawling park (officially two parks side by side) incorporates a variety of recreational features and connects with two interesting old mill villages, Dickeyville and Franklintown. High above the west bank of Gwynns Falls is Crimea, the former estate of the wealthy railroad heir Thomas Winans.

The original park, limited to the valley of Gwynns Falls, was added to the city's park system in 1908, acting on the Olmsted brothers' recommendation. Leakin Park, west of Gwynns Falls, includes the old Crimea estate and the forested Dead Run valley. The combined parks include two ball fields, two children's playgrounds, an Outward Bound camp and the Carrie Murray Nature Center, founded by Orioles baseball hero Eddie Murray. The woodlands are home to a great variety of urban wildlife; one of the Nature Center's missions is to rehabilitate wounded animals, particularly birds. The park's most unifying feature is the Gwynns Falls Trail, a fifteen-mile network of paved paths for hiking and biking that follows the two stream valleys and extends south, beyond park boundaries, all the way to Carroll Park—thus fulfilling part of the Olmsted vision of linking the city's green spaces. Unfortunately, the park's qualities of remoteness and easy access made it too handy as a dumping ground for trash, as well as for the bodies of people murdered elsewhere. This has given the park a bad reputation that it no longer deserves. In tandem with the development of the Gwynns Falls Trail, the city closed off the old, little-used park roads that used to facilitate clandestine activity. Crime is actually far lower in the park than it is in any of the surrounding neighborhoods. That said, it's always safer to travel *anywhere* with a group, whether on wheels or on foot.

Maryland Zoo in Baltimore

1 Safari Place, Druid Hill Park • West
(410) 396-7102 • marylandzoo.org • Admission Fee

One of the oldest zoos in the country, this venerable institution began in 1876 as the Baltimore Zoo. Over the course of 150 years, its mission and its design have reflected changing ideas about keeping, breeding and exhibiting animal specimens. In the nineteenth century and for much of the twentieth, zoos existed chiefly for human entertainment. Increasingly, and particularly since the 1960s, they have embraced the mission of public education and the preservation of endangered animal species. Up until the early twenty-first century, the Baltimore zoo's oldest exhibits still featured antiquated iron cages that offered their inmates little space, comfort or stimulation. A thorough redesign, begun in 2004, greatly advanced the zoo's commitment to more spacious, natural settings. At the same time, the zoo's entertainment functions are not neglected: a miniature railroad, a carousel and a variety of novel display structures are all designed with children in mind.

Altogether, the zoo occupies 135 acres within Druid Hill Park. Among its animal exhibits, several stand out as innovative and relatively progressive regarding animal welfare and educational value: the "Chimpanzee Forest" is a spacious hillside exhibit offering its inhabitants a degree of distance and privacy. The "Polar Bear Watch" includes a variety of arctic- and tundra-dwelling species, along with educational displays that present facts about the impacts of climate change. The zoo's habitats for lions, giraffes and elephants were expanded and improved in 2018–19.

The zoo's headquarters building, known as the Mansion House, was originally the country home of the wealthy Rogers family, who had owned the surrounding land since the eighteenth century. The core of the present building was built around 1801 as a Federal-style house. In 1863, after the Rogers estate became Druid Hill Park, architect John H.B. Latrobe surrounded the house with wide porches and placed a Victorian cupola on top. The porches were enclosed in the 1930s, essentially creating the building as we see it today.

Orianda House at Crimea

1901 Eagle Drive • West • Exterior Only

Here's a corner of Leakin Park with a fascinating history. Baltimore's nineteenth-century penchant for railroading quickly drew admirers, and Thomas and William Winans, sons of pioneering rail and locomotive builder Ross Winans, were two who took advantage. They traveled to czarist Russia in 1847 to construct rolling stock and a rail line between St. Petersburg and Moscow. Leaving William to finish the job (and eventually settle in Europe), Thomas returned to Baltimore in 1850, heavy with czarist cash. Alas, his exotic and palatial 1852 city home Alexandroffsky was demolished. The remaining legacy of apparently well-earned rubles is his stone summer home, the Italianate and porch-encased Orianda House, built in 1857 within the private nine-hundred-acre Crimea estate. The property also includes a unique board-and-batten Gothic chapel that Thomas's Russian-born wife, Celeste, had erected around 1859 for Crimea's Catholic workforce—many thought to have been Irish immigrants who'd fled the potato famine. (Celeste died in 1862 when she was thirty-eight; she has been described as the nation's first female philanthropist for the soup kitchen she opened in 1854 near Alexandroffsky.) The estate was gobbled up by Leakin Park, and the youth outdoor education program Outward Bound uses Orianda for offices and housing, although you can explore the grounds. Also in this part of Leakin Park, the Chesapeake & Allegheny Live Steamers model steam train club (www.calslivesteam.org) has track for its sundry trains, some of which are large enough to be ridden by adults and children during their periodic meets.

BIBLIOGRAPHY

Bentley, Helen Delich, and F. Key Kidder. *The Great Port of Baltimore.* Baltimore, MD: Media Two, 2006.

Bernie, Francis F. *The Amiable Baltimoreans*. Baltimore, MD: Johns Hopkins University Press, 1984.

Black, Catherine F., and James D. Dilts. *Baltimore's Cast-Iron Buildings and Architectural Ironwork*. Centreville, MD: Tidewater Publishers, 1991.

Blight, David W. *Frederick Douglass, Prophet of Freedom.* New York: Simon & Schuster, 2018.

Bowditch, Eden Unger. *Baltimore's Historic Parks and Gardens*. Charleston, SC: Arcadia Publishing, 2004.

Bready, James H. *Baseball in Baltimore: The First 100 Years.* Baltimore, MD: Johns Hopkins University Press, 1998.

Brugger, Robert J. *Maryland: A Middle Temperament, 1634–1980.* Baltimore, MD: Johns Hopkins University Press, 1988.

Chalkley, Tom, Charles Cohen and Brennen Jensen. *Charmed Life.* Baltimore, MD: Woodholme House Publishers, 2000.

Chapelle, Howard Irving. *The Baltimore Clipper. Its Origin and Development.* Hatboro, PA: Tradition Press, 1965.

Crenson, Matthew A. *Baltimore: A Political History.* Baltimore, MD: Johns Hopkins University Press, 2017.

Davis, Amy. *Flickering Treasures: Rediscovering Baltimore's Forgotten Movie Theaters.* Baltimore, MD: Johns Hopkins University Press, 2017.

Dorsey, John, and James Dilts. *A Guide to Baltimore Architecture.* 3rd ed. Centerville, MD: Tidewater Publisher, 1997.

Goldstein, Eric L., and Deborah R. Wiener. *On Middle Ground: A History of the Jews of Baltimore*. Baltimore, MD: Johns Hopkins University Press, 2018.

Graham, Leroy. *Baltimore: The Nineteenth Century Black Capital*. Washington, D.C.: University Press of America, 1982.

Headly, Robert F. *Motion Picture Exhibition in Baltimore*. Jefferson, NC: McFarland & Company, 2006.

Hirschland, Ellen B., and Nancy Hirschland Ramage. *The Cone Sister of Baltimore: Collecting at Full Tilt*. Evanston, IL: Northwestern University Press, 2008.

Holcomb, Eric L. *The City as Suburb: A History of Northeast Baltimore Since 1960*. Santa Fe, NM: Center for American Places, 2005.

Luke, Bob. *The Baltimore Elite Giants*. Baltimore, MD: Johns Hopkins University Press, 2009.

Naylor, Henry, and Caroline Naylor. *Public Monuments and Sculpture of Baltimore*. Baltimore, MD: self-published, 1987.

Olson, Sherry H. *Baltimore: The Building of an American City*. Baltimore, MD: Johns Hopkins University Press, 1997.

Owens, Hamilton. *Baltimore on the Chesapeake*. Garden City, NY: Doubleday, Doran & Company, 1941.

Papenfuse, Edward C., and Joseph M. Coale III. *Atlas of Historical Maps of Maryland, 1608–1908*. Baltimore, MD: Johns Hopkins University Press, 2003.

Pietila, Antero. *The Ghosts of Johns Hopkins*. Lanham, MD: Rowan & Littlefield Publishers, 2018.

Poe, Edgar Allan. *Tales of Edgar Allan Poe*. Introduction by Hervey Allen. New York: Random House, 1944.

Preston, Dickson J. *Young Frederick Douglass: The Maryland Years*. Baltimore, MD: Johns Hopkins University Press, 1980.

Rodgers, Marion Elizabeth. *Mencken: The American Iconoclast*. Oxford, UK: Oxford University Press, 2005.

Rukert, Norman G. *The Fells Point Story*. Baltimore, MD: Bodine and Associates Inc., 1976.

Shivers, Frank R., Jr. *Maryland Wits & Baltimore Bards*. Baltimore, MD: Malay & Associates, 1985.

Solomon, Burt. *Where They Ain't: The Fabled Life and Untimely Death of the Original Baltimore Orioles, the Team that Gave Birth to Modern Baseball*. New York: Free Press, 1999.

Starr, Blaze, and Huey Perry. *Blaze Starr: My Life as Told to Huey Perry*. Santa Barbara, CA: Preager Publishers, 1975.

Stockett, Letitia. *Baltimore: A Not Too Serious History.* Baltimore, MD: Johns Hopkins University Press, 1997.

Thistle, Maeve. *Sources in Context About the Baltimore Abolitionist Elisha Tyson.* Baltimore, MD: self-published, 2018.

Whitehorne, Joseph A. *The Battle for Baltimore 1814.* Baltimore, MD: Nautical & Aviation Publishing Company of America, 1997.

Zembala, Dennis M., ed. *Baltimore: Industrial Gateway on the Chesapeake.* Baltimore, MD: Baltimore Museum of Industry, 1995.

INDEX

C

D

E

F

G

H

I

J

K

L

M

N

O

P

Q

R

S

T

U

V

W

Z

ABOUT THE AUTHORS

Brennen Jensen has written about Baltimore for more than thirty years as a freelancer and for seven years on staff at the Baltimore *City Paper*. A former senior writer for the *Chronical of Philanthropy*, he has also written for National Public Radio, CityLab, *Residential Architect*, *Urbanite* and national lifestyle publications such as *Garden & Gun* and the *Local Palate*. He and his artist wife, Jill Orlov (and two spoiled rescue mutts), share an 1840s house in the city's Woodberry neighborhood.

Tom Chalkley is an illustrator and writer, a lifelong Marylander and a Baltimorean since 1979. He contributed to the Baltimore *City Paper* from 1978 to 2008 and co-wrote, with Brennen Jensen and Charles Cohen, the paper's "Charmed Life" column about Baltimore history, culture and characters.

Visit us at
www.historypress.com